HISTORICAL AND SOCIO-CULTURAL ASPECTS OF NORTH-EAST INDIA

About the Editor

Dr. Sikhamoni Konwar (Gohain Boruah) is presently Principal of Karmashree Hiteswar Saikia College, Guwahati (India). She did her schooling in North Lakhimpur, graduated from Cotton College in History (Major) and obtained her Master degree with specialization in ancient Indian history from Gauhati University. She was awarded JRF by Indian Council of Historical Research and received her PhD from Gauhati University on the subject "Charaideo: The Religious and Cultural Centre of the Ahom Royalty" in 2006.

She has the credit of contributing 22 research papers in the International seminars and 22 in National seminars. Her research papers and articles have been published in the proceedings of the seminars, in the reputed journals, magazines, souvenirs and local newspaoers. She has authored a book "Charaideo: A Cultural Heritage Site of Assam". She has also edited the book "Diversity and Integrity of North-East India".

She is a life member and is associated with North-East India History Association and served two consecutive terms in its executive body. Besides, she is also the life member of South and South-East Asian Association for Study and Culture and Religion (SSEASR), All India Oriental Conference, Indian History Congress, Kamarupa Anusandhan Samity, Indian Association for Asian and Pacific Studies also associated with International Associations of Historians of Asia (IAHA). Her major areas of interests are the history and culture of Assam.

HISTORICAL AND SOCIO-CULTURAL ASPECTS OF NORTH-EAST INDIA

Volume Two

Editor

Dr. Sikhamoni Konwar
Principal
Karmashree Hiteswar Saikia College, Guwahati

CONCEPT PUBLISHING COMPANY PVT. LTD.
NEW DELHI-110059

ISBN-13: 978-93-5125-196-5 (Set)
ISBN-13: 978-93-5125-197-2 (Vol. I)
ISBN-13: 978-93-5125-198-9 (Vol. II)

First Published 2016

Published and Printed by

Concept Publishing Company Pvt. Ltd.
A/15-16, Commercial Block, Mohan Garden
New Delhi-110059 (India)
T: 25351460, 25351794, *F*: 091-11-25357109
E: publishing@conceptpub.com, W: www.conceptpub.com
Editorial Office: H-13, Bali Nagar, New Delhi-110 015, India.

Cataloging in Publication Data--*Courtesy:* D.K. Agencies (P) Ltd. <docinfo@dkagencies.com>

Historical and socio-cultural aspects of North-East India /
editor, Dr. Sikhamoni Konwar.
volumes cm
Contributed articles.
Includes index.
ISBN 9789351251965 (set)
ISBN 9789351251972 (vol. I)
ISBN 9789351251989 (vol. II)

1. Folklore--India, Northeastern. 2. Values--India, Northeastern. 3. Moral education--India, Northeastern. 4. India, Northeastern--Social conditions. 5. India, Northeastern--Economic conditions. I. Konwar, Sikhamoni, editor.

GR305.5.N67H57 2016 DDC 398.209541 23

PREFACE

India is a multi-cultural country bound by the spirit of unity in diversity. And this socio-cultural phenomenon is much reflected in North-East India. The North-East India region consists of seven States of India known as seven sisters. It is the hub of cultural diversity in terms of ethnicity, language, literature, diasporas, migration etc. North-East is known as the anthropological museum of the country. Historically, North-East India is a strategic location for its proximity to India's international borders with four countries — China, Myanmar, Bhutan and Bangladesh. India's North-East region has distinct geographical unit connected with the rest of the country by only 24 km slender thread of the Siliguri corridor that connects with the country. North-Eastern state share 98 per cent land with International border, only 2 per cent with the mainland of the country. So, the North-East region is like a land bridge and Gateway to South-East Asia. Keeping this in view, it is pertinent to mention here that we thought of highlighting the rich historical and socio-cultural aspects of North-East India by publishing a collection of research articles in a book entitled The *Historical and Socio-Cultural Aspects of North-East India.* It is our earnest attempt to bring forth the historical and socio-cultural aspect of North-East India from an academic point of view. In recent years, we have noticed that ignorance about North-East India has degenerated into deep-rooted societal misconceptions about the region which needs to be transformed highlighting the basic facets of its history, culture, life-style, geography etc. The present book discusses various issues relating to North-East India and tries to project it in proper light. It is hoped that the present book will be beneficial to all concerned of the society, students, academicians and, above all, will pave the way for the assimilation of the North-East culture with the main stream in this era of globalization.

Most of the chapters are well researched. Scholars of high repute have contributed to this book of two volumes. We have also encouraged the younger and new scholars to contribute for these volumes.

It is my bounden duty to express my gratitude to the academic advisers and editorial board for entrusting me with the responsibility of editing the book and here I must admit my limitations.

I want to place on record my deep appreciation to the Academic Advisers, Members of the Editorial Board, all the fraternity of our College and Prof. Paromita Das and Mr. Ranjit Konwar who helped us in varied ways for the preparation of this book.

My sincere thanks are also extended to the esteemed contributors, who readily responded to our request, and other well-wishers, who have been source of support and encouragement. We apologize to our readers for our unintentional shortcomings, errors or omissions and commissions. Despite our best effort, we may not be able to cover the whole aspect of the historical and socio-cultural aspects of North-East India, as such many relevant aspects may have been left out. Finally, we would like to thank Concept Publishing Company Pvt. Ltd., New Delhi for their interest in the work.

Dr. Sikhamoni Konwar

CONTENTS

		Pages
	Preface	v
	Contributors	xi

SECTION III — Socio-Economic Scenario

23.	Assam's Linkage with South-East Asia: In Tai Context *J.N. Phukan*	203
24.	Marginal Visibility: Representation of Women of Assam in 19th and 20th Century Historical Narratives *Priyam Goswami*	214
25.	India's North-East: A Geo-Strategic Survey *S.P. Kar*	225
26.	Labour Migration and Economic Enterprise: The Nepalis in Assam *Lopita Nath*	246
27.	Frontier Markets and the Ahom-Jayantiya Relations *I.S. Mumtaza*	276
28.	Situating the Partition of 1947 Within the Frame-work of Post-Colonial Assam *Moushumi D. Pathak*	281
29.	Orphanages in Assam and Meghalaya: A Socio-Educational Study *Rosemary B. Choudhury*	287
30.	Tea Trouble: Tea Garden Labour Strike in Assam from 1921 to 1939 *Reeta Dutta Hazarika*	298
31.	Socio-Economic Change in Medieval Assam: The Case of the Paik System *Banasree Phukan*	307
32.	Customary Law in the North-East: Status of Women *Debajani Choudhury Kar*	314

33. Universalization of Elementary Education in Assam: Still a Dream 322
Tasrina Hussain

34. Use of Tobacco and Oral Cancer 327
Mrinmoyee Baruah

35. Assam Pradeshik Mahila Samity and Women's Empowerment in Assam 333
Kashmiree Gogoi Baruah

36. Socio-Economic Status of Scheduled Tribes of North-East India: Problems and Prospects 341
Faraz Ali Ahmed

37. Socio-Economic Analysis of the Elderly Population of Guwahati City 348
Indrani Kalita Choudhury

38. Development, Displacement and Social Movement in North-East India 356
Devajyoti Gogoi

39. Influence of Gandhism in the Socio-Political and Economic History of Assam 368
Nurul Islam

SECTION IV — Traditional Practices and Culture

40. Traditional Food Habits of Assamese People 377
Sunil Kr. Saikia

41. The Marriage Ceremony of the Ahom: Continuity and Change 383
Sikhamoni Konwar

42. Festivals of the Tiwas of North-East India: An Overview 392
Mowsumee Bordoloi Hazarika

43. Tihar and Bhai Tika of the Nepalese of Assam 401
Ranjan Kumar Bhatta

44. Traditional Dance Dramas of the Khamptis of Arunachal Pradesh: An Ethnographic Note 411
Rashmirekha Sarma

45. Religious Practices of the Mising People of the Majuli Island 419
Binita Pegu

46. Breaking the Patriarchal Myth: A Study of Naga Customary Laws 428
Rituparna Patgiri

47. Cultural Aspects of the Khamtis of North-East India 439
Prafulla Borah

Index 447

VOLUME ONE

SECTION I — Folk Culture and Tradition

1. Notions of Traditional Healing and Faith among the Dimasa 3
Ritu Thaosen

2. Rift in Mahapurushiya Order : A Critical Review 8
Biman Hazarika

3. A Relook into the Status of Tantric Goddess in Early Assam 17
Gargee Sharmah

4. Identity and Liminality in North-East India: A Study of the Ahoms in Colonial and Post-Colonial Assam 27
Rajib Handique

5. Hari-Hara in the Art of Assam 38
Deepi Rekha Kouli

SECTION II — Value Education and Culture

6. Ahom Culture 47
B.K. Gohain

7. Sankardeva's Philosophy of Culture 61
Jagadish Patgiri

8. Impact of Koch Rulers on the Temple Architecture of Assam 67
Paromita Das

9. Negotiating 'Change' and 'Space': Mamang Dai's *The Legends of Pensam* 71
Sweta Pegu

10. The Peripheral Cinemas of the North-East 79
Manoj Barpujari

11. Women in Early Nineteenth Century Assam 92
Manjula Phukan

12. Quit India Movement in Nagaon District: Some Observations 100
Akunthita Borthakur

13. Socio-Cultural Aspects of Bajali 105
Kanan Medhi

14. Tourism and Its Socio-Cultural Aspects of the North-Eastern Region 111
Tulika Chowdhury

15. Tribal Culture and Its Relevance in Planning in North-East India 115
Nivedita Brahma

16. English Language Teaching in Assam in Secondary School 134
Manoj Kumar Choudhury

17. Higher and Technical Education in North-East India 145
Daisy Nath Choudhury

18. Value Education in the Government Secondary Schools of Guwahati 157
Saswoti Baruah Bhuyan

19. Bhupen Hazarika: The Singer of the Man and Society 162
Anup Kr. Deka

20. Vaishnavism in Assam in the Pre-Sankarite Period 170
Marami Choudhury

21. The Sattras of Majuli: Its Art and Culture 179
Biju Rajkhowa

22. Socio-Economic Status of Tribal Population in the Light of Education 191
Gitika Das

CONTRIBUTORS

Banashree Phukan, Asst. Prof., History Department, Pandu College, Guwahati

Binita Pegu, Asst. Prof., Department of History, K.H.S. College

Dr. Debjani Choudhury Kar, Head, Department of Political Science, K.H.S. College, Sixmile, Guwahati

Devajyoti Gogoi, Research Scholar, Department of Sociology, Gauhati University, Guwahati

Dr. Faraz Ali Ahmed, Asst. Prof., Department of Political Science, K.H.S. College

Dr. I.S. Mumtaza, Department of History, Gauhati University, Guwahati

Indrani Kalita Choudhury, Asst. Prof., Department of Economics, K.H.S. College, Guwahati

Prof. J.N. Phukan, Department of History, Gauhati University (Retired)

Dr. Kashmiree Gogoi Baruah, Asst. Professor, Head, Department of History, K.H.S. College, Sixmile, Guwahati

Dr. Lopita Nath, University of Incarnate Word, San Antinio, Texas, U.S.A.

Dr. Moushumi D. Pathak, Associate Prof., Arya Vidyapith College, Department of History, Guwahati

Dr. Mowsumee Bordoloi Hazarika, Vice-Principal, Head, Department of Assamese, K.H.S. College, Sixmile, Guwahati

Dr. Mrinmoyee Baruah, Asst. Professor, Department of Political Science, K.H.S. College, Guwahati

Nurul Islam, Asst. Professor, Head, Department of Philosophy, K.H.S. College

Prafulla Bora, Research Scholar, Department of History, Assam University, Diphu Campus (Assam)

Prof. Priyam Goswami, Department of History, Gauhati University

Ranjan Kr. Bhatta, Head cum Asst. Prof., Department of English, K.H.S. College

Rashmirekha Sharma, Archaeological Survey of India, Guwahati Circle Guwahati (Assam)

Reeta Dutta Hazarika, Principal i/c, Narangi Anchalik Mahavidalaya

Rituparna Patgiri, Research Scholar, Department of Sociology, Jawharlal Nehru University, New Delhi

Dr. Rosemary B. Choudhury, Associate Prof., Head, Department of Education, Handique Girls College, Guwahati

S.P. Kar, I.P.S. (Rtd.)

Dr. Sikhamoni Konwar, Principal, K.H.S. College, Guwahati

Dr. Sunil Kr. Saikia, Writer and Former Director IIE, Guwahati

Dr. Tasrina Hussain, Head, Department of Education, K.H.S. College

SECTION III

Socio-Economic Scenario

23

ASSAM'S LINKAGE WITH SOUTH-EAST ASIA
In Tai Context

J.N. Phukan

The term North-East (North-east) India and South-East (South-east) Asia are modern European creations, created for Europeans. But soon these have been widely used and accepted by others including the states and nations involved therein. In other words, they are now widely accepted by all in references to wider coverage.

A look at the land boundary of India's North-East with South-East Asian countries, it immediately brings to notice that the erstwhile Assam, before the creation of Nagaland, Mizoram and Arunachal Pradesh, constituted a larger territorial entity which had direct land connection with Burma, presently Myanmar. However, we use the name 'Burma' for historical reasons. In ancient times Assam was called Pragjyotisa, then Kamarupa, and lastly 'Asam' (Assam). Today, however, Assam looks small without having direct land boundary with Myanmar.

Historically and ethnologically and also culturally, Assam had far wider and deeper relations with its eastern neighbour Burma (Myanmar).

At the outset let me recall that Assam was an old term that came into existence as early as the early thirteenth century CE from the time of the coming of the Tai Ahom, and has been in use for the last eight hundred years. It has been associated with a Tai group of people well-known as the Ahom or Tai-Ahom. They are ethnically and linguistically related to all Tai groups of people living in several countries of South-East Asia and southern China. But for Burma, a name derived from a people — Myanma (written Mranma), now called Bama (r), forms a nation in the regional grouping of South-East Asia. The term *South-East Asia, Asia East by South, Indo-China*, etc. are not indigenous terms, but are products of European perceptions designed to fit in their own concepts of things and mental panorama. Therefore, any attempt to examine historical relations of Assam with Burma (Myanmar) of present South-East Asia may be a misnomer apart from individual countries that constitute modern South-East Asia.

For many hundred years, the polities/kingdoms that are today within modern South-East Asia had been known and still known by their individual status such as Burma (Myanmar), Siam (Thailand since 1939), Cambodia, An-Nam and Lao (French Indo-China), Java, Bali, Sumatra, Malacca (Melaka), and others. These names provided more space to and emphasis on local, ethnic, and cultural identities rather than collectivism. In the Preface to the *Cambridge History of South-East Asia*, Nicholas Tarling, the editor, writes, "The title South-East Asia becoming current during Second World War, has been accepted as recognizing the unity of the region, while not prejudging the nature of that unity" (Vol. I, Cambridge). Some fifty years ago, George Mc T. Kahin of Cornell University, Ithaca expressed skepticism of bringing under one general term applying to so many countries with varied peoples, languages, cultures, political systems, and he writes "South-East Asia is not an area of great political homogeneity. Politically, as well as culturally its component states are more varied than those of Europe" (Preface to *Governments and Politics of South-East Asia*). Today, however, there is a strong shift from individual identification to collectivism, and 'South-East' or 'South-east' Asia has received wide acceptance in many spheres — political, national and international, academic, cultural, trade and commerce, etc.

In the same way, Assam is being overtaken by North-East India by inducting individual political units or States like Manipur, Kachari (Cachar), Jayantia, Tripura, Koch and others. Today, the seven States of the region namely Assam, Arunachal Pradesh, Manipur, Mizoram Meghalaya and Tripura are collectively called Northeast India or India's North-East. North-East is now in wide use in many official and non-official documents such as North-East Business Summit, North-East Cultural Centre, DoNER (Development of North-Eastern Region), North-Eastern Hill University, North-Eastern Regional Institute of Management, etc. Such a shift to a collective identity of the region has certain demerits as well. It somewhat overshadows and often put the local identities and cultural variations at the backstage.

Before engaging Assam's relation with South-East Asia, it will be in fitness of things to make reference to India's relations with South-East Asia that go back to a very long past, the beginning of which is a matter of speculation. But the relations started at some point of time and continued for many thousand years, and relations still persists. All of us know that India has contributed immensely towards the making of civilization and culture of South-East Asia both Hindu and Buddhist ways. In certain spheres, relations were so deep and widespread that some scholars viewed ancient South-East Asia an extension of India, or "Greater India", and some even called "Hindu Colonies in Far East". For a long time, this fascinating study involved many European and Indian scholars, who had brought out very rich and memorable works.

The early South-East Asian kingdoms included Champa, Funan, Srivijaya, Majapahit, followed by Dvaravati (in central and north-eastern Thailand, a distinctive cultural complex associated with Mon people by the name Dvaravati. "Little is known of its history, its geographical extent, even the location of its capital". A coin bearing the inscription "Lord of Dvaravati" was found, and is the only evidence of the name of that state. Flourished from sixth through nineth centuries), Hamsawati (the Mon State of Pegu, now Begu) was in Lower Burma.

These are only by way of reference in order to show continuity of South-East Asian kingdoms till the early thirteenth century. We, therefore, move on to our own area of Assam in relation to with South-East Asia.

Modern scholars have divided South-East Asia into two broad divisions, i.e. Mainland South-East Asia and Island or Peninsula South-East Asia, and I move to the first because it is here that Assam played its role. However, this area has an extension towards north and north-west where also the Tai have their land and strong connections. For instance, the Tai people have been in living in Vietnam's north and north-west, and there are also about 20 million Tai in China's southern region, particularly in Yunnan and Guangxi. This region may, therefore, be called an extension of Mainland South-East Asia, or even "Greater South-East Asia" (*Ethnic Groups of Mainland South-East Asia*, Frank M. LeBar, Gerald C. Hickey, John K. Musgrave, *et al.*, Human Relations Area Files Press, *New Haven*, 1964, p. 3).

The Tai in South-East Asia and Southern China

The Tai people today are very widespread over several thousand square kilometers and in geographical limit they are found 7° to 26° N. and 94° to 110° E. This region includes, either in part or whole, six sovereign countries — India, Myanmar, China, Vietnam, Laos and Thailand. David K. Wyatt, a very reputed historian on Thi history observes, "Within this vast region the Tai are the largest and most widespread population" and

"Their most visible representatives are the Thai (or Siamese) of Thailand". Although the designation "Thai" is applied to all people living in Thailand, but the ethnic Thai, Tai for our purpose, are living in Thailand from the extreme south to the north all along the Mekong River touching Laos, and from Aranya Pathet on the east to the border of Burma on the west. In the case of Laos, Lao People's Democratic Republic (LPDR). too, the Tai who called themselves Lao (or Lao Lum or valley dwelling Lao) are spread over the whole of the country, but more concentrated in the valleys. There are many people of Lao origin who have been living, due to historical reasons, in north-eastern Thailand (Isan), but are now Thai. The Lao people enjoyed supremacy in political power for several centuries. The Lao language is the national language (*lingua franca*) of Laos today as Thai in Thailand.

In Vietnam, there are more than six Tai groups inhabiting the country's north and southwestern regions, in the valleys of the Black River and its tributaries. The social scientists in Vietnam broadly designate them as Tay-Thai. But at the group level, they are known as Nung, Tho, Nang, Black Tai (Tay Dam), White Tai (Tay Khao) and Red Tai (Tay Deng), numbering a total of about 3 million.

Moving up to the north and north-west of Vietnam, in southern China, the Tai are inhabiting the Guangzi province, where they are called Zhuang (earlier Chuang). The Zhuangs are the largest numbering nearly 16 million. The whole province is, therefore, named as Guangzi Zhuang Autonomous Region. In the neighbouring Yunnan province to the west of Guangxi, there are nearly 2 million Tai (called Dai in Pin Yin), but their concentration is mainly in Dehong Dai-Singpho Autonomous Prefecture and Xishuangbanna (Sip Song Pan Na in Tai) Dai Autonomous Prefecture. These two regions touch northern border of Myanmar.

In Myanmar there are approximately 5 million Tai officially called Shan, a term inherited from the British colonial days. The term "Tai" is alien to Burmese official records. The Shan people are widely spread over northern, north-eastern, northern central region, and also in several pockets in the valleys along the middle course of the Chindwin River. The Shans are found also in the Tamu region in Myanmar across Manipur (India) border. They constitute the second largest ethnic group next to the Bamar (Burman) and almost all speak Tai as their ethnic language.

The Tai people who speak Tai language thus occupy a vast contiguous area in South-East Asia and southern China. All total the number of Tai people approximates about 75 million. This figure is quite big enough comparable in number to the French or the Germans.

Myanmar area	690,651 sq.km.	45,573,000 (2005)
Cambodia	172,511 sq.km.	9,287,000 (2005)
Laos	236,800 sq.km.	5, 500,000 (2005)
Thailand	513,998 sq.km.	65.000,000 (2007)
Vietnam	330,738 sq.km.	70,454,000 (2005)

Role of the Tai in Restructuring the South-East Asian Society

The Tai had played no role in making the ancient civilization of South-East Asia. In most part of Mainland South-East Asia where we find them today they were not there till about nineth-tenth centuries. Those who were there they lived in the fringe areas, either in groups under their own chiefs or as subjects of the major political powers. The Tai thus encircled the northern Mainland South-East Asia. This situation has not greatly changed even today.

However, the Tai people played an undeniable historical role in the making of modern South-East Asia. This can be understood in the light of development of events in South-East Asia between the nineth through twelfth centuries.

Dai-Viet: In 939 A.D., the Vietnamese threw off the one thousand years of Chinese shackle and became independent. But the Dai-Viet kingdom centered in the coastal plain and the Red River Delta had to face the Chinese in the north for survival. On the north-west lived the Tai people in the upland valleys who were gathering strength under their local chiefs.

Champa: During the nineth and tenth centuries Champa situated in the coastal belt of middle Vietnam had to fight for its existence against encroachment of its powerful neighbours like the Dai-Viet (Vietnam) in the north and Cambodia to the south and west.

Khmer Empire: The Khmer Empire centering the Angkor region was expanding rapidly during nineth and tenth centuries beginning with the accession of Jayavarman II in about 802. For the next two centuries, Khmer empire expanded in all directions.

Burma: In the nineth and tenth centuries, in Burma there was no great single empire. The **Pyu State** collapsed due to the pressure of Nan-Chao empire, and the Burman established a small state centered on **Pagan** in the mid-ninth century. In the coastal region arose a new **Mon** kingdom centered on Pegu.

Of these, two kingdoms — **Khmer** and **Pagan** — emerged as great powers during the eleventh and twelfth centuries. This was the golden age for these two classical Indianized empires. It was during this period

Angkor and Pagan attained their pinnacle of glory. It was the age of Suryavarman I, Suryavarman II, Jayavarman VII, Anoratha, Kyanzitha, the age of Angkor Vat, Angkor Thom, Bayon, the age of Pagan with its myriad temples.

But from the eleventh century, "the Tai had begun to become a part of the South-East Asian history when they formed their own kingdoms and empires".

The thirteenth century is a watershed in South-East Asian history. Till the early decade of the century, Pagan and Angkor flourished undiminished, but suddenly, in the words of David K. Wyatt, in the second quarter of the century, the imperial momentum and dynamic collapsed in Angkor and soon thereafter in Pagan. "By the end of the century, both those great empires were golden memories, no matter how potent, of a past that would never be recaptured". A similar view was expressed by famous scholar George Coedes who says that these kingdoms Champa, Pagan and Angkor had no longer the resilience to withstand a major shock, or even to survive a minor disturbance.

The transformation of Mainland South-East between the thirteenth century and the middle of the fourteenth century was associated with three significant developments: (1) The first and the most important was the movement of the Tai down from upland valleys onto the plains formerly dominated by major kingdoms at the same time founding regional centers of powerful new states stretching "all the way from the plains of Assam in north-eastern India to northern Laos in the east and to Nakhon Si Thammarat on the Malay Peninsula in the south" (David, p. 38). Another significant development associated with the rise of the Tai was the revivification of the Buddhism and foundation of Buddhist monastic institutions throughout the region. The third was the rise to power of the Mongols in China and the extension of China's influence on South-East Asia by diplomatic and military means. These three developments had brought basic transformation of politics and society in the region in question overshadowing earlier civilization.

Charles F. Keyes of University of Washington writes, "the ascendancy of the Tai was most dramatic in the period between the mid-thirteenth and the mid-fourteenth centuries. During this period, the Tai founded a number of new states in what are now Thailand, Burma, India, and Laos and also succeeded in becoming the rulers of a large part of Burma and in effecting the demise of the Khmer Empire".

Charles Keyes, however, has called the Tai "barbarians". These Tai who were to dominate South-East Asia since the thirteenth century were probably "barbarians", that is, they were neither "Indianized" nor "Signified" who introduced a new type of social structure. They were ruled by chiefly families and chiefs supporting the sons in expanding territories with necessary personnel and equipments. By this method, the Tai brought under their control large areas previously settled by other ethnic groups. The more the Tai expanded, the more they came into increasing contact with the earlier people of South-East Asia. In the process the Tai achieved political dominance, but they also received or adopted their culture in various ways.

The capture of the Mon kingdom of Haripunjay in northern Thailand by King Mangrai sometime 1293 brought that kingdom to an end. The founding of the kingdom of Lanna (Chiengmai) led to the emergence of a new historical tradition known as the Yuan that persist in Thailand even today.

The Sukhothai kingdom was founded by King Ramkhamhaeng (c.1279-99) against Khmer rule in the Upper Menam Valley where Khmer stamp of civilization and Buddhism were firmly established. From northern and central parts the Tai moved down, and finally in 1350, they became lords of the lower Menam valley. It was called Ayuthiya. In the struggle between Sukhothai and Ayuthiya, the latter ultimately triumphed. The Thai then pushed towards the heart of Angkorean Empire and finally occupied its capital.

In the north, in the central Mekong region the Lao Tai asserted to build a new state called Lan Chang which later came to be known as Laos.

The Tai played a key role in the transition of Burma from classical Pagan civilization to post-classical Burma. Pagan crumbled at the Mongol invasion for not receiving Mongol embassy, and the opportunity was seized by the Tai to occupy Pagan towards the end of thirteenth century. The Shan rule continued at Pagan for the next one and a half century. But the culture persisted with Theravada Buddhism of Pagan as the main prop. In Burma's several other areas, the Tai founded small principalities by chiefs often related to one big royal branch. These were Mong Kwang (Mogaung), Mong Mit, Hsen Wi, Hsi paw, Keng Tung, Khamti Lung, and others.

Thus, by the second half of the fourteenth century, the Tai had become political master of most of the northern part of the Mainland South-East Asia. Thus, there arose the Shan States of Burma, the Lan Chang Kingdom, Siam that gave a new direction of life and culture throughout the region. The modern South-East Asia owes its emergence to the Tai.

North-East India: People Across Border

North-East India's close neighbour is Burma and is separated by a long 1400 km. landmass touching four Indian States — Arunachal Pradesh (440 km.), Nagaland, Manipur and Mizoram.

It is most important to note that both sides of this long border are inhabited by people of the same ethnicity. This is due the fact that there has been movement of people from the east to west or southwest. This process of movement began long ago, and has continued to the recent time.

Starting from the extreme east the ethnic groups are —

The **Lisu** (Yubin — who are very little known outside). This name is synonymous with Li-hsaw, Li-shaw, Lisaw, Liso, Yaoyen, Yawyin, etc. The Lisu are spread over a wide area. They are found in Upper Salwin in Yunnan, in northern Thailand, and Northern Shan States in Burma.
The **Tai** (Ahom, Khamti, Phake, Aiton, Khamyang and Turung).
The **Singpho** (Kachin).
The **Naga** tribes.
The **Mizos** called Chin in Myanmar.

Each tribe/people living on both sides of the border shares common ethnicity, language, beliefs and customs, social institutions, food habits, economy, attitude of mind, etc. Formerly there had been unobstructed movements from either side. Today, they are separated by the international boundary. In spite of formal restriction of crossing the border at free will, they still continue, at a much restricted rate, border crossing, to maintain contacts with their kinsmen on social and economic matters.

What is noteworthy for us is that these people in North-East India are still linked to their homeland. Their traditions are still strong and the feeling of belonging to the same ethnicity gives them extra dose of strength. For instance, a number of pro-democracy supporters slipped the border to Mizoram and Manipur when the Army Junta in Myanmar had crackdown on pro-democracy supporters and found shelter in Mizoram and Manipur. The Kachin could cross the Patkai and stay on the Indian side without being recognized. Thus people from one side could mix with the people on the other side.

It is also important to note that far beyond the border people of the same origin or ethnicity are living in South-East Asia or adjacent Chinese territory. They share the same legend of origin, the same language, dress in the same way, eat the same type of food, reside in same type of house, they convey the same belief and customs, and even some have their relatives at a great distance. A Singpho living in Margherita or Miao faces no problem whatsoever, rather receives warm welcome from the Kachins of Myitkeina (the headquarters of the Kachin State), at a distance of about 450 km. from his home, or even beyond in China's Dehong Tai-Singpho Autonomous Prefecture of Yunnan. Again take the case of the tiny Lisu community now living in Bijoynagar circle (about 4,000) in the extreme east of Arunachal Pradesh. Their close kinsmen are living in Upper Irrawaddy region of Myanmar where they number more than 3,00,000, or in China's Yunnan Province numbering about 6,00,000, or in Thailand's well-known Golden Triangle region beyond the Mekong where they number more than 25,000 souls. They are really an international community. Thus a Singpho/Kachin has a vast area extending three sovereign countries. In the same way the Lisus have a hinterland that extends to four countries — India, Myanmar, southern China and Thailand. These are a few instances of people of North-East having connections with the people of South-East and southern China.

Tai

Coming specifically to the Tai of Assam including those in Arunachal Pradesh there are altogether six groups, i.e. Ahom, Aiton, Khamti, Khamyang, Phake and Turung. The largest majority is the Ahom whose number is computed between 2 to 2.5 million. The Khamtis number about 20,000 thousand while Aiton does not exceed 3,000 and the Phake is of the same number. The Khamyang comes to about 7000 and the Turung about 4000. The Ahoms entered Assam in the early thirteenth century. Others mainly in the mid-eighteenth century. Like the Thai of Thailand, the Lao of Laos, and the Shans of Burma, the Ahoms too contributed to the history, culture and civilization of North-East India.

The Ahoms, particularly the Ahom rulers maintained their social and political relations with the Tai (Shan) royal families of Hukwang, Mogaung, Bhamo, Mong Mit and even of the Chinese Shan State of Mong Mao. There are firm evidences of Shan princes as consorts of the Ahom kings. In the same way Ahom princes were given marriage to Shan rulers. The contact of the Ahoms with the Tai of Burma was not lost. We may surmise that it was through the Shan, the Ahoms could know the development in the neighbouring South-East Asia, if not in distance region. The land route by which Siu-ka-pha came to Assam and running through Mogaung connected the Ahoms with the Shans. Besides, some amount of products from Burma like ruby, jade, gold, silver, gems, Chinese silk, porcelain, and other articles came to the Ahom kingdom.

The Tai differ in several ways from those of other tribes like the Singpho, Naga, Mizo, Lisu. The Tai are valley dwelling people and practice wet rice cultivation while other tribes do swidden farming on hill slopes. The Tai are literate people, and barring the Ahoms, others are Hinayana Buddhists, having a monastery in every village with a monk who gives instruction in Pali. Pali Buddhism links them with all other Tai people in South-East Asia. The most important linkage between the Tai of Assam and those of South-East Asia is the language that is Tai language. A Tai of Assam who speaks Tai can converse with a Tai of Vietnam, or a Tai of northern Thailand or one is at home with the Shans of Burma. A person knowing Tai language can travel from Assam through Burma and then through Thailand and move upward to Laos and to Vietnam and move westward to Yunnan without even knowing any other language. This is really astonishing.

The next important linkage is Buddhism for those who are Buddhist Tai. Besides, they all share common origin, common beliefs and practices, common way of life, share many other cultural and social ways. All the Tai believe in vital energy called *khwan*, they worship their ancestors although the method of worship differ in certain cases. All believe in a variety of spirits called *phi* and propitiate them for keeping them contented.

No doubt the contact between them is very limited due to political compulsion, yet occasional social relations still continue between them. For instance, in 2001 I met a Khamti lady doctor at Muse in the Burma-China border where she has been practicing, and she told me that she is a relative of the Khamti Chief family of Narainpur in Lakhimpur, at a distance of 600 miles.

A strong bond of connection of the Tai of Assam with those of South-East Asia still exists. They are not only distant blood relatives, but also share common heritage and culture.

In the context of Look East Policy of the Government of India and the various measures taken for materializing this policy in certain spheres, the Tai connection with the South-East Asian people particularly with the Thai, Lao, Shan and even with Dai of Yunnan may be viewed as a golden thread. This thread could be explored and exploited to cement India's relations with South-East Asia. The Tai and other border people have a better opportunity to play a positive role in the direction of Indo-South-East Asian relations.

Scholars on South-East Asia

Among Europeans, include Aymonier (*Le Cambodge*, 3 vols.), Georges Coedes (*The Indianized States of South-East Asia, The Making of South-East Asia*), Louis Finot, Fergusson (*History of Indian and Eastern Architecture*), H. Kern, N.J. Krom, von C.C. Berg, J.C. van Leur, C.C. Berg, H.G. Quaritch Wales, The early Indian scholars who entered, who engaged in research on South-East Asia included Romesh Chandra Majumdar, K.A. Nilakantha Sastri, Phanindra Nath Bose (*Indian Colony in Siam*, Lahore, 1927), B.R. Chatterji (*Indian Cultural Influence in Cambodia*), Kalidas Nag, P.C. Bagchi, B. Ch. Chhabra, Himangsu Bhusan Sarkar, Nihar Ranjan Ray (*Brahmanical Gods in Burma*, 1932 and *Buddhism in Burma*, 1936), S.K. Saraswati, D.P. Ghosh, O.C. Ganguly (*The Art of Java*, 1927), Ananda K. Coomaraswamy (*History of Indian and Indonesian Art*).

REFERENCES

B.N. Mukherjee, *External Trade of Early North-Eastern India*, Vikas, 1992.

Charles F. Keyes, *The Golden Peninsula*, Macmillan, 1977.

D. Nath (ed.), *Reopening of the Stilwell Road*, MAKAIAS, New Delhi.

David K. Wyatt, *Thailand: A Short History*, Bangkok, 1982.

D.G.E. Hall, *South-East Asia*, London, 1955.

Foreign Affairs Office, Yunnan Provincial Peoples Government, *Minority Nationalities*, 1990.

Frank M. LeBar, Gerald C. Hickey, *et al.*, *Ethnic Groups of Mainland*, South-East Asia, New Heaven, 1964.

H.B. Sarkar, *Cultural Relations between India and South-East Asian Countries*, ICCR, Motilal, 1985.

N. Ganesan and Kyaw Yin Hlaing ed., *Myanmar: State, Society and Ethnicity*, ISEAS, Singapore, 2007.

Nayanjot Lahiri, *Pre-Ahom Assam*, Munshiram, 1991.

Nicholas Tarling (ed.), *The Cambridge History of South-East Asia*, 1992.

R. Panth, *Buddhism and Culture of North-East India*, Nava Nalanda Mahavihara, Nalanda, 2004.

Sachchidanand Sahai and Neeru Misra (eds.), *Mapping Connections Indo-Thai Historical and Cultural Linkages*, Mantra, New Delhi, 2006.

24

MARGINAL VISIBILITY: Representation of Women of Assam in 19th and 20th Century Historical Narratives

Priyam Goswami

"... to be deprived of a past is to inherit an impoverished present and a future sealed off from change".[1]

I

For long, women have been denied their rightful place in history. Historical discourses generally reflect the views of a patriarchal social system and treat women as incidental rather than an integral part of the historical narrative. As a result, the public role of women has been largely undermined. The history that is taught in schools and colleges casts men as dominant subjects. As such, the way the students understand the past will inevitably influence the way they think about the present and consider the future. Joan Wallach Scott in her book, *Gender and the Politics of History*, argues that history as a discipline has failed to reflect upon knowledge of the past, choosing instead to reproduce it.[2] From her perspective, studies of history have perpetuated a view of the past whereby men are well established as dominant and universal subjects, central historical actors who have come to represent moments of historical significance. Traditional historical writings have often rendered women invisible unless they were queens or empresses. Occasionally historical narratives singled out one woman for special attention, but by and large, issues that were intimately connected with the lives of women were generally overlooked and little was known about the ways in which women shaped, influenced, and made history. As a result they perpetuated the absence of women in our historical understanding and memory. The universality of male history is so normalized that until recently hardly anyone questioned the marginal visibility of women in historical narratives. With the socio-political changes of the late 1960s, however, historical enquiry has expanded to include a focus on race, class and gender. This literature has begun placing women's varied experiences worldwide in historical context and rather than perpetuating dominant narratives, today, attempts are being made to reread history and to represent what has always been there, but has been neglected, abandoned and forgotten. It is an attempt to perceive women in history less as a separate subject than as a way of thinking, a "strategy by which to focus on . . . that which traditional history has obscured". It is a route by which the habit of treating the history of women as anecdotal, merely a collection "of missing facts and views" can be bypassed And more than anything else, it is an intellectual exercise, calling into question "the claim to universality which 'History' generally assumes as a given" and identifying relationships of power that the powerful prefer to conceal.[3]

This chapter is an endeavour to probe into the missing women from the historical narrative of Assam and historicize their role in the struggle for freedom. An attempt will also be made to briefly draw parallels with the representation of women in the armed struggles in the recent history of Assam.

The nineteenth century is of particular significance in the history of Assam. The cumulative effect of English education, the growth of industries, trade and commerce, the development of the transport and communication network and, above all, the influx of new ideas, brought about radical changes in mindset of an elite section in Assamese society. A wide variety of issues were discussed and debated upon by the emerging intelligentsia and in the process, ideas and attitudes underwent a profound change. A significant development occurred in the realm of changing attitudes towards women, though opinions differed. A remarkable significance of this debate, however, was that it gave women a visibility which had been denied to them earlier. For centuries they had remained in the periphery of society and their problems had always been relegated to the background. The subordinated position of women had implied that their miseries and pain were not meant to be articulated, much less discussed in public. In their plea for the creation of a just social order for women, the reformers now brought issues related to women into the public space.

Towards the end of the century, however, debates on women's issues gradually lost its centrality and focus, making way for the larger issues of political nationalism. In Assam social conditions of the period were such that participation of women in political affairs was beyond comprehension. Hence, the question of female participation in the early political organizations like the *Jorhat Sarvajanik Sabha*, the Assam Association or the Surma Valley Conference did not arise. But by the second decade of the twentieth century significant changes had taken place. Education had produced a small section of "new women" whose interests went beyond the household. This generation of educated women acted. They articulated the needs of women, critiqued their society and the foreign rulers and developed their own institutions. Inspired by the activities of the *Bharat Mahila Parishad* (1904) and *Bharat Stree Mahamandal* (1910) (none of which had any branch in Assam), the women of Dibrugarh under the leadership of Hemoprova Das, formed the first women's organization in the province in 1915. Subsequently, similar organizations were set up at Nagaon and different other places. Although the objective of these organizations was socio-cultural regeneration[4] rather than political in nature, their importance lies in the fact that they served as the pioneering medium for the expression of "women's opinion". In the absence of a provincial organization, they used the platform of the Assam *Chhatra Sanmilan* (Assam Students' Association) and the *Asom Sahitya Sabha* (Assam Literary Society) to voice their opinions. Lakshmiprova Chaliha, Chandrakanti Das and Chandraprova Saikiani were the first women representatives at the Assam *Chhatra Sanmilan* session held at Tezpur in 1918. Unfortunately, very little of these early initiatives has been recorded.

In course of time women became an integral part of the Gandhian movement. He projected them as symbols of courage, intelligence, perseverance, robust independence and power and not as stereotypes of submission, subservience, self effacement, helplessness and patience. But Gandhi did not want to involve women in direct action. In fact, he inducted women because they were considered self sacrificing, able to endure pain and were essentially non-violent in nature. He did not visualize any fundamental division of labour or departure from normal social relations of a woman as wife and mother. And herein lies an inherent dichotomy in Gandhi's views on women.

Gandhi's call to women, nevertheless, had an immediate liberating effect and he was able to draw large numbers of women into the vortex of the struggle although he perpetuated the image of the traditional Indian woman. The fact that there was no material weaponry involved, made women equal, or perhaps even better fighters, campaigning, protesting, fasting and donating to the cause of freedom. As Geraldine

Forbes has commented, "the nature of their work influenced how women saw themselves and how others saw their potential contribution to national development".[5]

Assam was no exception to this general scenario. Initially, social conservatism stood in the way of the participation of women in the movement and active participation was limited to a small section of women like Bidyutprova Devi, Girija Devi (sister of Tarun Ram Phukan), Hemanta Kumari Devi, Dharmada Devi, Nalinibala Devi (wife, sister and daughter of Nabin Chandra Bordoloi), Pushpalata Das, Guneswari Nath and Chandraprova Saikiani, among a few others. All of them belonged to or had connections with families of Congress leaders. They organized meetings, both in rural and urban areas, to spread the messages of non-cooperation, *swadeshi* and constructive work. But their task was not easy. Very often they had to confront hostile situations, especially in remote rural areas, but the fact that they persisted despite threats to their lives on several occasions, is testimony to their commitment to the cause.[6]

Gandhi's visit to Assam in 1921 provided the much needed impetus to their work. His appeal went beyond "respectable" women to women marginalized by middle class society. As an example, the case of Mongri, a tea labourer mistress of a European planter may be cited. Mongri, alias Malati *mem*, was an alcoholic. She was so influenced by Gandhi that she not only gave up drinking, but subsequently also actively participated in the anti-liquor drive. Mongri died in a clash that occurred during the picketing of liquor shops and is in fact the first woman in Assam to be killed for participation in the Non-Cooperation programme. But the significant question is — how many people have even heard of her or know of her courage? In Godebori, a remote village in Kamrup district, Bhanumati Talukdar, a mother of three children, enrolled herself as a full time worker of the Congress. Referred to as *Volunteerani* Bai by the local people, Gandhi called her the Sarojini of Assam. Pramila Medak, of the Mishing community of Golaghat, remained an active worker despite being excommunicated by her community for defying social restrictions and joining the Non-Cooperation Movement. Mongri, Bhanumati and Pramila are just three stray examples. There were hundreds of others like them whose varied work and sacrifices have remained unrecognized and unrecorded.

Women's participation in the freedom struggle was at three levels: (1) women as part of the great mass of the people who joined the *satyagraha* programmes; (2) women as a small group who took up social issues like *khadi* or the problem of the *harijans*; (3) a small section who believed that the end justified the means and, therefore, had no qualms at adopting revolutionary methods. Gandhi used women's role in the *khadi* movement to convince men that women's participation was essential if *swadeshi* was to succeed. In fact, the spinning and weaving skills of the women in Assam strengthened his faith in their capacity to help the nation and themselves[7] and this immediately widened the scope of the movement drawing women from rural areas into it in large numbers. In Assam, most women concentrated primarily on propaganda and constructive work, but the very fact that they came out of their homes to take part in processions and picket opium shops and liquor dens was in itself very liberating.

In an attempt to bridge the rural-urban divide, women's organizations had been formed from time to time, but working as they did in isolated segments, it was extremely difficult for them to coordinate their activities in the absence of a provincial forum. Hence, they were compelled to use other platforms like the *Asom Sahitya Sabha* and *Assam Chhatra Sanmilan* to voice their opinion. With the passage of time, the necessity of an independent provincial women's forum that would enable women to express their views fearlessly and without any inhibitions was increasingly felt. At the initiative of Benudhar Rajkhowa, President of the 1926 session of the *Asom Sahitya Sabha*, and with support from others, a meeting was held at Bijni Hall, Dhubri, with the purpose of forming a provincial women's organization. Thus, the Assam *Mahila Samiti* came into existence in 1926 with Chandraprova Saikiani as its first Secretary. Subsequently, branches were set up all over the province.

Initially, the majority of the *Mahila Samitis* were middle class organizations and too urban to appeal to the greater section of Assamese women. In course of time, however, their efforts opened up avenues for innovative activities of social reform which in turn involved large sections of women at the local level.[8] Women's issues were articulated from time to time though their immediate concern appears to have been the mobilization of women for political agitation. They began to define their interests, propose solutions and take action. This indirectly shaped the movement for women's rights and legitimized their claim to a place in the governance of the province. Public and the private spaces no doubt continued to exist as separate categories, but the usual definitions of appropriate behaviour were redefined. Looked at from this angle, Assamese women had indeed taken a big stride forward.

The initiative taken by women inspired the younger generation of girls. In 1930, Pushpalata Das, along with Sarla Saxena, Punyaprava

Barua and Jyotsna Majumdar, organized the *Mukti Sangha*, to mobilize girls in the national movement. Their fiery speeches electrified young minds who pledged, in words written in their own blood, to fight for *Purna Swaraj*. The rapidly increasing membership and the activities of the *Sangha*, caused grave concern to the government and Pushpalata, who was then the Union Secretary, Panbazar Girls' High School, was expelled from the institution. The Government agreed to reinstate her on condition that her mother signed a bond guaranteeing her "good behaviour". Swarnalata, Pushpalata's mother, refused to give this undertaking. The support of her family emboldened her further and rather than defusing her spirit, the incident ignited the spark in Pushpalata's into a flame.[9] Inspired by her courage and commitment to the cause, several Student Committees started imparting training in martial arts for girls in order "to meet exigencies" in the ensuing Civil Disobedience movement.[10]

The call for Civil Disobedience in 1930 met with tremendous response in Assam as elsewhere in the country. With a large number of men behind the bars, women came out in thousands defying prohibitory orders to demonstrate their solidarity with the programme of the salt *satyagraha*. Women's power had been strengthened by the organizational activities carried out during the preceding years of the movement and the formation of the *Mahila Samities*. The main thrust of their activity during this period was their anti-opium campaign, which gained momentum as the days passed. The APCC Report of 1930 records with appreciation the tremendous participation of rural women, along with their urban counterparts, during this phase of the movement. In fact, even the British Prime Minister observed that he was not afraid of Gandhi, but of the innumerable illiterate women of India who bore the message of revolt in every household.[11] But despite their massive involvement in the movement, women often found themselves sidelined in the organizational work. The need for a women's wing in the Congress was being acutely felt. After a great deal of persuasion from women leaders like Vijaylakshmi Pandit, Mridula Sarabhai, Aruna Asif Ali and Sucheta Kripalani, among others, it was eventually decided in 1940 to set up women's wings as an integral part of the Congress at both the national and provincial levels. In Assam, the women's wing was set up in September 1940 with Pushpalata and Amalprova as joint secretaries. The following year, the All Assam Girl Students' Committee was formed at Shillong.

In the 1940s, women in general began to claim a more active role for themselves in the public space and fought with their male counterparts during the last phase of the struggle. This female activism was most visible during the "Quit India Movement". In the face of unprecedented police repression and with large numbers of men in prison, prominent women leaders took upon themselves the task of coordinating the activities. In Assam, Chandraprova Saikiani was one of the main guiding forces among women. While the majority of the women concentrated on programmes of reconstruction and, as Congress volunteers, also enrolled themselves as members of the *Saṇti Sena,* a small, but determined section was much more radical in their activities. Violence and sabotage were their weapons of choice. The "Quit India Movement", powered by the simple, but electrifying slogans of "do or die" and "*Bharat choro*" had unleashed an unprecedented fervour throughout Assam. Influenced by the revolutionary activities elsewhere in India, a section of Assamese youth took to militancy and justified their actions in the context of spiraling police atrocities on non-violent crowds. By 1943 there were as many as 32 underground volunteer camps at Bajali alone. Similar camps were also organized at different places of Kamrup, Darrang, Nagoan and Sibsagar districts. These local cells coordinated the activities of their members, many of whom were women.[12] In 1942, the *Mrityu Bahini*[13] (Suicide Squad) was formed to carry out subversive activities in a more organized manner. Women members no doubt pledged allegiance to the male leaders like Hem Chandra Barua and Sankar Chandra Barua, but a new image of female militancy presented itself. Kanaklata, Ratnabala Phukan, Buddheswari Hazarika, Khahuli Nath and Damayanti Bora were all active members of the *Mrityu Bahini* and were acclaimed as exemplary women among radical circles. But there were hundreds of others, ordinary women who, from behind the scenes, made immense contributions in hiding weapons, sheltering fugitives and encouraging men, using their domestic role to cover subversive and revolutionary activities. Many others worked as spies, money raisers, conspirators and saboteurs. Female militancy was a well known fact that had a romantic currency. But the recognition ended there. Society at large disapproved of those who had crossed the socially constructed boundary of feminine modesty by engaging in violent revolutionary activities. Such strong traditionalist moorings, in fact worked as strong deterrence to the social emancipation of women.

Gandhi's initial disapproval of the "secret methods and activities involving violence" and his insistence on the constructive programme led to a temporary slowdown in sabotage activities. A section of women led by Kalyani Dutta and Amalprova Das, both of whom visited strife torn Noakhali, took the initiative in working towards communal harmony.

We have observed the varied nature of women's participation in the freedom struggle, but significantly, even after six decades of Independence, much of their contribution remains unrecognized. Ironically, the Congress leaders themselves paid little attention to women's contribution and except for allowing them some symbolic presence, never included women in any decision making process. It is not surprising, therefore, that representation of women in the historical narratives has been found to be very selective. In writings on the freedom struggle in Assam, the activities of only a handful of women are repeatedly cited. Pushed to the periphery, the majority of the women who contributed to the movement are only marginally visible. Unfortunately, this phenomenon is also evident in the representation of women in the struggles of post-independence Assam.

II

In recent years North-East India has become a hot bed of multiple conflicts. Starting with the Naga separatist movement in the 1940s, conflicts have proliferated in most of the states in the region especially since the late 1970s. The nature of these conflicts is such that the methods of warfare penetrate into towns, villages and homes of the common people. The use of systematic force through insurgency, reduction of democratic space, rape, violations of human rights, etc. have resulted in perpetuating fear and insecurity and thereby fragmenting the emotional fabric of the community.[14]

Anuradha Dutta argues that there are certain common, structural, institutional and psychological features which have combined to form the preconditions for insurgency in the region. Among these, she mentions unequal distribution of wealth, poverty, underdevelopment, poor governance, collapse of the traditional social structure, rampant corruption, confusion generated by modernization and factionalism.[15] Assam, too, has been plagued with violent social and political movements over the past several decades. The multi-ethnicity of Assam has been attacked from a narrow ethnic position of identity politics and armed opposition groups, formed on ethnic lines, have emerged in recent years to push forth their demands for greater autonomy. In fact, today there are as many as 34 insurgent groups, large and small, operating here. The result is that this once peaceful state has become a cauldron of violence, terror and insecurity.

In such conflict situations, women suffer in a variety of ways, irrespective of whether they are direct participants or are outside it. In any case, the majority of the victims are civilians and because of the large number of victims among the civilian population, the volume of refugees and internally displaced persons has increased enormously in recent years. Uprooted population groups, particularly women and children, live for years in camps with limited access to vital resources. The lack of attention to their particular needs, attacks and acts of violence in the camps perpetuate their insecurity.

It is important to note here that the women in Assam cannot be classified as a homogenous category of analysis because of the tremendous diversity in ethnic populations as well as economic and social differences. But underlying this diversity are certain common features — basic attitudes, social prejudices and male dominance — which usually act against the woman and marginalized her at every level. In what ways have these impacted on her performance? What has been her role in the circumstances? Is she an active participant in the peace building process or is she a mute spectator? Have her efforts at peace building been recognized? What role does she play in the decision making process? Has the female combatant been able to find the rightful recognition within her respective organizational set up? Is her voice heard at all? These are certain important questions that need to be addressed because these women have shaped, influenced, and made history and without their perspective our historical understanding and memory of the conflicts will remain deficient and imperfect. It is unfortunate that not much study has been done on the singular contribution of women in Assam towards understanding the dynamics of armed conflict and violence in society perpetuated by counter-insurgency measures.

Women can play and have been playing a prominent role at various levels in all the phases of conflict in Assam. During a conflict period the threat of violence is extremely high. Fear and insecurity, distrust and suspicion, the destruction of livelihoods, loss of family and death are just a few example of the problems confronted. In the circumstances, it is the ordinary women in the village who have had to bear the main brunt in a strife torn society. She is compelled to play multiple roles — that of a mother, a bread winner and even a social activist in view of the proliferation of societal evils like alcoholism, drug abuse, sexual promiscuity and HIV/AIDS, among others. It is the woman who takes the strain of keeping the family together during such times In fact, a woman's survival strategies in this context proves her resilience and creativity. It is ironical that in spite of her significant contribution the ordinary woman is more often than not sidelined and her work remains unacknowledged.

In Assam, several women's initiatives have emerged from time to time in an effort at peace building. The *Matri Manch, Anchalik Mahila Sajagata Samiti, Chapar Anchlik Mahila Samiti*, All Bodo Womens' Welfare Federation, among a host of other NGOs, have attempted to create frameworks of activism to intervene in the cause for the protection of women's interests and campaign for peace. Through targeted actions and training in the fields of peace building and human rights, the organizations have been able to raise awareness among the affected and have succeeded in encouraging them to demand for their rights. The psycho-social support provided by women to victims of violence, trauma management and reintegration of widows and former combatants into society has helped in preventing social and economic isolation.

Conclusion

Women's leadership and civic engagement has historically led to positive and progressive social change in most communities. Women's participation in decision making is particularly crucial in conflict ridden situations in all its three phases — before, during and after the conflict. When women's voices are heard, recognized and recorded as valuable, more sustainable economic and social stability can be achieved. In this context, Elizabeth Rehn has observed that "it is crucial that women's voices are heard and their work on the ground is recognized, valued and supported. Decisions should be made with them, not for them".[16] The international declarations have affirmed a woman's right to participate in politics; peace building and the economic development of their societies, but none-the-less, women continue to be systematically excluded from official peace talks and decision-making processes. This negates a democratic process and prevents women from participating in events that directly impacts their security and leadership options.

In both armed struggles as well as peace-time initiatives, women find themselves at the receiving end. Although women often leave the confines of their homes to sustain struggles, they are not accorded decision-making powers and remain marginalized. The mobilization of women for the purposes of furthering the cause of a struggle and then pushing them to the vestiges of public memory is a common feature even today. Will the historical narratives of tomorrow give adequate representation to the women of today? Or will they be reduced to mere footnotes in any historical narrative? This remains to be seen.

NOTES AND REFERENCES

1. K. Lalita *et al.*, "We Were Making History . . .", Life Stories of Women in the Telangana People's Struggle, 1989, p. 19.
2. Joan Wallach Scott, *Gender and the Politics of History*, New York, 1999, p. 17.
3. Linda K. Kerber, in Foreword of Gerda Lerner, *The Majority Finds Its Past: Placing Women in History*, University of North Carolina Press, 2005.
4. Their main objective was the upliftment of the Assamese society, particularly of women and children, in educational, cultural and economic matters. A significant thrust area was activity related to making women self reliant and in this respect, their initiative in setting up of *sipini bharals* (weavers' stores) was commendable.
5. Geraldine Forbes, *Women in Modern India*, Cambridge, 2004, p. 122.
6. Dipti Sharma, *Assamese Women in the Freedom Struggle*, Kolkata, 1993, p. 66.
7. *Young India*, 7 September 1922.
8. The general aim of the *Mahila Samities* was to cater to the all round development of women in Assam. With this end in view their activities centred round female education, sanitation and heath care, child care, and economic self-reliance.
9. D. Sharma, *op. cit.*, p. 136.
10. *Asomiya*, 10 May 1931, cited in D. Sharma, *op. cit.*, p. 147.
11. Puspalata Das, "Women Satyagrahis and the Quit India Movement"in Arun Bhuyan ed., *Nationalist Upsurge in Assam*, Guwahati, 2000, p. 150.
12. For details refer D. Sharma, *op. cit.*, pp. 269-81.
13. Membership to the *Mrityu Bahini* was conditional. Both men and women between 18 and 50 years who were physically fit were eligible, but only those with total commitment to the cause were inducted under an oath of secrecy.
14. For details refer, Triveni Goswami, *Role of Women as Peace Builders*, Guwahati, 2006, pp. 9-12.
15. Anuradha Dutta and Ratna Bhuyan (ed.), *Genesis of Conflict and Peace: Understanding North-East India*, Vol. 1, New Delhi, 2007, p. 17.
16. E. Rehn and J. Sirleaf, *Women, War and Peace: The Independent Experts: Assessment on the Impact of Armed Conflict on Women and Women's Role in Peace Building*, New York, 2000.

25

INDIA'S NORTH-EAST: A Geo-Strategic Survey

S.P. Kar

North-East India has a unique geo-political position. The region consists of seven full-fledged States of India,[1] but is bounded in its north, east, south and west by other independent countries, except for a narrow corridor[2] that connects it with the rest of the country. By its very geographical location, it has inherited an extremely strategic spot, encircled as it is by an unstable and unpredictable environment. It faces China (the world's second biggest military power) in the north, Myanmar (a hotbed of insurgency with myriads of 'rebel groups' at work at cross purposes) in the east and Bangladesh (a relatively immature democracy with a number of *jehadi* groups on the prowl) in the west and south-west. The only succour for the region is the placid existence of friendly Bhutan on its north-west.

The most notable aspect of the history of Sino-Indian relations has been China's unfailing duplicity in its dealings with India; the stories of *Panch Sheel*,[3] armed aggression against India in 1962, border talks spread over decades, periodic skirmishes on the international border between the two countries, China's territorial claims over Ladakh and Arunachal Pradesh, diversion by China of the water of the Brahmaputra in its higher reaches, China's active support with arms and logistics to Indian insurgents, clandestine arms trade, and many other issues bear out her manipulative diplomacy and geo-political games. It has now become a test of India's patience and wits to deal with the Chinese, particularly because they are hardly amenable to reason. 'Denial' and 'bullying' are two instruments of foreign policy for them. This is more so because India admittedly is a soft power.

The North-East is a special target of China's military power and economic clout that it has been able to acquire in the last sixty-four years of an autocratic communist regime. They are now calling Arunachal Pradesh as 'southern Tibet'. They even objected to India's President and Prime Minister visiting Arunachal Pradesh. They didn't allow IAS officers of Arunachali origin to visit China along with other Indian officers. They have built up a massive military presence in Tibet, said to be of the strength of 2,00,000 soldiers[4] and backed by an infra-structure of thousands of kilometres of rail-track and surface roads right up to and parallel to the entire length of the MacMahon Line and the borders with Sikkim and Bhutan. They have constructed a good number of air-fields and air-bases in Tibet itself with hundreds of warplanes deployed therein. They have positioned in Qinghai province (Inner Tibet) their inter-continental ballistic missiles with nuclear warheads aimed at Indian 'targets'. They send in spies to places in Arunachal Pradesh to subvert the loyalty of the tribes there. They engage with the Bhutan Government 'to settle' the kingdom's northern border, basically to punch a hole in India's defence across the Chumbi valley. They provide shelter to India's fugitives — the likes of Paresh Barua, Anthony Shimrey, *et al.* — and help them to continue insurgency in the North-East with a steady supply of arms. They dump Indian market with their low quality industrial products manufactured in Yunnan province. They indulge in 'cyber war' to get at our defence secrets. All these have a long and developing history.

Background

Geographically, India meets China across the territory of Tibet. Tibet was an independent country till it was subjugated by China in 1950. The language, culture, rituals and heritage of Tibet have always been distinctly different from those of China, but very close to Indian ethos. Indian and Tibetan scholars and pilgrims used to exchange visits to each other's country from time immemorial. Mount Kailash and Manas Sarovar, though located in Tibet, have always been visited by Indian pilgrims, while Nalanda and Bodh Gaya in India, among other places, were perennial attractions for the Tibetans. The status of Tibet as a sovereign country gets reflected from the fact that it had participated as such in the first Asian Relations Conference held in New Delhi in April, 1947.[5] Tibet used to issue passports and visas till its occupation by the Chinese in 1950.

India's relation with Tibet used to be regulated by the Indo-Tibetan Convention of 1904. Under it, the British Indian government had established a mission at Lhasa (Tibet's capital) and three trade agencies at Gyantse, Yatung and Gartok in Tibet. The convention also provided for a trade agreement between the two countries; and also deployment of two military detachments and maintenance of Post and Telegraph services in Tibet by India. India naturally inherited these rights from the British when she became independent in August 1947. By an Anglo-Chinese treaty in 1906, the Indian rights in were recognized by China. In the 1914 Simla conference attended by the representatives of the governments of British India, Tibet and China, the boundary between India and Tibet in India's North-East was negotiated and defined in terms of the MacMahon Line going, by and large, on the crest of the watershed of the Himalayas. India, since then, has been respecting the Line as the international border between India and Tibet.

Following the communist take-over of the mainland China in 1949, the Chinese government lost no time in laying claim of sovereignty over Tibet and gained full control over the country by the end of October, 1950. India under the leadership of the then Prime Minister, Pandit Nehru, made grave errors in her foreign policy and acquiesced in the occupation of Tibet by the Chinese. Despite timely warnings by Sardar Patel, Rajendra Prasad, Dr. B.R. Ambedkar and other top leaders of the country, Nehru allowed the Chinese to consolidate their occupation of Tibet. In no time, India withdrew her military mission as well as the civilian personnel manning P&T services, etc. from Tibet, thus unwittingly allowing the Chinese to reach up to MacMahon Line in the north-east India. (This was in addition to their occupation of huge chunks of Indian territory in Ladakh in the west and Barahouti, etc. in the middle sector.)[6]

In those critical years, Pandit Nehru was totally unmindful of the possibilities of the Chinese communists turning into India's strongest adversary. Even as early as September 1949, "a Chinese magazine accused the Indian Prime Minister of aiding imperialist designs for the annexation of Tibet" (*With Nehru in Foreign Office*, by Subimal Dutta, p. 76). At the same time, "the Communist radio asserted that Tibet was a part of China and the British and the American imperialists, and their Nehru, are plotting a coup in Lhasa for the annexation of Tibet" (*India, from Curzon to Nehru and After*, by Durga Das, pp. 294-95, 1969).

The 1950s saw some unreal bonhomie between India and China even as the latter was scheming to expand territorially into Indian territories. *Panch Sheel*, a concept of peaceful co-existence of nations, dominated the outward face of India-China relations since 1954, while the Chinese had no compunction in raising claims after claims on Indian territories.

"The Five Principles of Peaceful Coexistence, known in India as the *Panch Sheel*, are a set of principles to govern relations between states. Their first formal codification in treaty form was in an agreement between by China and India in 1954. They were enunciated in the preamble to the "Agreement (with exchange of notes) on trade and intercourse between Tibet Region of China and India", which was signed at Peking on 29 April, 1954. This agreement stated the five principles as:

1. Mutual respect for each other's territorial integrity and sovereignty,
2. Mutual non-aggression,
3. Mutual non-interference in each other's internal affairs,
4. Equality and mutual benefit, and
5. Peaceful co-existence".

By 1959, small skirmishes between the border forces of India and China became a regular occurrence. Meanwhile, the Dalai Lama, the spiritual and temporal ruler of Tibet, had to flee his country following the violence perpetrated by the Chinese occupation forces in Tibet. He entered India in March 1959, through Tawang, a small locality on the tri-junction of India, Bhutan and Tibet. India granted the Dalai Lama political asylum, a fact that annoyed the Chinese immensely. Pandit Nehru made his last ditch effort to remain conciliatory to the Chinese in the parleys he had with Chinese premier Chou-en-lai in April 1960, but the Chinese showed an extreme degree of intransigence.

The Flashpoint

The most critical area of land-space, so far as the geo-political threat to north-east India is concerned, is decidedly the State of Arunachal Pradesh, which was previously known as the North-East Frontier Agency (NEFA). It is the biggest of all the north-eastern States, having an area of 83,743 sq.km. and a population of 10,97,968 (2001 census). It has about 82 tribes and sub-tribes. Owing to the high mountain ranges that separate the narrow valleys and the turbulent rivers that cut across the valleys largely from the north to the south, its administrative districts (earlier called Divisions) are generally not accessible to one another except through the Assam plains.[7]

Tibet borders the entire northern boundary of Arunachal Pradesh. The north-western parts of the State were under the control of the Monpa kingdom of Monyul that flourished between 500 BC and 600 BC. Subsequently, the said area came under somewhat loose control of Tibet and Bhutan, especially in its northern areas. Then the area moved over to Ahom, and later British, control. Very little is known about the history of the rest of the State.

Chinese Aggression of 1962

After Tibet's military occupation by China in 1950, India and China came face to face — eyeball to eyeball — so far as the borders between the two countries were concerned. Despite India's friendly gestures towards China ever since the establishment of the Communist regime there, the latter refused to recognize the MacMahon Line[8] — the historical boundary line between Arunachal Pradesh and Tibet. Tension started growing between the two countries since the mid-1950s on the validity of the said Line as also that of the control over other areas in the western Himalayas, right up to Ladakh in J&K. Gradually, but inevitably, a battle of nerves ensued between the two countries, which culminated in an armed aggression by China against India in October 1962. Though China later vacated many of the areas occupied by it in Arunachal Pradesh (then called NEFA) during the aggression, the myth of inviolability of the great Himalayan barrier on our northern borders no longer remained valid.

The border of Arunachal Pradesh with Tibet was breached in depth by the Chinese Army in 1962 at places and in areas wide apart from one another, — from Tawang and Sela Pass in the west to Longju in the middle and Walong in the far east. The aggressors had stopped a little short of the Assam plains in this venture. The persistence even now of the Chinese Government with their claims on many parts of Arunachal Pradesh makes the situation — the defence of the entire North-East — a matter of concern for India.

Geography of the Area

The said border, which, in effect, is India's border with China in India's north-east, is dominated by the Great Himalayas. The great mountain, including its lower ranges and foothills, has a width of nearly 300 km on the average, extending from the tri-junction of Bhutan, Arunachal and Tibet to Kibithoo, the easternmost point on the border. The Brahmaputra, flowing eastwards as the Yarlung Tsangpo from a middle point in Tibetan Himalayas,[9] takes a big bend[10] and enters Arunachal Pradesh as the Dihang (also known as the Siang); it then flows southwards across the State and takes yet another bend before descending on to the Assam plains to flow westwards as the Brahmaputra. The Lohit, the Subansiri, the Noa Dihing, the Kameng and the Tirap are some of the other big rivers that flow through Arunachal Pradesh and join the Brahmaputra at different points. All these rivers and their tributary streams emerge from the overlooking snowy peaks and are fast-flowing with crystal clear water.

Brief History

The British Government, which took charge — though it was a nominal charge — of the entire North-East following the Treaty of Yandaboo in 1826, left the mountainous region of what is now Arunachal Pradesh virtually untouched and sustained it as a 'forbidden land', because they wanted it to remain more or less as a 'buffer zone' between this remote part of India on one hand and Tibet and China on the other. The British policy of keeping the land in total isolation from the mainstream life and development process[11] was slowly discarded when a first batch of pioneers — volunteers handpicked by the first Prime Minister of India Jawaharlal Nehru — went to the then NEFA in December 1953. In the words of Markot Ramunny, a Deputy Advisor to the Governor of Assam and Development Commissioner for NEFA (1957-59), the Central Government "approached the problem of administering and developing 'the hidden land', destroying nothing of its culture and tradition and denying nothing to the people".[12] In pursuance of the policy, a track was opened in September 1958 through the land of Monpas. In a graphic description of the pioneering efforts that commenced in the 1950s to remove the artificial curtain that kept the area isolated, Ramunny writes:

"Monpas are Buddhists. In the olden days, every third child in a family was sent to the monastery to become a Lama. The most prominent building in any village was the Gompa with its beautiful paintings. At the entrance and exit, every village had the 'kakalings'. These had beautiful ceilings with figures of the Buddha and other incarnated Lamas, Dalai Lama's (image among them) being the most prominent. Along the village paths, there were longish rectangular-roofed stone structures known as 'manes' with prayer wheels inside. People always kept to the left of the mane, invoking the blessings of the Holy Spirit inside. A month's supplies for 10 officers and staff were carried by porters. The administrative trail was long. In all, about 50 people moved from village to village, climbed peaks, went down valleys, crossed rivers on rickety wooden bridges, and waded through rivulets to reach Tawang. Most of the places we visited then would be missing from the tourist itinerary today as the road has been laid along the easiest gradient".

Amongst the most prominent tribes in the State, the Akas, the Nishis and the Mishmis live primarily in the districts of Subanasiri, Siang, Lohit, etc. The Singphos mostly live in Tirap and Changlang, the easternmost districts of the State, as well as in the contiguous Margherita sub-division of Tinsukia district of Assam. The Singphos had helped the British pioneers into the area to get acquainted with the luxuriant growth of tea plants in upper Assam. The discovery of tea by the British in this part of the country motivated the rapid colonization by them of this distant land. The Singphos also had a history of giving a long fight in localized skirmishes against the British rulers. During the Second World War, the hardworking Singphos came out in big numbers to help General Stilwell construct the 1725 km long Stilwell Road from Ledo to Kunming in a record time. The valley of the Burhidihing river is largely inhabited by the tribe, along with Tangsa, Apatani and other smaller tribes. Singphos are also found in comparatively big numbers in the Kachin and Chin hills of Myanmar and have a close interaction across the international borders with their kith and kin in both the countries.

The State of Development

The state of development in Arunachal Pradesh, in respect of roads, communication, electricity, schools and so on, was, to say the least, primitive at the time of India's independence. Indeed these primary requirements of life did not even exist in the entire region, thanks to the 'hands off' policy the British Government had pursued in respect of most of the hill regions of the North-East. Ramunny had recorded at some time in the 1950s that "the older generation seemed to be unaware of (the existence of) India". Terrace farming (mainly of maize) and sheep rearing were the basic occupation of the simple people. Garments were made of the wool from the sheep. At higher altitudes, yaks were in use. The inhabitants of this unpolluted land were, however, conscious of the need for manuring the soil for cultivation; they thus would take all the ash from the kitchen to the field. Toilets were so constructed that the night soil would collect in baskets kept below the ground. Once in a month, these were taken out to be spread as manure in the fields. Cattle dung was also used extensively as manure. The villagers grew plenty of vegetables. Drinking of *laupani*, a kind of cereal beer has been an age-old practice. The people were very hospitable to guests. However, as Toynbee observed elsewhere, the entire region comprising the present Arunachal Pradesh "stood still for centuries".

As a logical consequence of the frontier policy of the British in the North-East (that kept the frontier population absolutely isolated during the entire period of their rule), some of the tribes in the interior areas of Arunachal Pradesh remained highly suspicious of outsider plainsmen, who ever made it bold to make an attempt to explore their home space. Even a friendly approach to them by outsiders evoked a violent response. The following incident bears testimony to the situation that obtained in the years following India's independence.[13]

It was in late 1953. In the northern part of then undivided Siang Division (later divided into East and West Siang Districts) and astride the Subansiri River, an un-surveyed area of a few thousand sq. kilometers that abound with high-altitude mountains, deep valleys and virgin forests just on the south of the MacMahon Line, was sought to be explored by the administration. The area was home to a fierce Thagin tribe, which has been resisting, rather violently, the para-military Assam Rifles in the latter's attempts to penetrate the valley and establish contact with them. Ominously, there were also reports of a number of foreigners (purportedly Tibetan or Chinese) having visited the area more than once. The reports added that these foreigners had distributed presents among the Thagins and asked them to resist Indian administrative control.

In view of the development, the administration decided to send in a strong column of the Assam Rifles[14] to the area to investigate the information received and to allay the fears of the Thagins. On October 22, 1953, the column reached the Achingmori camp, erected ironically for it by the local Thagins. Finding the disposition of the tribals not at all hostile, the troops took it easy and got engaged wholeheartedly in settling down in their new home in the new environment, posting a minimum number of sentries in a routine fashion. The locals, meanwhile, steadily gathered at and near the new camp in enormous numbers, plausibly to collect token gifts of salt, etc. as was the practice in the tribal areas.[15] Even as the Thagins were gathering in such big numbers right in the camp compound, the A.R. personnel remained too busy in their chores to read the dangerous development. Then, abruptly, on a given signal, the collected crowd attacked the sentries and after quickly hacking all of them down, fell upon the rest of the party. There was little chance for the unarmed A.R. personnel (they having kept all their arms under the guard of the sentries) to retaliate or even flee. In the one-sided massacre that ensued, the commander of the column and most of the troops, including the civilian component of the group, were brutally killed. At the same time, some personnel were taken hostage by the attackers while the whole lot of government property and arms and ammunition, which the column had with it, were also carted away.

Following the incident, the Government of India mounted an operation compelling the offenders to release the surviving hostages and return the looted arms, ammunition and other properties. However, the matter was dealt with by the authorities with appropriate understanding of tribal susceptibilities within the framework of the policy laid down by Pandit Nehru for winning them over, rather than going for punitive measures as was normally done by the British government in similar cases.

The Himalayas do not form an insurmountable wall against China in this segment, though the terrain remains one of the most difficult ones of the world. It has a good number of passes and routes across the mountain ranges through which both Tibetans and Arunachalis used to have barter trade and cultural intercourse, though to a very limited extent. Here lies the strategic importance of the State, given the history of a border war between the countries in the 1960s.

It is of significance to North-East India that so far as trade possibilities are concerned, the areas in Tibet situated across the borders of Arunachal Pradesh and Sikkim are comparatively thickly populated. According to age-old practices, people on either side of the Indo-Tibetan border go fairly deep into each other's territory for small scale trade, in some cases for barter trade.

Strategic Frontier

Some of the traditional trade routes, between Arunachal Pradesh on one side and Tibet and Myanmar on the other, are, at the same time, strategically very important. The inherent danger in the situation is that while these routes serve as passages for economic activity essential, to a large extent, for the survival of the tribes living astride them, the same routes could as well be used by the hostile neighbours to send in spies and agent provocateurs for subversive propaganda and other harmful activities. Thus, these routes, if made fully operational, might pose a danger to the region from national security point of view.[16]

In the first half of 2009, perception developed from the ground situation on the Arunachal part of the Indo-Tibetan border that China has been developing its strike capabilities across the border by strengthening its military infrastructures including airfields and deploying additional divisions dangerously close to Indian borders. This naturally makes our defence in the eastern Himalayas vulnerable and a matter of concern. Keeping the fluid situation in view, the Indian Defence Ministry proposed to take over the airstrips built in Arunachal Pradesh after the 1962 Chinese aggression, to be under the exclusive control of the Indian Air Force. The Airstrips are located at places like Walong, Mechuka, Tuting, Bijoynagar, Along, Zero, Tawang and Pasighat and are used for carrying troops and supplies to the inaccessible areas. According to press reports,[17] as a back up to the chain of Arunachal airstrips, the airfields at Tezpur and Chabua in Assam are to be upgraded and used as bases for Sukhoi-30 warplanes for defence of the region. Besides, the air bases at Bagdogra, Hashimara, Jorhat, Kalaikunda, etc. will be modernized to strengthen the defence of the region.[18] Reports further say that the Government of India have decided to locate two more Divisions of the Army in Arunachal Pradesh in the near future.

Strategic Trade Routes to Tibet and Myanmar

1. *Dibrugarh-Tezu-Walong-Kibithoo-Kahao-Rima-Chamdo*

Kibithoo is a crossing point from Tibet, very low in altitude-1,371 m Kahao is on the Lohit as it enters India. Rima (Zayui) is in Tibet, just about 10 km from the international border. The famous Rima gap is within 100 km of the courses of three great rivers — the Salween (Myanmar), the Mekong (Vietnam) and the Yangtse (China). The distances covered in the route are: Tinsukia (Assam) to Tezu = 137 km, Tezu to Hayuliang = 103 km, Hayuliang to Walong = 103 km, Walong to Kibithoo = 30 km, Kibithoo to Kahao = 1.6 km. This will become the fastest all-weather route to the Tibetan border from the Indian plains after a bridge on the Lohit is completed.[19] Known as the Walong sector, this section of the border was a scene of intense fighting between the armies of China and India in 1962. For some time, Walong — a small garrison town — went under Chinese occupation during the border conflict. Its location is of high strategic value.

The stand-off between India and China in this sector in late 2009 generated a lot of uneasiness among the people inhabiting the area, especially in the proximity of the international boundary. The last Indian security post here is Chaglagam, which is manned by the Indo-Tibetan Border Police (ITBP). An hour's track from the post is the last Indian village, called Taflagam, some 60 km south from the MacMahon Line.

The Taflagam villagers felt unsafe after they discovered the evidence of Chinese incursions in early 2009 in the mountainous forests of uninhabited Phomphom, 30 km south of MacMahon Line. The area is so tricky that the actual border still lies a good three-day track away from the last inhabited village of Taflagam. The Indian security forces do patrolling in this area — the area being so difficult that it takes a good 16-day long range patrolling (LRP) to cover the distance between Chaglagam and the MacMahon Line. The 60 km track, passing over mountains that rise up to 13,000 feet, includes stop-overs at seven camps before the troops spend two days at the final point close to the border.[20]

Patrolling by the Indian security forces hardly reaches the actual border in this sector. It has been reported that the Phomphom incursions by the Chinese were actually discovered by hunters from the local Arunachali villages. They said that the Chinese had stripped off pine barks and painted "China" in red on the trees' exposed surface. Indian soldiers brushed off the writings by the Chinese whenever they saw them. There were the Hadera and Glai Takru passes, right on the border, where the Chinese had built up mule tracks and dirt bike-roads astride the MacMahon Line. On the Indian side, it's a eight-day walk from the border to the first usable road. A 57 km road from the district headquarters Hayuliang to Chaglagam was constructed as recently as 2006. The inaccessibility of and insecurity in the area has been compelling the villagers to migrate inwards, away from the Tibetan border.[21]

China's claim that the territories that constituted Arunachal Pradesh belonged to China created a lot of misgivings in the State. Chinese agencies had, in recent times, gone so far as to brand Arunachal Pradesh as 'southern Tibet'. This naturally has angered India, especially the people of Arunachal, formidably. Though for all practical purposes, it could be a diplomatic ploy by the Chinese government to exact concessions in the border dispute in the Ladakh sector, the Arunachalis have become a great deal restless about it. The All Arunachal Pradesh Students' Union, in a reaction to the Chinese provocation, did a bonfire of Chinese goods at Itanagar and other places and warned traders against dealing in them. It is reassuring that the ire of the students got directed towards various items of use made in China, because the illegal trade in Chinese goods conducted through the cross-border routes posed an economic danger to the State and the country even otherwise. Besides, these uncharted trade routes could well be used to send in saboteurs into the region. The action of the students' union reaffirms the people's patriotic feeling — their sense of belonging to India — which is our real asset in the so-called territorial dispute with China. The students went so far as to ask the Central Government "whether it was keen to protect the territorial integrity of the country".[22]

2. *Dibrugarh-Ledo-Pangsu Pass (937 m)-Mytkina (Myanmar)-Kunming (Yunnan, China)*

This is the alignment of the Stilwel Road, constructed during the Second World War (1939-45) by the allied powers to keep the Nationalist Chinese forces of Generalissimo Chiang-Ki-Shek supplied with munitions and food. This was necessitated by the exigencies of war following the conquest of the entire South-East Asia, including its maritime routes, by Japan. With its solid foundations still intact, the road now requires some major repairs and fresh construction of bridges to make it operational. Both Kunming and Calcutta (now Kolkata) are about 1,700 km from Ledo.[23]

3. *Dibrugarh-Roing-Anipi-Mipi-Yongop La-(all having altitude of an average of 3,000 m) to Shuden Gompa (4,175 m)*

The Idu Mishmis of this region visit Tibet very often.

4. *North Lakhimpur-Along-or Passighat-Yingklong-Tuing (590 m)-Gelling (1,220 m)-Kepang La (,1915)-Kemteng-Gya Dzong (2,775 m)*

Shimong Adis living in this region also have their kith and kin in Tibet.

5. *North Lakhimpur-Along-Mechuka-up the Yagyap chu-Nepar La or Nyug La (4,700 m)-Migyitun-Kyim Dzong*

Pachakshiri Membas who inhabit this region are known as Moinbas in Tibet.

6. *North Lakhimpur-Dapporijo-Nacho-Taksing (2,400 m)-Limeking-Lhontse Dzong*

Essentially, it is a trade route by which items like Tibetan ornaments, especially brass carved bells, known locally as 'majes', used to be brought in.

7. *Tezpur-Bomdila-Tawang-Bam La (4,332 m)-Tsona Dzong*

This route is very close to Bhutan. Chinese goods are unofficially imported into Arunachal in large quantities by this route and *via* Melee La in

Bhutan. The Chinese Army had made a massive thrust through this route in 1962 and had almost reached Tezpur in Assam plains, but for the unilateral cease fire they declared on November 20, 1962. Lhasa (3,607 m), the capital of Tibet, is about 600 km along this route from the Arunachal-Tibet border. The Tibetan spiritual ruler Dalai Lama had entered India in 1959 by this route and received political asylum.

Historical Importance of Ledo-Kunming Route

A traditional trade route, this route basically follows the water course of the river Burhi Dihing and its tributary, the Tirap, across the Patkai ranges on the north-eastern corner of India's border with Myanmar. The Burhi Dihing river system flows down to the Assam plains and meets the Brahmaputra. It was by this route that groups of Mongoloid people from East Asia had been coming to North-East India since time immemorial. Tai adventurers from the kingdom of Mong-rimong-ram (situated in the China-Myanmar-Thailand border region) had started their westward journey in 1225 A.D. under the leadership of prince Su Ka Pha, and reached Tipam in Assam in 1228 A.D. after crossing the rivers (the Salween, the Irrawaddy and the Chindwin) and the deep gorges in upper Burma and the mountain passes of the Patkai ranges. They travelled through the famous Pangsu Pass to land in the Burhi Dihing basin.

The strategic nature of the route becomes obvious from the fact that even in modern times, during the Second World War, General Joseph Stilwell of the US Army constructed, roughly along the route of Sukapha's historic journey, a new road (named after himself) to maintain war supplies from India to China.[24] Starting from Ledo, it touched Lekhapani, Pangsu Pass, Nong-pong, Nog-yang Lake, Bhamo, Mytkyina and Kunming, the last place being the capital of China's Yunnan province.

In recent times, there has been a strong demand voiced in the North-East, especially in Assam and Arunachal Pradesh, for rebuilding the 1,736 km Stilwell Road that has 57 km in India, 1,040 km in Myanmar and remaining 639 km in China, to facilitate trade and commerce across the borders. Reports say China has already developed the road on their side and in fact been continuing the road's reconstruction process into Kachin province of Myanmar from their end. However, India has virtually shelved the idea of re-developing the road in view of the Kachin highlands being a hub of Indian and Myanmarese rebels. Even Myanmar did not favour the idea as the road would give the rebels "better access into the area".

Historically, this route had a lot of peace-time utility in trade as well as in migration of people from one country to another in the region. The road alignment was also used in military incursions. The Burhi Dihing played a significant role in the making of Assam's history. The Buddhist Tai communities, like Khamtis, Phakes, Aitons, Khamjangs, Turungs, Doanias, *et al.*, are believed to have entered Assam through the course of the river during the later part of the seventeenth century. The unspeakably barbarous Burmese aggression on the Ahom kingdom in early 19th century also took place through this route.[25] Another similar route of historical significance is the Tamu-Morey route across Manipur-Myanmar border.

Presently, these two primary routes from the North-East going eastwards are regarded as having enormous potential for trade, commerce and cultural activity among India, China, Myanmar, Thailand, Malaysia, Singapore and other South-East Asian countries. There is a strong feeling among some people in the north-eastern States of India that enhanced trade with the said countries would contribute significantly to a vibrant economic growth of the entire South and South-East Asia. Tourism, among other things, is cited as a possible medium that could generate a lot of revenue in and people-to-people exchanges among the countries concerned. It could be a golden gate to the Orient. In this connection, the proposed *Asian Highway* and the *Trans-Asian Railway* is supposed to connect the North-East with the entire South-East Asia. The introduction of an Air India flight between Guwahati (Assam) and Bangkok (Thailand) in 2001 is considered as a step forward in the whole scheme of things. However, this sentiment perhaps ignores the intricate geo-strategic interests of India on its eastern borders. Our efforts should be to achieve connectivity with China and the South-East Asian countries without disturbing the balance in our strategic interests.

Sikkim

Gangtok-Nathu La[26] (4,420 m)-Yatung (in Chumbi Valley)-Paro Dzong-Gyantse-Lhasa

This is a very strategic trade route that opens up to Tibetan China not only the northern Bengal, but also the entire North-East through the narrow Siliguri corridor. In effect, the entire north Indian plains remain exposed to China through this key-hole across the snow covered mountain wall. In 1965, during the Indo-Pakistan war, China, as an ally of Pakistan, had threatened to open up a front against India at Nathu La to ease the

Indian pressure on the then West Pakistan. The nature of the threat posed by China was aptly described in the following report published in the TIME news magazine dated September 24, 1965:

> "The focus of India's attention last week shifted to its Himalayan border in the north. There, while the war with Pakistan continued in bloody obscurity, Red China sharpened its knife for India's back. In Peking, India's charge d'affaires was roused at one o'clock in the morning with a court summons to the Foreign Ministry, where he was handed an ultimatum. In brutal terms, the note gave the Indian Government three days 'to dismantle all military structures along the Sikkim border' or else take the grave consequences'.

Ever since fighting broke out in Kashmir, China has been verbally encouraging Pakistan and denouncing Indian 'aggression'.

Should China seize Sikkim, it would be in a position to close the narrow neck of land linking India proper with the State of Assam and the North-East Frontier Agency, as well as open a route from China to East Pakistan".

Presently, China evinces a good deal of interest on this route in view of the fact that Kolkata (Calcutta) port — and for that matter the Bay of Bengal — is just about 1,400 km from Lhasa by this route. Indian traders, however, lack enthusiasm about it and thus it remains in doldrums. Despite problems, Nathu La could well be used for promoting domestic tourism

One of the reasons why the Chinese would be interested in the above trade route is that its use will ensure cheaper supplies to Tibet. In contrast, bringing in supplies from mainland China takes longer time and is more expensive.

Yunnan Province of China

The Chinese province of Yunnan, situated to the north-east of Upper Myanmar, has a significant presence in the region, particularly because of its proximity to north-east India. Yunnan is ethnically most diverse in the People's Republic of China. Thirtysix out of China's 56 officially recognized ethnic groups live here creating a cultural mosaic. The Chinese have been using it as a centre for opening up the country's access to south and south-east Asia and the Indian Ocean. Besides, its peculiar location could be put to use to remote-control and materially support ethnic and other types of turmoil in Assam and its sister states to keep

India busy with local insurgencies, cultural conflicts, and so on. This would dampen the pace of India's economic development and weaken its growth as a military power. Yunnan is mountainous, especially in its north and the west. The ethnic affinity among the numerous tribes in Yunnan, upper Myanmar and north-east India, as also their attitudinal similarities, is likely to be a determinant factor in the evolving geo-politics of the region.

Strategic Use of Yunnan Province

China has a wide design for the India's North-East. It also backs several rebel groups in the CHT of Bangladesh and Kachin-Chin areas of Myanmar. If all these inaccessible areas are joined up with the insurgency-laden States of Manipur, Nagaland, Tripura, Meghalaya and Assam in India, it forms a compact corridor connecting Yunnan with Sittwe (formerly Akyab) port on the Bay of Bengal. As it is, the old Burma Road connects the Chinese province with the centre of Myanmar at Mandalay. As a matter of fact, on one hand, these areas are already bubbling with illicit trade in arms, drugs, wild-life products, etc., and on the other, consumer durables manufactured in Yunnan are pushed through the same areas to Indo-China peninsula, the South-East Asia and mainland India.

The record of China's Yunnan province being a refuge of NE rebels got confirmed from the reports in the media circulating since late 2009 that ULFA C-in-C Paresh Barua had slipped away to Yunnan (or the nearby areas of Kachin province of Myanmar) after the anti-terrorist crackdown initiated by the Bangladesh government on return to power of pro-India Prime Minister Sheikh Hasina in 2008. Reports said that China, for its own geo-political exigencies, provided Barua facilities to have a safe haven at Ruili in Yunnan and move about freely in the northern Kachin areas of Myanmar, where she wields considerable influence so far as the local rebels are concerned. In fact, China had brokered peace between the Kachin and Wa rebels on one side and the Myanmar government on the other, and in turn, availed itself of a solid bargaining power to make the area a safe haven for sundry rebel groups from north-eastern India, like the NSCN (K), the ULFA, Meitei outfits, et al. The motive behind China's clandestine networking with the Indian rebels lies in its desire to cause instability in the vulnerable N.E.—a situation that would surely weaken the India's' internal and external security.[27]

The history of China's conduct in relation to India, especially in respect of the affairs of north-east India, has been one of hostility since the early 1950s. The Naga rebels were provided by them with arms and training in guerrilla warfare right back at the time when an armed rebellion broke out in the then Naga Hills district of Assam (1955). They had used some Arunachal tribesmen to show them the routes through the mountains of the State during the aggression they committed on India in 1962. Rebels from Manipur were imparted training in guerrilla tactics at Lhasa in the 1970s. Rebel Mizos were given lessons in arms by Chinese instructors in Chittagong Hill Tracts in the mid-1960s.

A PTI report dated December 19, 2009 said that the Arunachal Pradesh government had claimed that North-east militants, including ULFA, were getting arms and ammunition from China. "The Centre is also aware of it. ULFA and other militant groups of the North-East are procuring arms and ammunition from China", State Home Minister Tako Dabi told reporters on the day on the sidelines of a function at North-Eastern Police Academy (NEPA) at Umsaw (Shillong).

He said the militants, particularly those of ULFA, were using Arunachal Pradesh as a 'corridor' to China.

Though Dabi denied the presence of permanent ULFA camps in Arunachal Pradesh, he said "they use Changlang and Tirap districts in the State as sanctuaries".

Asked what steps the government was taking against the militants, Dabi said, "the government is on alert. Para-military and army personnel have been deployed in adequate numbers in the areas".

Routes for Gun-running

Owing to the all-pervading influence acquired by China in the area, the Myanmarese military junta ruling the country for several decades maintained a studied silence about the Indian rebels on its soil, despite the diplomatic prodding of the Indian government to take action against the said rebels. China herself maintained a cordial liaison directly with the Indian rebels holed up in Myanmar and allowed the PLA help them with arms supply and training facilities. An NE rebel leader was reported to be shuttling freely between Ruili in Yunnan and Muse, Bamo and Laiza in north Myanmar. In the arms deals struck with the Chinese, the said leader reportedly transported the Chinese arms and ammunition from Ruili to Bamo, and from there routed the supply to different destinations through the Irrawaddy and its tributaries. It is to be mentioned here that China has been reported in recent years to have built a number of highways from different locations in Yunnan, especially from Kunming, to reach out the interiors of northern Myanmar, particularly Kachin and Thailand.

The newly conceived rail link between Chittagong in Bangladesh and Kunming in Yunnan under the Trans-Asian Railway (TAR)[28] has left India worried. The Bangladesh government has been reported to have sought Chinese help to connect Chittagong with the TAR. Once undertaken and completed, this project is bound to open up India's eastern flank more widely to various activities, open or clandestine. Among other things, tiger trade and smuggling in illicit drugs and arms involving India's North-East and its neighbourhood would automatically have a boost. With the international rail link being operational, travel by India's insurgents to and from the guerrilla training camps in Kachin and the Chin Hills as well as collection of arms supply by them from international gun-runners would be a comfortable job.

China's Geo-Economic Eminence and Threats Therefrom

Ever since Mao Zedong proclaimed the founding of the People's Republic of China in 1949, it has been in a relentless march towards becoming a formidable world power — a status it admittedly acquired before the end of the first decade of the twentyfirst century. Capitalizing on Mao's legacy, Deng Xiaoping, Mao's political successor, unleashed an economic miracle in China in the closing decades of the last century and now, the new China thus created is glorying in wealth as well as in power — economic, political, strategic and diplomatic — flowing from the wealth acquired. Taking a capitalist route, Communist China has acquired a terrible economic clout as the world's "busiest factory and energy-user" — a fact that makes it a main player in virtually all the international financial institutions also. China is now up for expansion of its nuclear power plants in the coming decade (2010-2020) three times as many as the rest of the world combined. This expansion is bound to strengthen its economy with no parallel in the world. This overwhelming influence that China has already gained over the years has very cleverly been put to use by its leaders to gain strategic advantages across Asia, particularly *vis-à-vis* India, both on Indo-Tibetan borders and the Indian Ocean rim in South Asia.

In this connection, the remarks of William Dalrymple, a prolific American writer who had widely traveled in India's neighbourhood in recent times, are very significant. He said in an interview with the Times of India[29] that in the south Asian neighbourhood, the most interesting geo-political phenomenon was the way China was literally encircling India. The Chinese were busy making deals with India's neighbours. Chinese presence in all the countries neighbouring India had been increasing dramatically. This was, he said, posing a formidable danger to the territorial integrity of India.

China too has internal problems with some of its minorities in Tibet, Xinjiang, etc. but has, by and large, been able to control the problems by unrestrained use of military power. She considers India as a rival in its quest for natural leadership of Asian countries. Thus the rulers of China have unabashedly developed Tibet — as a matter of fact the process has been continuing — as a base for any possible military adventure across the Himalayas — should they feel the necessity to do so — for upholding their long-term policy of expansion in and domination of the entire continent. This is entirely in disregard for human rights of the affected minorities, international conventions governing relations between sovereign nations and existing treaties entered into with her by India and Tibet. The economic clout China enjoys has muted the United States, Russia, the U.K., Canada and other western powers towards the aggressiveness she displays in respect of the autonomy question of Tibet, rights of Uighars in Xingjiang, sanctity of India's northern borders, etc. It was strange that though the US recognizes the validity of the autonomy claims of Tibet, President Barack Obama avoided seeing the Dalai Lama during the latter's visit to that country in late 2009, lest a meeting between the two leaders annoyed the Chinese.[30] The ambivalent attitude of the Obama administration to the rising Chinese threat to Asian security on land, in air and on sea makes the region south of the Himalayas vulnerable.

NOTES AND REFERENCES

1. Euphemistically known as Seven Sisters.
2. The 20-40 km-wide Siliguri corridor is extremely tenuous, being in a striking distance from militarized Tibet under Chinese occupation.
3. Adoption of the principles of *Panch Sheel* accompanied with the slogan of *Hindi Chini Bhai Bhai.*
4. According to a report, the Chinese are in a position now to mobilize on a short notice a half-a-million-strong army in Tibet. India, on the other hand, took cognizance of China's war-like preparations only lately. We are still talking in terms of raising two additional mountain divisions for Arunachal Pradesh and placing four fighter squadrons of Sukhoi 30 variety, two each, at Tezpur and Chabua. Full road connectivity with and 'advance landing grounds' for helicopter gunships near the various strategic points on the MacMahon Line are still a far

cry. No one really knows if our nuclear warheads are at all in place to counter the ones deployed (by the Chinese) in their Qinghai province aiming at us.

5. The conference was held at the initiative of Pandit Jawaharlal Nehru, then vice-president and foreign minister of the Interim Government of India.
6. Nehru revealed his mind in 1954 when he said: "What right does India have to keep a part of its Army in Tibet, whether Tibet is independent or a part of Chına?" [Brig J.P. Dalvi, *Himalayan Blunder*].
7. Construction of a trans-Arunachal highway extending from Tawang on the Bhutan-Tibet border to Tirap district in the state's extreme southeast on the Patkai Bum, which will criss-cross the mountains and valleys across all its districts, has now been planned.
8. The MacMahon Line is an imaginary line running along the watershed of the eastern Himalayas from the meeting point of Bhutan, Tibet and Arunachal Pradesh to the tri-junction of Myanmar, Tibet and Arunachal Pradesh. It connects the crests of the highest mountain peaks between Tibet and Arunachal Pradesh and has been the official border between Tibet and India, east of Bhutan. The line was decided upon in a conference of the representatives of British Indian Government, Tibetan Government and Chinese Government at Simla (Shimla) in 1914. It drew its name from Sir Henry MacMahon, who represented the British Government in the conference.
9. The lake Manasaravar is the place from where the river originates.
10. Known as the Great Bend, located near the Gogring village in Arunachal Pradesh.
11. This policy was partly administrative in nature. The British had introduced an "Inner Line" system in 1873, which prohibited the entry of plainsmen into the Frontier territory, so that the tribal life and culture in it did not get influenced by outside cultures and practices. The British also took care to keep the primitive tribes away from the plains to protect the plains people from occasional raids by the tribes.
12. Ramunny, Markot, "Arunachal Ambience", *Frontline*, October 15-28, 1988.
13. Palit, D.K. Maj. Gen., *Sentinels of the East: The Assam Rifles*, Palit and Palit, New Delhi, 1984.
14. The Assam Rifles is the oldest para-military force in the country. Raised in 1835 as the Cachar Levy and having gone through a lot of transformation in the interim years, it has, by now, gathered tremendous experience and a standing as a tribal-friendly Force to deal with conflict situations in the North-East. It is deployed almost entirely in the seven sister States of the region.
15. The British had introduced a system of befriending tribes in the North-East by offering different types of gifts to the 'gaonburas' (the heads of tribal villages) and others concerned whenever a senior government official, like the Deputy Commissioner of the district for example, happened to visit their location. The Indian Army and Para-Military Forces, like the Assam Rifles, followed the practice right through with good results. This has always been a good medium for manifestation of the Administration's goodwill to the simple-minded tribal people.

17\. *Asomiya Pratidin*, June 11, 2009.

16\. Presently some of these routes are being used for encouraging tourism, including eco-tourism, which fetches a good volume of incomes for the local people.

17\. *Asomiya Pratidin*, June 11, 2009.

18\. *The Times of India*, January 21, 2010.

19\. This road links up with that leading to Chengdu (Sechuwan) (Yunnan). Thus this has a tremendous trade and tourism potential.

20. *The Telegraph*, October 25, 2009.
21. *Ibid.*
22. *The Telegraph*, February 9, 2010.
23. A strong demand is now being raised in the North-East, especially in Assam and Arunachal Pradesh, for the re-opening of the Stilwell Road as a part of India's 'Look East Policy' to facilitate trade and commerce with Myanmar, Yunnan province of China, Thailand and other countries beyond. The state governments concerned are very much with the demand. The question, however, remains how much it will further add to the trafficking of arms and drugs from South-East Asia and China to North-East India. An operational Stilwell Road might as well add to strategic difficulties for India in the event of a future armed conflict in this region.
24. By 1943, the Japanese Imperial Army had conquered and brought under its occupation the whole of South-East Asia and the seaboard east of China. The Allied Powers had, therefore, to maintain by air war supplies to the Chinese Army from airfields in Assam. That was becoming too difficult in the situation, given the volume of requirements in China and the frequent crashes of transport planes over the hump across the mountainous terrain of Arunachal Pradesh and Northern Burma. The Allies, therefore, constructed in a record time a road from Ledo to Kunming for the purpose.
25. The Burmese army, coming from Ava, the then capital of the Burmese kings, crossed over to the Assam plains several times through this route. Incidentally, they also withdrew from Assam by the same route.
26. In 1904, Sir Francis Younghusband led a British Expeditionary Force from Gangtok (Sikkim) to Lhasa (Tibet) through the Nathu La Pass situated between Sikkim and Bhutan. It is a part of Sino-Indian Silk Route between South Asia and Tibet. Remaining closed since the 1962 Chinese aggression, it re-opened in July 2006 after 44 years.
27. China's secret liaison with the newly emerging Maoist groups in India, especially in the North-East, remains more or less under wraps till now. It will add a further dimension to the problem in the region in the near future.
28. The TAR is a project under the UNESCAP (UN Economic and Social Council for Asia and the Pacific).
29. *The Times of India*, December 27, 2009.
30. President Obama later met the Dalai Lama on a subsequent occasion.

26

LABOUR MIGRATION AND ECONOMIC ENTERPRISE
The Nepalis in Assam

Lopita Nath

"It is impossible for anybody who has lived in Assam for the last sixteen years, not to have noticed the remarkable number of Nepalis that are seen all over the province, particularly in the Assam Valley, the Hill districts and the frontier tracts. . ., there has been a great infiltration of Nepalis eastwards from Nepal. . .", wrote an Intelligence Officer to the Assam Government in 1946.[1] The process of immigration of the Nepali people from the hills of Nepal to the valleys, plains and again the hills of North-East India, Sikkim, Burma, Malaya and as far as Mandalay, etc. started about two centuries ago and continues till date. Largely generated by the colonial intervention, the linkages established during the colonial era provided the basis for much of the migration even in the post-colonial era.

In North-East India and Assam, the *Nepali* speaking people who are variously denoted as Nepali or *Gurkha*,[2] presents the widest possible variation in terms of occupation, expectations, aspirations and status in the region. Primarily, the Nepalis came in search of a living, taking up all kinds of work although in the past, they have gravitated towards the armed services and private security in addition to dairy farming and agriculture. A large number of these early migrants who came in the first rushes of the colonial period have become domiciled in the region, have assimilated with the land, and are permanently settled in some job or more commonly as a dairy farmer. They have never seen Nepal and have no wish to do so. They are committed to establishing an identity for themselves here. Then, there are other Nepalis, who came in the early part of the twentieth century, who although are more or less established here in paid jobs or as dairy farmers, have land and relatives in Nepal, either through matrimonial or fraternal alliances. They come and go and maintain links with Nepal, although they prefer to stay here. Finally, there are large groups of migrant labourers, who constantly move back and forth, continuing till date, between their home in the Nepali Hills and their place of work or business in the region. These three categories together constitute the bulk of the Nepali population in North-East India.

The one common factor among the majority of these Nepal speakers is their dependence on dairy farming even in the present times. Even the larger sections of the temporary migrant labourers are engaged in the industry. Except for the original graziers and herdsmen, who came around the last part of the nineteenth century, the larger section of the Nepali speakers in the region have undergone a transition from labouring in mines or plantations or any paid job (as household help or clerics) to dairy farming. Today most of the milk or ghee requirements of the region are met by the Nepali dairy farmers.

Often host societies value the work that the migrant workers give, but give little thought to the human beings behind that work, be they domestic workers, factory hands, or small entrepreneurs. But the human cost they face is real, difficulties in coping in alien land, discrimination and difficulties in integration. They remain in the margins of the society. Even the Nepalis in Assam and elsewhere in the country, despite the primacy of their trade and business and the almost complete dependence of the regions population on them for their dairy requirements, they maintain a marginal economic and social status in the region. They live almost in a kind of cultural shadow without full recognition of their rights and credit to their contributions in a land, which they have served for two centuries. This has in recent times led to ethnic assertions for establishing their identity and defining their status.

The primary purpose of this article is to lend truth to the hypothesis that the Nepali labourers/dairy farmers belonged to the landless milieu in Nepal, and that they were original labour migrants, who turned to dairy farming. The chapter shall also look into the operational dynamics of their business in the region. Last, but not the least attention will be devoted to migration networks and linkages, which stand between the macro and the micro dimensions. Finally, the long span of migration will be seen in its proper historical and social context with proper integration of theoretical understanding with empirical research.

Nepali Labour Migration — 16th-19th Century

Although, migrations from Nepal into North-East had been trickling in even before it was opened by the colonialists in 1826, their numbers were small, the borders seemingly overlapping;[3] and going by available historical evidence, these early migrants completely assimilated into the early Assamese society.[4] It was only in the colonial context after the first Anglo-Nepal war (1814-16), and the deployment of the Gurkhas (Nepali soldiers) that major Nepali migrations took place in the region. However, although this was primarily a colonial move, it was prompted by the conditions in Nepal, which began in the sixteenth century and became more intense by the eighteenth and nineteenth century.

It was as early as the sixteenth century that changes occurred in Nepal in the mode of production and pattern of property ownership. Nepal, had an ethnically diverse population with migrants over time from Mongolia, Tibet and China from the North and the Indo-Aryans from the South. Hagen (1916: 60) called Nepal the "ethnic turn-table of Asia".[5] With the immigration of the Indo-Aryans in the sixteenth century (who were believed to be mostly Brahmins and Rajputs fleeing from the religious tyranny of the invading Muslims) the communal mode of production, and transhumant pastoralism and shifting cultivation practiced by the Tibeto-Burman settlers,[6] yielded to a settled intensive agriculture.[7] Lowland fields and lower slopes were terraced and irrigated for wet-rice cultivation.[8] This forced the ethnic groups, who had inhabited the lowland areas up the hillsides, to less productive lands in response to the gradual acquisition of the more productive land by high caste Hindus. Thus, by the sixteenth century, there emerged a high caste Hindu landlord class strengthening their position in the society. A class structure based on the ownership of land and labour began to develop. Anthropologists conducting research in Nepal, like Caplan,[9] McDougal.[10] Poffenberger,[11] have remarked that this process resulted in a concentration of wealth and land in the hands of high caste families and a corresponding loss of land, wealth by tribal groups and people of low caste like the Gurungs and Magars.

Volume 64 of Regmi Research Collections published from Kathmandu, remarks that an order by Prime Minister Jang Bahadur Rana to Colonel Krishnadhwaj Kunwar in 1850, June, regarding 'emigration from the Eastern Hill region' says "We have received reports that you are leaving your *Kipat* (communally owned) lands and going abroad because of the pressure of money lenders and the oppression of amalis (court officials) revenue collectors and government officials. . .". This document supports the view that to a large extent it was direct and indirect pressures of state taxation which led to initial out-migration soon after the establishment of the unitary Nepali State.[12] The Gurkhali state not only brought all *Kipat* land under state ownership, but also imposed a tax or rent called *raikar*,[13] and engaged the majority of the cultivators in the cultivation of the these lands. The policy of making land Grants—*Birta* and *Jagir*[14] to the high castes depriving the low caste Gurungs and Magars, led to the emergence of a landlord class. The landholders employed peasants to cultivate their lands, mostly in the Terai, and in return appropriated higher rents and larger shares of production. Regmi and others argue that this caused disparity in access to resources and overall depletion of the land and forest resources.[15]

The States demand for revenue seems to have been related initially to finance the Gurkhali states expansionary wars and then for the consolidation of the territory conquered and with the rise of the Ranas for the upkeep of the unproductive elite class.[16] To fill in their labour requirements for army, administration, construction works (forts, palaces, temples, etc.) as well as needs of the royal palaces, the Government resorted to *Corvee*, "the time honoured system of exacting works from its subjects on a compulsory basis".[17] The *Corvee* system called *Jhara*[18] became a severe hardship for the peasants of Nepal (in the eighteenth and nineteenth centuries) and also downgraded their economic position as in some households agricultural production declined due to the shortage of labour.[19] In this system the Gurungs and Magars, were used mainly in the army, peasants belonging to Indo-Aryan groups for transportation and other supplementary work,[20] while the high caste groups generally enjoyed exemptions from Corvee though at times they were also required to render free labour.

Land relations in Nepal further deteriorated during the period of the Ranas (hereditary Prime Ministers), who ruled from 1846-1951. At the same time, the passage of the *legal code in 1854*, inaugurated caste based system, whereby the members of the occupational castes (the untouchables), who were also artisans were denied access to education and government service, ignoring their artisan skills. This system forced these people into the lower classes, not only in terms of social prestige, but also in terms of economic position. In addition, the excessive burden of tax or *corvee* obligations imposed by the government pushed many materially and culturally rich ethnic groups into a precarious position.[21]

Ludwig Stiller, in his 'Silent Cry' had observed that the increasing expansion and consolidation of Nepal had been achieved "without weighing the cost in terms of human suffering for one's own people".[22] The grim poverty of the people accentuated by building economic pressures and oppressive land and labour policies and the resultant obnoxious rural indebtedness and loss of land threatened the very survival of the low-income groups.[23] Thus, for the Nepalis, migration was the only way out of their misfortune and they soon made their way to Sikkim, Darjeeling, Assam, Bhutan and beyond. This was made easy by the economic transformation of the North-East following the British occupation. The early British adventurers were greeted with vast expanses of uninhabited wastelands throughout the province interspersed with thick forests of sub-tropical trees and cane; a "dreary and desolate wilderness that seemed totally devoid of man, beasts, or birds, a death like stillness everywhere prevailed, broken only by the occasional barking or halloo of the ooluck or ape".[24] It was the discovery of the tea plant that put to rest all doubts about the economic prospects of this new land frontier. Opened to capitalist exploitation, the period from 1826-1873 was a period of transition for Assam's pre-capitalist economy into its colonial phase.[25] All the inputs of production for the expanding modern economy, except land, were brought in from outside the province; capital and enterprise from the metropolis and labour from the other provinces. Migrants as soldiers, labourers, agriculturists, graziers, petty traders and also English educated job-aspirants were actively encouraged by the colonialists to take advantage of the new opportunities and enterprises, that imperialism opened up on the eastern frontier. While most of the non-indigenous population was from nearby Bengal, there was also a smattering of Marwaris, Biharis and also Nepalis.

The nineteenth century portrait of the North-eastern frontier framed by the colonial patronage, presented an attractive picture to the Nepali highlander. Without land to either cultivate or graze his cattle, discriminated against by the high caste and the ruling families both in terms of employment and opportunities, burdened by taxation in Nepal, the Nepalis found North-East India an easy and feasible getaway. The most common avenues were the Gurkha army and the jobs in the forests and plantations. In the colonial period the primary cause of migration was for survival and sustenance. The Census Reports recorded an increase of the Nepali population in Assam from 21,347 (35%) in 1901 to 88,306 (1.02%) in 1931 (See Table 26.1: Growth of Nepali Population in Assam).

Table 26.1: Growth of Nepali Population in Assam

Year	*No. of Nepali Population in Assam*	*Percentage*
1901	21,347	0.35
1911	47,654	0.67
1921	70,344	0.94
1931	88,306	1.02
1951	1,01,338	1.26
1961	2,15,213	1.98
1971	3,49,116	2.38
1991	4,32,519	1.93

Source: Census of India Reports, 1901-71; 1991. M. Hussain, 1993:258.

In the post-colonial period, the Nepali population increased significantly, nearly doubling in the years 1951-1971. Numerically, they rose from 1,01,338 in 1951 to 3,49,116 in 1971, indicating a nearly 3.5 times growth in these twenty years (See Table 26.1). The reasons were not far to find. The earlier trends of migration found formal manifestation in the Indo-Nepal Friendship Treaty of 1950, the Tripartite Delhi Agreement of 1951 and the revised Indo-Nepal Agreement of 1956. All these, particularly Article 7 of the Indo-Nepal Treaty of 1950, ensured equal rights and privileges in terms of residence, ownership of property, employment, occupation and movement on a reciprocal basis for both nationals of India and Nepal in both the countries. The non-requirement of a visa or passport for entry into either country and the understanding that there was no legal preventive steps in controlling migration, facilitated the movement into the North-eastern corner of India. In the 1960s and 1970s the eradication of malaria from the Nepal Terai and the official encouragement for highlanders to colonize these jungled plains provided an outlet for migratory pressures. The Terai forests got used up, but the continuing need for the peasantry to find means for sustenance and survival, burst through the open Indo-Nepal border to take advantage of the work opportunities available in the modernizing economy of independent India. Industrialization and the development of roads (particularly after the Chinese Aggression of 1962 in NEFA and Assam) and other public infrastructure also threw up a great demand for unskilled labour, very effectively provided by the willing Nepali worker. Among other things, the growth of an Indian middle class through the 1950s and 1960s created household jobs like *darbans* (gate keepers) and kitchen help, which were provided by the Nepalis. Higher income levels[26] and better educational facilities also encouraged exodus to the North-East India.

Table 26.2: Demography of the Nepalis in North-East

States	*1951*	*1961*	*1971*	*1976*	*1981*	*1991*
Arunachal Pradesh	NA	10,610 (25,000)	30,912 (85,000)	NA	45,508	NA
Assam	1,01,338*	2,15,213 132,925*	3,49,116 353,673*	NA	NA	4,32,519
Manipur	(2860)	13,571	26,381	(36,604)	37,046	
Meghalaya	NA	32,288 (6000)	44,445 (10,111)	NA	61,259	
Mizoram	NA	2042 (2000)	NA (4000)	NA	5983	
Nagaland	NA	10,400	17,536	NA	24,918	
Tripura	NA	1696	2107	NA	2190	

Source: Timsina, 1992. Figures in brackets from Dutt, 1981 and figures in asterisks from Sinha, 1982.

In the recent times, migration into Assam was considerably dependent on a chain network created by the early migrants. The presence of a large population of Nepalis in different parts of the region employed in the Assam Rifles in Shillong, Indian Oil Corporations in Duliajan and the Assam Oil Corporation in Digboi, in trade and business all over the region and particularly as agriculturists and dairy farmers encourages newer migrants into the region. These networks thus had a multiplier effect. The links between the migrants and the area of origin have thus persisted over generations. Even though remittances may fall off and visits home decline in frequency, but familial and cultural links remain. Migration of the Nepalis has thus continued along the established chains, making it almost a self-sustaining process.

Profile of the Nepali Migrant in Assam — 19th-20th Century

"There is a hill; send up a Gurkha",[27] seemed the most appropriate profile of the Nepali migrant in the North-Eastern frontier. But the Nepali migration into Assam, spanning over almost two centuries took on different dimensions at different periods of history. In the pre-colonial times the early matrimonial alliances led to the movement of a number of Nepali Brahmin priests, Chettri warriors, farmers, herdsmen and artisans from Nepal to Assam. These early migrants, who completely assimilated into the Assamese society, formed a part of the historical process of the time.

In the colonial context, the Gurkhas were the first major wave of Nepali migrants to Assam. They first came in the wake of the Treaty of

Sagauli (1815-16) in 1817, when 1000 Hindustanis and Gurkhas took part in the Sylhet operations as a part of the Cuttack Legion, later known as the Assam Light Infantry. Thereafter, following the Anglo-Burmese war of 1824-26, the Gurkhas described by Lord Bentinck as "brave and energetic" and 'the most eligible' came to replace the Manipuris in the Company's forces in the North-east. And within a period of six years (1833-1839) nearly one-third of the battalions in the Assam Light Infantry came to be composed of Gurkhas. Beginning 1835 the 'Cachar Levy', which eventually grew into the 'Assam Rifles' liberally enlisted the Gurkhas. Whether it was the Sylhet or the Shillong plateau, Naga Hills or the Lushai Hills, Chittagong Hill tracts or the Sadiya Frontier tracts, the Bhutan wars or the Manipur rebellion, the Gurkhas constituted half the Assam rifles and were always there in operation. As early as 1865, the Nepalese *Khukri* replaced the short sword and the crossed *Khukri* became the emblem of the Assam Rifles.[28] The eastward thrust into the new area was made by the British with the Nepalis as their vanguard. These soldiers were recruited mostly from the Western and Central Hills of Nepal among the low-caste Magars and Gurungs, who suffered from low economic positions at home, as well as discrimination for high ranks in the army during the Rana regime. Other ethnic groups recruited were the Chettris, Rais, Limbus, Tamangs, Thakuris, Sunwar and others from the East.[29] It was only during World War II that a small number of Brahmins and Newars were recruited. A career as a soldier was highly respected not only enabling men to escape from a life of poverty, but also the remittances sent home either as salaries or pensions became a family's only source of income.

In the eastern frontier of India, the Gurkhas played a crucial role in the unification, consolidation and reconstruction of the region. The then Chief Commissioner of Assam, Bampyfylde Fuller made a statement to that effect. "It was fortunate for the Government of the province that on these emergent occasions it could rely upon a garrison of regular troops that include the Gurkha Regiments".[30] "The Gurkhas were useful for any odd and sundry jobs, as well as specialized jobs assigned to them. A capable, cheerful and alert people and are essentially a virile race. Though quick tempered and keen to resent an injustice, they are remarkably willing and loyal, if treated with consideration. . . . Though small in stature, these Nepalese have big hearts. . . . Naturally vigorous, excitable and aggressive, they are very law abiding. . .", these comments recorded by L.S.S. O'Malley, editor of the Bengal District Gazetteers, aptly described the Nepali migrant in the North-eastern frontier.[31] After release from service, they settled down in and around the district towns and strategic location on the hills. The Assam Rifles rehabilitated its Gurkha soldiers in various sites at Sadiya in Assam, Mantripokhari in Manipur, Aizwal in Mizoram, Mokakchung in Nagaland and also at Arunachal Pradesh, Meghalaya and Tripura.[32] Compact pockets of Nepali settlements in different parts of the region have emerged. Most of these residents have displayed a tremendous capacity of assimilating with the local people contract marital alliance and also become a part of the local economy. These settlers with their peasant background and military training have acquired the image of loyal citizens with pro-establishment attitude towards the Government. "Gurkha soon evolved as a brand name for integrity and loyalty as the batman to the British officer became the prototypical household help".[33] The arrival of the Gurkhas encouraged their brethren to come and settle in the North-east.

A second wave of the Nepali migrants became a source of brawn encouraged to migrate eastward along the Duars to Assam Valley and the far eastern hills from present day Arunachal all the way to Northern Burma as a consequence of British colonial expansion. The various expeditions against the 'tribes' of the North-East, large scale lumbering and clearing of forest lands for settlement, agriculture and plantation required hardy as well as pliant labourers. The Nepali migrants unlettered and unexposed perfectly fitted this need and they were attracted in large numbers to the forests, road construction sites, mines, fields, plantations and so on. In the later part of the nineteenth century and early twentieth century, the Nepalis worked as labourers in the tea gardens throughout the province and in the oil refineries at Margherita and Digboi and in the coal mines and saw mills in Upper Assam and Meghalaya.[34] The Nepali migrants of the last part of the nineteenth and the first quarter of the twentieth century were practicing herdsmen and dairy farmers. Just like the 'Gurkha', the '*Khuntiwallah*' (*Khunti* — temporary herdsmen's sheds; *wallah* — man) became the prototypical milkmen or dairy farmer among the Nepali migrants. Side by side with working in the mines refineries and plantation, these Nepalis laid the foundations of their own economic base as pastoralists and dairy farmers. A great number of these graziers were of the non-martial class.

The migration from Nepal once it began followed a dynamic of its own and accelerated and grew through the twentieth century and upto the present. In the post-colonial period, the bilateral agreements played a major role in labour migration to the region and did much to improve the social security and rights of migrant workers and their families. Further the reasons for migration now had intensively changed as the conditions in Nepal were no longer as it was in the nineteenth and early twentieth century. While in the colonial period they migrated to escape the economic and political exploitation, in the post-colonial period, they moved with great hopes and expectations for a better future. Thus, since the push factors were not so intense, the migrants made a conscious and rational choice to move. Further, with the existing networks already laid down by the earlier migrants, it was easier for the new migrants to find a footing in North-East India. The post-colonial Nepali migrant was of significance to the local economy because of their availability for any type of chore. With the expansion of construction works, commercialization, advent of modest industrialization and extension of transport and communication, there was an increasing demand for the semi-skilled brawn. The versatility of the Nepali besides an agricultural labourer, grazier or pastoralist, as a porter, watchman, gardener, driver, mechanic, plumber, cleaner, pony cart driver, bus conductors, etc. made them easily available to any private or corporate agency for any work on a modest payment. Unlike their pastoralist and soldier-farmer counterparts, the semi-skilled urban Nepalis are scattered in the townships keeping in view of the availability of such jobs they are engaged in.[35] There is little competition from the local indigenous communities because such specializations in which they have developed skills are limited in supply locally. The urban Nepalis lead a near cosmopolitan life in which their expenses are in tune with their income. They do not attract the envy of their non-Nepali neighbours because they rarely add to affluence.[36]

In the twentieth century, Nepali migrations also increased to take advantage of the better educational facilities and the employment opportunities that might follow. They are the newly emerging category of urban White Collar Nepalis. Second or third generation migrants with their newly acquired education and hold over the local language they have friends, patrons and enemies among the local community and are affiliated to various organizations in the North-east. They compete with the local people for the scarce white-collar jobs. They settle in the urban areas in the region and assimilate with the host community.

Beginning with the extension of the British interest, the Nepali migration to Assam spanned over two centuries. With the changing needs and times, the character of the migrant also changed. What looms large throughout this brief sketch is the industrious, enterprising and assimilative nature of the Nepali migrant. In Assam, the popular image of the Nepali is that of a smiling, ever ready and always obliging

Bahadur. indicating his aspirations for a better life. Since, they were first economic migrants, the Nepalis in Assam had always displayed a tendency to move to areas, which is economically profitable or where opportunities are available. The Nepali population in the region thus floats, from one urban center to another and find employment partly, fully, occasionally and even seasonally in various professions.

Nepali Dairy Farmers in Assam

A significant feature of the economy of North-Eastern region is the ubiquitous presence of the Nepali dairymen in the hills, open grasslands and in the plains and outskirts of the urban areas. These Nepali herdsmen and marginal farmers trickled down to Assam at least from the last part of the nineteenth and the first quarter of the twentieth century. The primary cause of the migration of these graziers was the lack of grassland to graze their cattle in Nepal,[37] when the lowland fields and lower slopes were terraced and irrigated for the cultivation of rice.

"We are originally dairy farmers. We lived in a hilly place in Nepal, but that place was hardly suitable for dairy farming. Searching for an easy and suitable land, we came to Assam and established ourselves here", we were told by most of the dairy farmers in the region.[38]

In land-abundant Assam, peasants enjoyed from time immemorial the traditional right to graze their cattle freely in the village commons and neighbouring forests.[39] The vast wastelands, which doubled up as excellent grazing reserves and the undulating topography made it easy for the Nepali herdsmen to migrate eastward. They, thus settled in the middle hills eastward from Nepal and with similar climatic conditions as prevailed in their places of origin it was just an extension of their natural habitat.

In the Brahmaputra valley, the Nepalis initially settled in the grazing reserves, i.e. the Chapari areas. The Burha Chapari of Tezpur was declared a professional grazing reserve as early as 1881,[40] which facilitated professional dairying by the Nepali migrants. The grazing area of the Nepali community spread from the Baraimala to Bhavani Devi *Than*, classified under the Mahajan (moneylender) of the area.[41] In the Goalpara division of Assam, 105 meters of reserved forests were left open for the grazing of cattle by the Nepalis in return for assistance in the fire protection.[42] The Nepalis had also settled in the *Char* (midstream sandbars) areas. A number of *Chars* bearing names of Nepali origin[43] found in the Nagaon, Morigaon and Nalbari districts are believed to have been inhabited by the *Khuntiwallahs* or the Nepali milkmen.

Under the British regime, the right to freely graze cattle was encroached upon to bring forth additional revenue to the exchequer. Although initially an insignificant source of revenue, with the steady rise in the immigration and settlement of the Nepali graziers, it soon became an expanding source. In the unclassed forests, the ryots were allowed unlimited grazing free of payment for their plough and domestic cattle, but Nepalis rearing cattle for dairy farming were charged for the grazing privilege.[44] These duties were collected "entirely from the Nepali herdsmen, who obtained steady and lucrative rate for the dairy produce in the numerous tea gardens of the province".[45] The grazing fees, which was introduced per head of horned animals in 1888 was gradually increased by the years so much so that it caused resentment among the graziers.[46] The increase in the number of buffaloes taxed more than doubled the revenue collected.[47] The total revenue of ₹ 2,77,000 collected in 1919-20 from grazing fee was accounted for by only one and a quarter lakh of cattle actually assessed. The overwhelming bulk of these cattle belonged to 6,319 professional graziers of whom, excepting a few hundred, all were Nepali migrants.[48] It was noted early in the Administrative Report of Assam 1912-13 that a large number of professional graziers had migrated from the adjoining areas of Jalpaiguri owing to the rise of grazier fees in that district.[49] This led to new rules of taxation in 1917. In 1937 a total revenue of ₹ 2,82,356 was realized from a total of 2,69,460 acres of Reserved grazing ground;[50] in 1939-40 of the total estimate of ₹ 3,53,115, only a sum of ₹ 2,47,052 (70%) could be collected.[51]

The available historical data and statistics on the Nepali herdsmen and graziers during the colonial period adds up to the fact that they had emerged as a prominent economic group among all the Nepali settlers in the region, contributing to the colonial exchequer. The Government thus, made it possible for their easy settlement and movement. This in turn encouraged further immigration of the Nepalis into the province.

Who Are the Nepali Dairy Farmers Today?

To a casual reader, every Nepali in the N.E. is identified as a dairy farmer or the *dudhwallah* (*dudh* — milk, *wallah* — man) and/or as a Gurkha. Even the District Gazetteer records that, 'the Nepalese for the most part were graziers, who keep large herds of cows and buffaloes. They have penetrated deep into the interior of the district and have established *khunties* (herdsmen's temporary sheds). Some have taken to cultivation also.[52] Firstly, the word Nepali needs some qualification. "The word Nepali . . . represents a culturo-linguistic denomination".[53] The Nepali migrants, actually belong to the tribal ethnic communities (non-Bahun) and the Newar community in the Kathmandu valley in Nepal. While in Nepal, the many castes and sub-castes — Newar, Rai, Chettri or Gurung — assert their own ethnic identities. Once out of Nepal, in the North-East and elsewhere in India, they tend to identify themselves as a single Nepali (Gurkhali in Darjeeling) community. As Sinha writes that, "As far as the plains from the Bengal Duars to the Barak Valley are concerned, in terms of Nepalese settlement, a distinct trend may be noted. The less skilful and marginal farmers and pastoralists turned to pastoral grazing on the hilly and forested tracts of the region".[54]

In a report to the Foreign Secretary of the Government of Assam on May 13, 1930, the Chief Secretary to the Government of Assam informed that, "The greater number of numerous Nepali graziers in Assam are Jaisis and Upadhyaya Brahmins or Chettris of non-martial classes".[55] The graziers in fact belonged to a separate social category than those, who had settled after retirement from service. The caste background of this category were "mainly Magar and Gurung and there were hardly any Brahmin or Chettri".[56] This fact has often been corroborated from the accounts of the present day dairy farmers in the course of our field study. They are mostly Brahmins (Sharmas, Upadhyayas and Jaisis) and Chettris.[57]

Animal keeping or livestock farming constituted a traditional off-farm occupation of the people of Nepal, since the early times, even before the immigration of the Indo-Aryans to Nepal. Livestock comprised one of the main components of the subsistence production system of the village, since this formed a strong link in the flow of energy from forest or pasture to farming and to the human diet. The ethnic hill tribes, i.e. the Gurungs and Magars practiced Transhumant pastoralism[58] and in the early 1940s, kept a considerable number of cattle, buffaloes, goats and sheep.[59] In the past until 40-50 years ago, almost every household had a herd of animals each consisting 10-20 cows and 10-15 buffaloes managed jointly by two or three families. The main objective in keeping cattle was to generate income both cash and kind; cows and buffaloes for milk and farming and sheep for wool needed in making blankets and other woollen clothes. But with the employment and recruitment of the Gurungs in the army service their access to cash income had increased after 1940s.[60] This in turn led to a decline in their dependence on livestock. By the 70s and 80s, livestock were managed by retired army men and their family members, who did not go to the army,[61] Gurungs were also found to hire oxen from others to plough land as they could afford it because of their access to off-farm income.[62] Buffaloes were kept for milk production for consumption.

This was not the case with the Brahmins and Chettris. Their non-recruitment in the army had left them largely dependent on land and livestock for their subsistence. In a study conducted in Nepal,[63] the Brahmins and Chettris were shown to own more animals than members of other ethnic groups. Brahmins followed by Chettris owned a large proportion of cows and oxen. The cow was viewed as symbolic in Hindu religion and as Brahmins were more inclined to religion, they kept more cows. In the later years (1980s and 1990s) the practice of borrowing cows in lieu of cash or kind for religious purposes reduced the need for ownership. Ox was required for ploughing the land and since Brahmins and Chettris practiced intensive cultivation in large areas of land, they owned more oxen. In the later years (1990s), Brahmins and Chettri ethnic groups, which did not have access to cash income often raised buffaloes for milk production. Some families sold milk in local tea shops, but the market for milk was small in the village itself until the 1990s. In due course milk was converted to Ghee (Clarified Butter), which could be stored for a long time and could be easily transported relatively long distances. In order to earn off-farm income, Brahmins and Chettris sold milch buffaloes, which they raised calves to milk producing age, to people residing near the towns.

Brahmins and Chettris were thus, more dependent on livestock and dairy farming. As mentioned earlier, the social and economic situation in Nepal, left the Brahmins and Chettris without much land to cultivate. A privileged section in Nepal and non-occupational ethnic group, they remained a class of landless milieu in Nepal. And unlike the Gurungs, who migrated to increase their cash income, the Brahmins and Chettris fell back on livestock farming. And when they began to migrate east in search of a better livelihood, it was also as herdsmen and graziers.

It has been mentioned that in the North-East, a large number of retired Gurkha soldiers and settlers have taken to dairy farming. Henry Cotton, the Chief Commissioner of Assam, noted as early as in 1898 that many of the retired Gurkha Sepoys, who had settled down in Assam, preferred cattle grazing to cultivation. Already having had a tradition of cattle farming, the hill ethnic groups — Gurungs and Magars, who were mostly serving in the army, found it easy to take to dairy farming after retirement and settlement in the North-eastern regions.

The Nepali dairy men and cultivators, in the western regions of Assam, i.e. Kamrup had originally come as soldiers in the Gurkha army or for as unskilled labourers and later shifted to dairy farming. In the course of our field work, Min Raj Joshi, former President of Brihattar Guwahati Gopalak Sanstha, told us that, "My father came from Nepal, when he was seven years old to Guwahati, joined the British Army and went to Nagaland. After the war. . . . Left the army, came to Guwahati during Second World War, when there was a big demand, he was engaged in milk supplying and bought cows with a loan of ₹ 300 from one Chandi Charan Bharali of Maligaon area in "57". Ram Prasad Joshi, Min Raj Joshi's father became an established dairy farmer. They later shifted to Noonmati area and has about 30/35 cows in Panikheti area.[64] There are others as well. Our local milk supplier, Narayan Sharma[65] also came to Assam from Baglung in Nepal. He was, however, born here as his father was a dairy farmer in Milanpur, Guwahati. Having returned to Nepal, he came back to join the Assam rifles, but since he could not get appointment, turned to dairy business. In these regions, the dairymen although settled here with a flourishing business, have their connections with Nepal. Matrimonial relations and fraternal relations, with a part of the family having migrated back,[66] is at the root of these relations. They have land here as well as in Nepal, and a part of the profits are sent back as remittances to Nepal. These men are motivated more by economic interests than any in their residence in Assam.

In the eastern regions of Assam (Lakhimpur, Dibrugarh, etc.) the dairymen are original dairy farmers and are third/fourth generation migrants. They are bonafide settlers of the region and have almost become indigenous to the area, where they have settled. They have no links with Nepal and their business is developed and marketed here. Their returns are also utilized here. Some, those who are educated are effectively employed as teachers or in some government posts. Ramji Chetry, a 4th generation migrant from Muga, a hilly place of Dhankuta district of Nepal and living in Ouguri Nepali gaon, Jaji, in Jorhat district of Assam, is a cashier of Jorhat Government dairy farm, while his wife is a teacher.[67] He also has 8 acres of land, where he grows paddy.

The dairy farmers in Assam belong to two distinct category: (i) Those, who own land and cattle; (ii) and those, who supply milk. The first category belong to the upper caste Jaisis and Upadhyayas and have large farms. They rear the cattle and produce milk, but do not supply on a house-to-house basis. The second category belongs to the Chettris and in some cases Magars, Gurungs, Thapas, etc., who are only milk suppliers. Not finding employment in the army, or elsewhere, they had taken to milk supply as an easy alternative. They do not own land or cattle. Having established contacts with the prospective customers, they buy the milk from the producers and supply it on a door-to-door basis. Their customers for the most part are individual households, sweetshops and restaurants and hotels. These milk suppliers are known as *Paikari* or not owning cows. In Guwahati alone there are about 220 *Paikari* dairy men.

Table 26.3: Showing the *Paikari* Milkmen in Greater Guwahati City (from Silpukhuri, Paltan Bazar and Bonda Areas)

No. (Approx.)	*Their Origin*
80	Tezpur
50	Nepal (Land here as well as in Nepal)
90	Nepal (No land/house, etc. here, but only for business)
Total 220	

This above Table 26.3 has been based on field investigation. These men are engaged in the business only.

A noticeable trend in the Nepali dairy farming industry is the ease with which the people from other professions make their shift to dairy farming. As mentioned earlier, the Nepali herdsmen and farmers moved out of Nepal in search of new opportunities. The only capital he carried with himself was his personal qualities as a cheerful, perseverant and sturdy hand, his ubiquitous *Khukri* and readiness to do anything to make a living.[68] With such temperament, they had easily combined in themselves a number of roles as dairymen, sharecroppers, agricultural labourers, porters, smith, carpenters and errand boys and today even as teachers, clerks, peons, etc. Ghanashyam Sharma, a dairy farmer in Guwahati told us, "I was a Chowkidar in the Survey of India Office in Guwahati; when I was transferred to Tezpur in 1985 (he joined in 1975), I resigned and turned to dairy farming". Another Mr. Chettri was a young Chowkidar for a group of flats in Beltola Guwahati. He left his job and joined the dairy business. This follows in many cases. Besides the fact that it is a traditional occupation and comes naturally, the importance of social networks here play a major role. Family members or friends already in the business provide the support needed to start the business. The availability of cows on loan, or milk and the ready market makes the transition from service to dairying easy.

Socio-Economic Status of the Nepali Dairy Farmers in Assam

The Nepalis since their migration to the Assam had taken up dairy farming as their primary occupation. The colonial government observing their interest in cattle rearing had variously aided and supported the farmers in their endeavour. In the post-independence period, the concept of milk producers' cooperative society became very popular in Assam.[69] In a majority of these the Nepali community has a dominant role. There are many cooperative societies in Assam alone,[70] of these the Sitajakhala Dugdha Utpadan Samiti (Sitajakhala Milk Producers Society) alone produces 5,000 litres of milk per day. Total milch-cow population in Assam is about 21 lakh. Average daily milk production is more than 20 lakh litres.[71]

Besides, there are individual producers as well. Mr. Tulsi Upadhyaya has about 200 buffaloes producing about 300 to 500 litres of milk. His farm is situated at Brahmaputra Chapari and he sends his milk to Dibrugarh. Ramji Chetry with 150 buffaloes and 200-350 litres of milk sends his milk to Tinsukia town from his farm at Dhola, on the outskirts of Tinsukia. There are others, who are only traders. Homlal Sharma, collects about 150 to 200 litres of milk and sells it in Gogamukh town. Most of them reported a profit of about 50 per cent with some loss. There are smaller producers with less than 100 or even less than 50 cows; some even have as many as only 10 or 12, producing about 30-50 litres of milk per day. These farmers supply milk in the vicinity of the area they live, cutting down on transport costs. Ghanashyam Sharma, such a small producer, calculated an income of average ₹ 5,000 per month,[72] Narayan Sharma, a *Paikari* milkman reported a monthly profit of ₹ 3,000-4,000. While in the earlier instances, the money is spent here, in the case of the *Paikari*, the remittances are sent to Nepal to be used there. This does not benefit the local economy.

Those, who are producers here face a lot of obstacles to their business. They can be listed as: (a) defective breeding policy of the Government, as in the artificial insemination programme, low quality semen is used; (b) where quality is good, the cost is very high; (c) good breed is not given; (d) cannot control prices; (e) cannot meet the demands; (f) fluctuating production; (g) diseased and malaria prone areas; (h) labour intensive. In Guwahati alone, where the monthly demand is for 5 lakh litres of milk, the total production is only 1 lakh litres. This leads to ways and means of supplying the demand — by mixing skimmed milk and water. Since, this does not meet the required standards laid down by the government, which is 1.2 per cent solid and fat (s&f), (Assam milk has 3.5% s&f), 80 per cent of the milk suppliers have adulteration cases over them.[73] This is, however, done by the suppliers and not the producers, who would never allow adulteration of their own farm milk. Their problem is, however, increased by the influx of the cooperative and other company's, ready to drink milk packets into the market. Although, they do not admit to losing business on that ground.

Assam has thus, emerged as a very lucrative area for the Nepali dairy farmer. As mentioned earlier, having established themselves economically, the Nepali immigration into the region continued as a chain migration relying on the network already laid down by the previous migrants. There was already an uncle or a brother here, already in the business and ready to help the nephew or brother, get some opportunity here. The present day migrants turn to the 1950 Indo-Nepal Friendship Treaty, which gave them a legal *locus standi* to engage in business, to acquire property, to settle themselves, seek employment and to move freely anywhere in India they like. This Treaty gave a formal sanction to their residence in the region as well as a status in the multi-cultural, multi-ethnic society of Assam.

But behind this facade looms, the larger question of the ethnic identity of the Indian Nepalis. As observed by Glazier and Moynihan, "ethnic identities have replaced occupational identities as a source of self-esteem; ethnic loyalties are increasingly affected by political events pitting one ethnic group against another; ethnicity has taken the role of religion as a means of establishing one's identity".[74] Milton Gordon (1964) referred to ethnicity as a 'sense of peoplehood' created by common race, religion, national origin, history or combination of these.[75] Yet, it should be noted that cultural factors may change over time due to contact and assimilation, but a sense of separateness and distinctive ethnicity persists. Ethnic groups may thus become behaviourly assimilated while yet maintaining a strong sense of ethnic identity. Migrant groups, as in case of the Nepalis have remained as ethnic minority groups in the larger cultural complex of India. Contact and acculturation raise hopes, but numerous barriers still block ethnic minority groups from entrance into full range of opportunities in the larger society. The word 'Nepali' in the Indian mind immediately associates Indian Nepalis with the country Nepal, which hurts the social, political and economic standing of the Nepali speakers of India. "The confusion is exacerbated to the detriment of Indian Nepalis and their social standing, because their open border between the two countries allows unrestricted passage for labour exporting Nepal to send out migrant labour to India. Thus, the continuous recharge of the Indian market by the out-migrating people of Nepal reinforces the belief among Indians that all Indian Nepalis are also citizens of Nepal", writes Subba.[76] This predicament was exacerbated by the provisions of the Treaty of 1950. Even though Nepalis settled in India prior to the adoption of the Indian Constitution of 1950 were declared natural citizens of India, the general notion of other Indians is that of Indian Nepalis are immigrants, as there was no way to differentiate Indian Nepalis from those, who settled in India after 1950 and those, who continue to come down from the hills of Nepal into India. Pre-1950 documents to prove domicile was never considered necessary. Indian Nepalis, by and large are even not aware of the treaty and its created difficulties and take all humiliation, harassments and even cases of mass eviction from the North-east as fated.

This feeling of a relative deprivation in the society has grown by the years. As early as 1903-04, a proposal was made to declare Kaziranga as a reserve forest, but its final constitution was delayed due to the presence of a large number of buffaloes belonging to Nepali graziers. The Chief Commissioner remarked "it is at present used as a grazing ground and the presence of a herd of tamed buffaloes in this locality means that sooner or later cattle disease will spread into the Game reserve and interesting fauna of the province will be destroyed. The entire object of existing reserve will in fact be nullified". Following this, the British Government ordered all the graziers of Kaziranga to vacate their grazing lands within 24 hours in 1920. While the forest rangers and foresters burnt the household of the graziers, the latter, terrified by the atrocities looked for an alternative. Again in 1942, to accommodate the Muslim immigrants from Bengal. . . . All[77] the grazing reserves, which according to notification should have been freed of the encroacher, have been allowed to be overrun by the immigrants. . . . Riots and bloodshed in which the local graziers and local men are always work off, are becoming daily occurrences".

These deprivations and harassments, in fact led to the first assertion of ethnic identity of the Nepalis in the North-East. The Tezpur Graziers Association came into existence in 1933 at Singri, with Chabilal Upadhyay, a grazier and a Mahajan as a founder President to take up the cause of these evicted Nepali graziers.[78] The objective of the Association besides protecting the graziers and grazing lands, was the preservation of social integration between the Assamese and Nepali communities.[79] During the same period, another crisis was created, when the names of a large number of domiciled Nepalis were deleted from the voters' list. The Assam Graziers Association under the leadership of Prasad Singh Subba, protested against the move and tried to get the names included as under the then political situation in Assam in the 1940's exclusion of names from the voters' list implied possible eviction and deportation. In 1944, the serious problem of eviction faced by the graziers, led the Governor to place the matter before the State Assembly. And in 1944, Saadullah Muslim League Coalition Government threw select professional grazing reserves open for settling immigrants.[80]

The Nepali move to maintain their distinct identity led to conflicts, which were generally struggles for recognition of higher economic and social status and political power. During the Freedom Movement, they aligned themselves with the All India Gurkha League and the organizations of the movement in Assam and the North-East to carry forward the struggle for the assertion of their rights.

The state, time and again stood forth as a protector of their rights. In 1947, with the constitution of tribal belts and blocks, the Nepali graziers were given protected class status, which remained in practice upto 1969.[81] But there have also been instances of large deportation of the Nepalis from the North-East in the late 1960s. Again in the 1970s-80s and the 1990s, the nativist and separatist insurgency movements that have rocked Assam and the entire North-East, have brought the identity of the Indian Nepalis into question. The rhetoric of the Assam Movement in order to legitimize its demands labelled the Nepalis as Foreigners along with the immigrants from Bangladesh and demanded deportation. Large-scale deportations also did take place with instances of occasional violence and harassments. Again during the Bodo Movement, to establish their majority in the Bodo-dominated Areas, the Bodos resorted to an ethnic cleansing campaign, harassing and displacing Nepalis in the BAC (Bodo Autonomous Council) Areas along with the Santhals and Bengalis. In both these cases, the attacks were unwarranted. The Nepalis in Assam, a minority group socio-economically marginalized and making every effort to integrate themselves with the host community, economically and socially, have at no point of time, even numerically posed a threat to the dominant Asamiya ethnic identity. In the same way, the Nepali population in the BAC areas, which is only 2.5 per cent on an average, is in no way large enough to constitute a threat to the Bodos. It was only in 1996 that the Government of Assam restored the protected class status in respect of occupation of land in protected belts and blocks with effect.[82]

Although at present the situation had calmed down, the political status of the Nepalis in the North-East has remained as confusing as ever. In Assam after the Assam Accord of 1985, all foreigners entering without valid travel papers after 25th March, 1971 (30th July, 1976) for the Nepalis as the date for the imposition of the (RAP) Restricted Area Permit were to be considered illegal migrants,[83] while the same time, the 1950 Treaty continued to grant the Nepalis a reciprocal right to settle in India (with no-time bound curtailment). Going by the Central Government directive, the IMDT Act was not applicable to Nepalis entering India with or without travel papers.[84] Supported by the Treaty Agreement, Indians or Nepalis did not require identity papers to enter into each others countries till date.

This political uncertainty has also reflected their economic and social status. The Nepali community in the North-East live with a constant threat to their property and personal security, because the administrative machinery of either country could not care less about their well-being. This has also brought into sharp focus the tension between the Central Government's recognition of their right to stay in India and the post-colonial 'sons of the soil movements' construction on them as illegal migrants after 1971 (1976). Even among them, there seems to be no doubt as to the illegality of the post-1976 migrants and demand the abrogation of Article 7 of the 1950 Treaty, sealing the border or/and issuing passport and visa to detect the foreign Nepalis. But the significant most constructive move was to assert their distinct identity. As Subba points out "In what is essentially a defensive strategy, their leaders have sought to establish them as a distinct group within India and also distinguishes them from the Nepalis of Nepal".[85]

These assertions are more oriented towards defining their economic and social status. These threats have also put their economic and social security under strain. Inspite of contributing much to the economy and almost monopolizing the dairy farming industry, they are still a marginal community economically. In the same way, inspite of the occasional abrasions, society has more or less made space for them, but has not given them their due. Moreover, the political situation manages by and large to keep them a marginalized community.

This is reflected in the position of the dairy farmers. Inspite of their status in the industry, they still maintain a low profile. In many cases, we have noticed a shift to the industry, from well-paid established jobs with a possibility of an upward mobility, by the Nepali community. Is it because their upward mobility is blocked? Or is it because of their cultural complex of being an Indian Nepali unsure of their future status? The answer is a combination of all three, but more because of the culture of living a marginalized submerged life and that the ease and comfort in a profession, which by tradition has been theirs for years. Any affluence or an upward mobility in the society will bring them to notice, which they can ill afford for their economic and social security.

Conclusion

The Nepali Labour Migration once it started followed a dynamics of its own, and is an ongoing process. The reservoir of theories and conceptual frameworks have indeed helped in the understanding of the process, but the extreme diversity of the movement, in terms of forms, types, processes, actors, motivations, socio-economic context and so on, constantly revealed by empirical research, the dynamism manifested by an ever-changing reality, contrast with the limitations of theory building.

There can be no doubt that a large section of the labour migrant emerged from the landless section in Nepal. And although there has been some movement of Nepalis back to Nepal, to take advantage of the economic advantages in Kathmandu, by the educated of Darjeeling and the North-East in the past few decades, the flow into India and the North-east is much greater in comparison. This move continues despite continuous reports about how the Nepalis are harassed, humiliated and even evicted from their home and hearth in some parts of India and the North-east. While there are instances of rich Nepalis moving to the Gulf region, as well as South-East Asia, the poorest among them still come to India and the North-east primarily for work and the possibility of sending some earnings to the impoverished homestead back in Nepal. In the nineteenth and early twentieth economic reasons brought Nepali speakers out of Nepal; today, however, employment opportunities cannot adequately explain all of the movement. Although primacy of economic motives is a factor, the issue of social security is also a factor. The fallout of the Maoist 'people's war' has seen a rise in the number of Nepalis fleeing Nepal mid-hills. In the North-east, inspite of the occasional abrasions in the 1970s and 80s, "the depth of the demand and intensity of feeling against the Nepalis were definitely not as vociferous as against the East Pakistanis/Bangladeshis".[86] Again as remarked by a Political scientist that although the Nepalis are immigrants, "in the assertion of the rights of the indigenous peoples' *vis-à-vis* immigrants that have affected the entire region since the Assam Movement, the Nepalis are not always seen as migrants".[87] Some credibility to this statement is lent by the recent directives of the Central Government on deportation of foreigners and the enforcement of the IMDT Act, where no mention of the Nepalis are made.[88]

That they still continue to live, work and develop their business here is one more evidence of a feeling of security. The Nepali dairy farmer in the entire North-East, is the personification of the entire process of migration, that began nearly two centuries ago. They have integrated in themselves the whole gamut of human and social attributes that have enabled them to integrate in a cultural complex far away from home. The continuing viability of their labour intensive and manually operated dairy business, in a fast developing economy and the impact of globalization, is not only due to their monopoly over the business, but also the support from the society as a whole. This has been merited by their sincerity, devotion to duty, reliability and adaptability and assimilative nature.

That the open-border between India and Nepal will continue to foster cross-border movements, it cannot be denied. Inspite of demands for abrogation of the 1950 treaty and sealing the border to rule out further migration, the presence of a large community of Nepali people in the Indian/North-Eastern frontier will always serve as an emotional bonding to come here. What remains for the Indian side is to continue to make space for them in an economy and society to which they already have large contributions.

NOTES

1. Report No. 61/24, April, 1946 of the Central Intelligence Office, Government of Assam, cited in A.C. Sinha, "The Indian North-East Frontier and the Nepalese Immigrants", in *Himalayan Environment and Culture*, Simla, IIAS, 1990, p. 148.
2. Gurkha/Gurkha (some 48 miles distant from Kathmandu) was one of the 24 hill states, Chaubisi Raj, the central province of what is now known as the Kingdom of Nepal. The inhabitants were of Mongolian origin and warlike. The chieftainship of Gurkha fell into the hands of a family of Rajput origin who had immigrated due to Moslem invasion. They of the Gurkha dynasty was Dravya Shah, a descendent of the Raja of Chitor in North-West India, son of the Raja of Lamjung who ascended in 1559. Another was the Raja of Kaski. Gurkha has given its name to the ruling race while Kaski and Lamjung are territorial titles of the Maharaja of Nepal. Prithvi Narayan Shah who ascended the throne in 1742, with the aid of his warlike Gurkhas dominated the 24 states and became master of the whole valley. The soldiers recruited by the British for their armies came to be called Gurkhas. Government File No. 26C of 1929, Confidential B March 1929, Nos.269-271, Serial No. 287, *Treatise on Nepal By Lieut. Colonel Terence Keyes*, Simla, Government of India Press, 1928. Government File No. 382, Confidential B, Sept. 1934, Nos. 7-14, *Memorandum on Nepal* (Part I), *Who's Who in Nepal*, (Part II), Lieut. Col. C.T. Daukes, C.I.E., Simla, Government of India Press, 1933.

3. In the eighth century, the extent of the empire of the King of Kamrupa, Sri Harsha Deva, as referred to by K.L. Barua, and accepted by scholars and historians of Bengal and elsewhere, was over nearly half of Northern India from Sadiya in the East of Ayodhya in the West and from the Himalayas in the North as far as Bay of Bengal and Ganjam to the South. K.L. Barua, *Early History of Kamrupa*, Shillong, 1933, pp. 111-13. Dr. Hutton also mentions Assam's relations with Mithila (North Bihar) and Buchanan refers to Purnea and Mithila as the same place and denotes this place as a portion of the dominion of Gurkha. Maheswar Neog (ed.), *Studies in the Early History of Assam*, Assam Sahitya Sabha, Guwahati 1973, pp. 312-13.
4. K.L. Barua has remarked that the process of assimilation going on in Assam since time immemorial, "Explains the complete fusion of Gaudiya, Utkal, Dravidi, Kamrupi, Maithile, Kanaujia, Marwari and Nepali Brahmins in the Assamese Brahmin Society of the present days." K.L. Barua, *My Reminiscences* (ed.) Maheswar Neog.
5. Hagens (1916) classification of the people of Nepal, *Source:* Toni Hagen, 1961, "Nepal", p. 61, cited in J. Adhikari, *The Beginnings of Agrarian Change: A Case Study in Central Nepal*, Kathmandu, 1996, p. 58.

Tibeto Nepalese Races			*Indo Nepalese Races*	
Tibetan Group	*Ancient Nepalese*	*Group*	*Indian Group*	*Nepalese Group*
Bhotiyas	Newars	Rais	Indians	Brahmins Kshatriyas
Sherpas	Tamangs Gurungs	Limbus Buras	Garhwals	Khas
Thakalis	Magars Sunwars	Rukhas Tharus	Kumaons	Chettris Thakurs

6. The Tibeto-Burman settlers practiced the communal mode of production characterized by pastoralism and swidden cultivation with production based on kinship relations and community solidarity. Property relations were characterized by communal ownerships. This system was called Kipat and survived until the 1950s in some villages in eastern Nepal inhabited by the Kirati people, like the Rai and the Limbu. M.C. Regmi, *A Study of Nepali Economic History, 1768-1846*, Delhi, 1971, p. 27.
7. *Ibid.*
8. Jagannath Adhikari, *The Beginnings of Agrarian Change: A Case Study in Central Nepal*, Kathmandu, 1996, p. 67.
9. Lionel Caplan, *Land and Social Change in East Nepal: A Study of Hindu-Tribal Relations*, Berkeley, C.A. University of California Press.
10. Charles McDougal, *Village and Household Economy in Far Western Nepal*, T.U. Press, Kathmandu, 1968.
11. Mark Poffenberger, *Pattern of Change in Nepal Himalaya*, MacMillan, Madras, 1980.
12. T.B. Subba, *State of Nepal*, 2002, p. 121.
13. The *raikar* land tenure system implied lands under direct control and management of the government and the cultivators were under control of the government. Only the government was entitled to collect land tax and levy any other taxes on them. Krishna B. Thapa, *Main Aspects of Social, Economic and Administrative: History of Modern Nepal*, Kathmandu, 1995, p. 121, Regmi, 1978.
14. Birta means land grants made by the King to individuals, usually on an inheritable and tax-exempt basis. *Jagir* means the land assigned to government employees

and functionaries, or *jagirdars*, in lieu of their emolument. M.C. Regmi, *Thatched Huts and Stucco Palaces*, New Delhi, 1978, pp. 161-62.

15. Regmi, 1971.
16. T.B. Subba, *State of Nepal*, 2002, p. 121.
17. Regmi, 1971, p. 102.
18. *Jhara* labour was used for military purposes as well as other state services. Such labourers were not only required to leave their villages for service in distant places, but were also required to furnish arms and equipments they had. The villagers enroute to war zones were also required to supply arms, ammunition, etc. within their village boundaries. This relay system called *hulak*, although meant to minimize the *Jhara* system, it was considered a burden to the villages on the route to the battle front. Regmi, 1971, p. 110.
19. Adhikari, p. 69.
20. During the process of unification, the Corvee labour was made universal in 1799 to meet the chronic labour shortage.
21. An example are the Tharus in the Terai, who were required to provide one member per family for corvee work for hunting trips or royal palace. To minimize the effects of this obligation, these Tharus developed a joint family system, so that many Tharu families has 50,100 or even more than that number. Further, under the Ranas, any sign of good living among them was considered a sign of savings and their house and property were confiscated. As such these settlers of the Terai never attempted to save, as their savings could not be utilized, but were consumed as feasts. Their position thus became economically vulnerable.
22. Ludwig Stiller, *Silent Cry*, Sah Yogi Prakashan, Kathmandu, 1976, p. 66.
23. N.R. Shrestha, *Landlessness and Migration in Nepal*, Colarado West View Press, 1990, pp. 292-97.
24. Cited in Sanjib Barua, *India Against Itself*, 2001, p. 44.
25. Anindita Dasgupta, "Othering of the Not-so-other: A study of the Nepalis in Assam", in A.C. Sinha and T.B. Subba (ed.), *The Nepalis in North-East India: A Community in Search of Indian Identity*, Indus Publishing Co., Delhi, 2000, p. 231.
26. In 1975, the per capita income of the Nepalese people were $115, while it was $136 in India, $6294 in US, $3664 in UK. Central Bureau of Statistics, H.M.G., *Nepal: Statistical Pocket Book*, Nepal, 1982, p. 210.
27. Cited in A.C. Sinha, *The Indian North-East Frontier and the Nepalese Immigrants*, 1990, p. 226.
28. Shakespeare, *History of the Assam Rifles*, 1977, 23.
29. Ethnic Background of the Gurkha soldier in the British army in First World War (1914-18) were as follows. J. Adhikari, p. 85.

Ethnic Group	*%*	*Ethnic Group*	*%*
Magar	35	Tamang	6
Gurung	17	Thakuri	3
Chettri	16	Sunwar	1
Rai	12	Others	3s
Limbus	7		

30. L.W. Shakespeare, *History of the Assam Rifles*, Macmillan Co., London, 1929.
31. L.S.S. O'Malley, 1907 (Reprinted ed.) 1985, *Bengal District Gazetteer*, Darjeeling, New Delhi, p. 44.

32. Of such sites Assam alone has thirteen, Manipur eight, Mizoran and Nagaland seven each, Arunachal Pradesh three and Meghalaya and Tripura one each. Some of these sites are as old as hundred yeats.
33. K.M. Dixit, *Lowly Labour in the Lowlands.*
34. Table showing Nepali Labourers employed in the Tea gardens, saw mills and oil refineries in Assam.

Year	*Total*
1897	179
1898	231
1899	188
1901	272*
1902	102
1903	184*

*These include figures for Bombay and Nepal.
Source: Report on labour immigration into Assam, 1898, 1899; Resolution on Labour Immigration into Assam, 1902-03, 1903-04, Shillong.

35. A.C. Sinha, 1990, p. 231.
36. *Ibid.*
37. The difficult terrain made life miserable and unprofitable for the farmers and graziers, who constituted 90 per cent of Nepal's labour force. Inspite of satisfactory harvest the farmer still faced hardships because of the considerable uphill distance from his village, to transport produce to the nearest urban market. They often migrate to the lowland Terai and since that region is also unsuitable because of the loo, they make a beeline for India and the North-East. Aṃena Nora Passah, "Nepali Christians in the Khasi and Jaintia Hills of Meghalaya", in Subba and Sinha (ed.), *The Nepalis in North-East India: A Community in Search of an Indian Identity*, Delhi, 2002, p. 279.
38. Interview with Tulsi Upadhyaya, 52 yrs., dairy farmer in Sisimukh Nepali Gaon, Dhemaji District, Assam.
39. A. Guha, *Planter Raj to Swaraj*, 1988, pp. 91-94.
40. Cited in Purushottam Bhandari, *Freedom Movement and Role of Indian Nepalis*, Jagiroad, 1996, p. 42.
41. The Baraimala center was under the Mahajan Bidyapati, while the Ama Chapari under the leadership of Chabilal Upadhyaya. Sajal Nag, "Fei-sation of the Nepalis of North-East India", in Sinha and Subba (ed.), 2002, pp. 184-93.
42. *Progress Report of Forest Administration in the Province of Assam*, 1895-96, p. 13.
43. Names like Forse Tapu, Rani Tapu, Shordar Tapu. The name '*Forse*' in Nepalese meant pumpkin or '*mitha lao*' in Asamiya. An officer of the Forest Department mentioned that there were large pumpkin plantations there. Another explanation offered was that the char was named after a popular and rich milkman or *Khuntiwallah*, whose name was *Forse*. In other words, the name *Forse Tapu* stood for *Forse Khutiwallah's Char*. Similar explanations are offered for the other names. What emerges from these stories and names is that the *Chars* with Nepali names had been settled earlier than those with Asamiya or Bengali names, Dasgupta, A. (2001): *Emergence of a Community: Muslims of East Bengal Origin in Assam in the Colonial and Post-Colonial Period*, Unpublished Thesis, G.U.

44. In the year 1892-93, 13,025 buffaloes and 1,162 cows paid grazing fees amounting to ₹ 6,772. Progress Report of Forest Administration in the Province of Assam, 1892-93, p. 10, cited in Tejimala Gurung, *op. cit.*
45. *Ibid.*
46. In 1888, the fees was 8 *annas* per annum per head of buffaloes and 4 *annas* per head of cows. In 1907, it was raised to ₹ 1 per buffalo and still higher in 1912 and continued to ₹ 3 per buffalo and *annas* 6 per cow, in 1917, in the Assam Valley, Garo Hills and N.E. frontier. In the Hill districts, a rate ranging from ₹ 4 to ₹ 6 was in force since 1917, cited in A. Guha, 1988, pp. 91-92.
47. No. of buffaloes taxed: 1895-1920.

Year	*1895*	*1900*	*1905*	*1910*	*1915*	*1920*
No.	15,640	18,735	24,346	40,000	42,000	86,325

Revenue Collected: 1916-1921

Year	*1916-17*	*1917-18*	*1919-20*	*1920-21*
₹ 1,000	183	342	277	341

Source: A. Guha, 1988, p. 92.
48. A. Guha, 1988, p. 93.
49. Report on the Administration of Assam 1912-13, p. 5.
50. Extract Revenue Department, No. 79R, dt. 8 January 1938, p. 2.
51. Report on the Land Revenue Administration of the Assam Valley division for the year 1939-40, p. 10.
52. K.N. Datta, *Assam District Gazetteer: United Mikir and North Cachar District*, Guwahati, 1979.
53. Subba, 1997, p. 40.
54. A.C. Sinha, "The Indian North-East Frontier and the Nepalese Immigrants", in *Himalayan Environment and Culture*, Shimla, IIAS, 1990, p. 229.
55. *Ibid.*
56. T.B. Subba, *op. cit.*, p. 40.
57. Unless otherwise noted this and other quoted comments are taken from interviews with Nepali dairy farmers, 3rd and 4th generation migrants in various places in Assam.
58. The Transhumance system of raising sheep was followed by the Gurungs in the past, about 50 years ago. Sheep used to be moved from lower to higher altitudes and *vice-versa* according to the season. During summer season (June-August) sheep were taken as high as 5,600 m and during winter (December-February). They were brought down to the village at 1,900 m. This practice had ceased by the 1990s. J. Adhikari, p. 191.
59. *Ibid.*, p. 188.
60. One of the main features of army service, past and present is that Magars, Gurungs, Rais and Limbus, but not Brahmins and Chettris have been the men mainly involved. Gurungs and Magars have been preferred for their military bearing and skill. Members of these ethnic groups were compelled to join the army for their low economic positions and discrimination within the country for high ranking military positions during the Rana regime. J. Adhikari, p. 85.
61. *Ibid.*, p. 18.
62. By hiring oxen they were relieved of the burden of maintaining oxen during the lean farming season. *Ibid.*, p. 184.

63. Table showing percentage of households owning livestock in 1988-1989. *Ibid.*, p. 183.

Ethnic Groups	*Cows*	*Buffaloes*	*Oxen*	*Goats*	*Poultry*
Brahmin	61.3	72.6	72.6	75.8	40.3
Gurung	20.0	63.3	25.0	8.3	71.7
Chettri	35.0	57.5	47.5	42.5	55.0
Occup. Castes	29.7	32.4	24.3	18.9	51.4

64. Interview with Min Raj Joshi, 50 yrs., President of the Greater Guwahati Gopalak Sanstha, Guwahati.
65. Interview with Narayan Sharma, 25 yrs., Milk Supplier in Guwahati.
66. Interview with Min Raj Joshi.
67. Interview with Ram Chetri, 45 yrs., a dairy farmer in Jorhat.
68. A.C. Sinha, 1990, p. 230.
69. Purushottam L. Bhandari, "Evolution and Growth of the Nepali Community in N.E. India", in Sinha and Subba (ed.), 2002, p. 121.
70. Some of the societies are: Tezpur graziers, Biswanath Chariali, Singri, Barpuja, Monaha, Chandrapur, Amerigog, Banda, Birkuchi, Dudhnoi, Rampur, Bokajan, Athgaon, North Jamuguri, sadiya, etc. *Ibid.*
71. *Ibid.*, pp. 121-22.
72. Interview with G. Sharma, aged 50, Guwahati.
73. Min Raj Joshi.
74. Nathan Glazer and Daniel P. Moynihan (ed.), *Ethnicity: Theory and Experiences*, Harvard University Press, Boston, 1976.
75. Milton Gordon, *Assimilation in American Life*, Oxford University Press, New York, 1964, p. 24.
76. *Ibid.*, p. 130.
77. Agni B. Chetri, *Itixaxar Adharat Asamar Nepali*, 1996, Guwahati, p. 109.
78. P. Bhandari, *Freedom Movement and the Role of the Indian Nepalis*, Assam, 1996, pp. 87-91.
79. *Ibid.*
80. Guha, 1988, p. 282.
81. Vide Memo No. RSD-26/64/PT/15 dated 17th June, 1969 cited in Purushottam L. Bhandari, "Evolution and Growth of the Nepali community in N.E. India", in T.B. Subba and Sinha (ed.) 2002, p. 121.
82. Vide Memo No. RSD-17/85/PT-1/2 dated Dispur 19th March, 1996. *Ibid.*
83. The Minutes of the Joint Action Committee of Assam Nepali Organization held on 9.9.1985.
84. The Illegal Migrant Determination by Tribunal Act was incorporated in 1983, which ensured that the genuine Indian citizens belonging to the minority communities could not be harassed in search and detection of foreigners. A. Dasgupta, p. 244.
85. Tanka B. Subba, *Ethnicity, State and Development*, Vikas, New Delhi, 1992. Cited in A. Dasgupta, p. 245.
86. M. Hussain, *The Assam Movement—Class, Ideology and Identity*, Manak Publications, Delhi, 1993, p. 261.
87. Sanjib Barua, *India Against Itself*, 1999, p. 53.
88. "Centre, States Strike deal on Identity cards", *The Telegraph*, January 8, 2003. "Launch Special Drives to Detect Foreigners", *The Assam Tribune*, January 8, 2003.

BIBLIOGRAPHY

Adhikari, Jagannath (1996), *The Beginnings of Agrarian Change: A Case Study in Central Nepal* (Kathmandu: TM Publication).

Administrative Report of Assam 1912-13 (Shillong, India: Government of Assam).

Baruah, Sanjib (2001), *India Against Itself: Assam and the Politics of Nationality* (New Delhi: OUP).

Bhandari, Purushottam L. (1996), *Freedom Movement and Role of Indian Nepalese, 1800-1950* (Jagiroad, Assam: Mrs. Rama Bhandari).

Bhandari, Purushottam L. (2003), "Evolution and Growth of the Nepali Community in North-East India", in A.C. Sinha and T.B. Subba (Eds.), *The Nepalis in North-East India: A Community in Search of Indian Identity*, pp. 106-23 (New Delhi: Indus Publishing Co.).

Bista, Dor B. (1980), *People of Nepal* (Kathmandu: Ratna Pustak Bhandar).

Caplan Lionel, *Land and Social Change in East Nepal: A Study of Hindu-Tribal Relations*, Berkeley, C.A. University of California Press.

Census of India, 1931, Vol. 3, Part 1 (Shillong: Central Publication Branch, Calcutta).

Census of India, 1932, Vol. 3, (Shillong: Central Publication Branch, Calcutta).

Central Bureau of Statistics (1982), *Statistical Pocket Book* (Nepal: H.M.G.).

Chetri, Agni B. (1996), *Itixaxar Adharat Asamar Nepali* (A historical perspective of the Nepalese in Assam) (Biswanath Chariali, Assam: Sri. Satyabrata Chetri, Galia).

Chettry, G.K.N. (2003), "The Nepalis of Manipur: Movement and Settlement", in: A.C. Sinha and T.B. Subba (Eds.), *The Nepalis in North-East India: A Community in Search of Indian Identity*, pp. 304-20 (New Delhi: Indus Publishing Co.).

Dasgupta, Anindita (2003), "Othering of the Not-so-other: A Study of the Nepalis in Assam", in A.C. Sinha and T.B. Subba (Eds.), *The Nepalis in North-East India: A Community in Search of Indian Identity*, pp. 230-49 (New Delhi: Indus Publishing Co.).

Dasgupta, Anindita (2001), *Emergence of a Community: Muslims of East Bengal Origin in Assam in the Colonial and Post-Colonial Period*, PhD thesis submitted to Guwahati University, India.

Datta, K.N. (1979), *Assam District Gazetteer: United Mikir and North Cachar District* (Guwahati: Government of Assam).

Dixit, Kanak Mani and Shastri Ramachandran (ed.). *State of Nepal*, Himal Books, Nepal, 2002.

Extract Revenue Department, No. 79R, 8 January, 1938 (Shillong: Government of India).

Guha, Amalendu (1988), *Planter-Raj to Swaraj: Freedom Struggle and Electoral Politics in Assam 1826-1947* (New Delhi: Peoples Publishing House).

Gurung, Tejimala (2003), "Human Movement and the Colonial State: The Nepalis of North-East India under the British Empire", in A.C. Sinha and T.B. Subba (Eds.), *The Nepalis in North-East India: A Community in Search of Indian Identity*, pp. 172-84 (New Delhi: Indus Publishing Co.).

Holly, Gayley (2002), "Gyanendra's Test: Nepal's Monarchy in the Era of Democracy", *Harvard Asia Quarterly*, Winter, VI:1. pp. 3-4.

Hussain, Imdad (2003), "Soldiers and Settlers: Recruitment of Gorkhas", in A.C. Sinha and T.B. Subba (Eds.), *The Nepalis in North-East India: A Community in Search of Indian Identity*, pp. 67-105 (New Delhi: Indus Publishing Co.).

The Kathmandu Post, 29 September, 2003, Kathmandu, Nepal.

Massey, D.M.; Arango, J.; Hugo, G.; Kouaouci, A. and Taylor, J.E. (1998), *Worlds in Motion: Understanding International Migration at the End of the Millennium* (Oxford, Clarendon Press).

Nag, Sajal (2003), "Fei-zation of the Nepalis of North-East India", in A.C. Sinha and T.B. Subba (Eds.), *The Nepalis in North-East India: A Community in Search of Indian Identity*, pp. 184-93 (New Delhi: Indus Publishing Co.).

Nath, Lopita (2004a), *Cross Border Labour Movements: The Nepalis in North-East India*. Paper presented at the Workshop on Labour Migration in an Earlier Phase of Global Restructuring, Xiamen University, China, sponsored by SEPHIS, 18-20 April, Unpublished.

Nath, Lopita (2004b), "Migrants in Flight: Conflict-induced Displacement of Nepalis in North-East India", *Peace and Democracy in South Asia Journal* (www.pdsajournal.com).

Nath, Lopita (2003a), "Conflict Afflicted Nepalis of Assam: The Reality", in A.C. Sinha and T.B. Subba (Eds.), *The Nepalis in North-East India: A Community in Search of Indian Identity*, pp. 208-229 (New Delhi: Indus Publishing Co.).

Nath, Lopita (2003b), *The Nepalis in Assam: Ethnicity and Cross Border Movements in the North-East* (Kolkata: Minerva Associates Publications Pvt. Ltd.).

O'Malley, L.S.S. (1985), *Bengal District Gazetteer* (Facsimile reprint of 1907 original) (Darjeeling: New Delhi).

Progress Report of Forest Administration in the Province of Assam, 1892-1893 (Shillong, India: Government of Assam).

Progress Report of Forest Administration in the Province of Assam, 1895-1896 (Shillong, India: Government of Assam).

Regmi, M.C. (1978), *Thatched Huts and Stucco Palaces* (New Delhi: Vikas Publishing House).

Regmi, M.C. (1971), *A Study in Nepali Economic History, 1768-1846* (New Delhi: Manjishri Publishing House).

Report of the Special Officer Appointed for the Examination of the Professional Grazing Reserves in the Assam Valley, 1944, Guwahati, India. Unpublished report held in Guwahati Assam Archives.

Report on the Administration of Assam 1912-13. Unpublished report held in Guwahati Assam Archives.

Report on the Land Revenue Administration of the Assam Valley Division for the year 1939-40. Unpublished report held in Guwahati Assam Archives.

Sinha, A.C. (2003), "The Indian North-East Frontier and Nepali Immigrants", in A.C. Sinha and T.B. Subba (Eds), *The Nepalis in North-East India: A Community in Search of Indian Identity*, pp. 31-52 (New Delhi: Indus Publishing Co.).

Timsina, Suman Raj, *Nepali Community in India*, New Delhi, 1992.

Todaro M.P. (1969), "A Model of Labour Migration and Urban Unemployment in Less Developed Countries", *American Economic Review*, March 1969; (1976) International Migration in Developing Countries, Geneva, International Labour Office.

Sinha, A.C. and T.B. Subba (Eds.) (2003), *The Nepalis in North-East India: A Community in Search of Indian Identity* (New Delhi: Indus Publishing Co.).

Shrestha, N.R. (1990), *Landlessness and Migration in Nepal* (Colarado: West View Press).

Stiller, Ludwig (1976), *Silent Cry* (Kathmandu: Sah Yogi Prakashan).

Subba, T.B. (2003), "Nepalis in North-East India: Political Aspirations and Ethnicity", in A.C. Sinha and T.B. Subba (Eds.), *The Nepalis in North-East India: A Community in Search of Indian Identity*, pp. 54-66 (New Delhi: Indus Publishing Co.).

Subba, T.B. (2002), "Nepal and the Indian Nepalis", in Kanak Mani Dixit and Shastri Ramachandaran (Eds.), *State of Nepal*, pp. 119-36 (Kathmandu: Himal Books).

Thapa, Krishna B. (1995), *Main Aspects of Social, Economic and Administrative History of Modern Nepal* (Kathmandu: Ratna Pustak Bhandar).

Tucci, Giuseppe (1962), *Nepal: The Discovery of the Malla* (Trans. Lovett Edwards) (London: George Allen & Unwin).

Whelpton, John (2005), *A History of Nepal* (United Kingdom: Cambridge University Press).

27

FRONTIER MARKETS AND THE AHOM-JAYANTIYA RELATIONS

I.S. Mumtaza

The westward expansion of the territory brought the Ahom into the relations with the Jayantiyas, the western neighbour of the Kacharis. With the Jayantiyas the Ahoms had, in addition to the political relations, a commercial relation, too. For the purpose, the Ahoms maintained some markets at different points of their frontier between the two kingdoms. In this article an attempt has been made to study the circumstances that led to the establishment of markets at the frontier and the impact of the political relations on these markets as well as on the commercial relations.

In 1605, the Jayantiya king, Yasamanik (c.1605-1625) sent envoys to the Ahom court to establish a relation with the Ahom king, Siu-seng-pha (1603-1641).[1] The chief object of this mission, on the part of the Jayantiya king, was to take revenge on the Kachari king, who had given him and his predecessor serious cause of displeasure.[2] Unable to offer any effective resistance to the Kacharis, Yasamanik endeavoured to embroil with the Ahoms and thereby to punish them. With this end in view, he urged the Ahom king that "give us protection against the Kachari king, who has been making preparation to destroy us".[3] He not only requested for assistance, but also he was ready to submit himself to the Ahom king by offering two of his daughters to him (Siu-seng-pha). As Siu-seng-pha accepted the Jayantiya king's offer, a political relation between the two with submission was established.[4]

Soon after the establishment of the political relations, the Jayantiya king made a request for a plot of land on the bank of the Kallang river, which was within the jurisdiction of the Ahom kingdom, for the purpose of establishing a market there.[5] It being a matter of serious kind, the request was discussed at the Ahom Royal Council. After a thorough discussion on the request, the Councilors came to the conclusion that a market could be established only on conditions: firstly, the plot of land should be on the frontier area of the Ahom kingdom so that the people of both the kingdoms could trade there, secondly, if the Jayantiya king could supply fuel wood, fish, dear as tribute for the market, then only a market would be established. The Jayantiya king, Yasamanik, agreed the conditions and a market at Phulaguri on the Ahom frontier and a place about 4 km to the north-east of present Raha town on the bank of the Kallang river, was established under the supervision of an Ahom official to trade by the traders of both the territories. According to L. Devi the Jayantiya king supplied these commodities to the Barphukan till 1667 when the office of the Barphukan was shifted to Guwahati.[6] This market was followed by a few more markets established at different important points like Salna, Sonapur and so on at the frontier of the Ahom kingdom.[7]

A closer study of the relations between them it is reveals that these markets were continued to be the centre of trade till an amicable political relation existed between the two kingdoms. Any disturbances in the political relation had its affect on the frontier markets, and these were closed for the Jayantiya traders. The political relations, again, depended on the behaviour of the Jayantiya king, and any violation in the existing norms and procedures was considered by the Ahom rulers as an attempt of throwing off the Ahom allegiance. Hence, this strategic office was handled with iron hand as in the incident happened during the reign of Jayadhvaj Singha (1648-1662). Soon after the accession to the Jayantiya throne, Yasamattarai (c.1647-1669) sent a verbal message that instead of five letters[8] addressed to him alone from the Ahom court, he should write to the Ahom king, his ministers to the Ahom ministers and his governor to the Ahom governor.[9] This proposal was interpreted by Jayadhvaj Singha as an attempt to throw off the Ahom allegiance. This brought the cessation of all communications between the two kingdoms. As a measure of punishment, the frontier markets were closed for the Jayantiya traders, and a number of Jayantiya traders were arrested.[10] Facing severe hardship due to the closure of the frontier markets, Yasamattarai in 1655 sent his envoys obeying existing norms and procedures to the Barphukan with a request to re-establish the relation with the Ahoms.[11] This led to the renewal of relations and the Jayantiya traders were allowed to trade in the frontier markets. Another incident for the closure of the frontier markets was occurred in the first quarter of the eighteenth century. In 1708, following the sending an army[12] by the Ahom king Rudra Singha (1696-1714) to the Jayantiya kingdom all the frontier markets were closed for the Jayantiya traders. The Ahom army in their expedition captured the Jayantiya king Ram Singha with his elder son Barkowar and brought to the Ahom kingdom. Ram Singha died in his captivity at Rangpur, and Barkonwar was made king, and then sent to Jayantipur.[13] Before his departure, Barkonwar promised to send people to serve under the Barphukan at Guwahati and an annual tribute.[14] With the re-establishment of an amicable political relation the markets at the frontier were opened for the Jayantiya traders. This situation, however, did not continue for long, as Barkonwar was unable to keep his promise, the frontier markets were closed and remained so till the later part of Siva Singha's reign. The closure of frontier markets had caused the Jayantiya traders considerable financial hardship. During this period, the Jayantiya king, without keeping his promise, requested repeatedly for re-opening of the markets.[15] In 1724 Barphukan replied to the visiting Jayantiya envoys that if the Jayantiya king sent tribute regularly, as he promised earlier, the markets would be opened permanently, otherwise not. He further said that Phulaguri was inside the Ahom kingdom and the market would be established wherever it was convenient for the Ahoms. There would be an official meeting between the officers of both the kingdoms, then only the Jayantiya traders could trade there.[16] Afterwards the Jayantiya king sent annual tributes regularly and the markets at frontier were opened for the Jayantiya traders, and continued the relations till the end of the Ahom rule.

The chronicles are silent regarding the list of articles transacted at these markets. However, stray references of the seventeenth and eighteenth centuries to the trade of the Ahom kingdom and the Jayantiya people throw some light on it. Shehabuddin Talesh, who accompanied the Mughal general Mir Jumla in his invasion of the Ahom kingdom in 1662-1663, says ". . . a group of Aashamese used to come near the border of Guwahati . . . to carry out business brought products like gold, musk, aloe-wood, pepper, *Sazaj* and silk clothes and bartered them for salt, sulphur, brimstone and some other Indian goods imported by the traders of Guwahati".[17] Jean-Baptiste Chevalier, "one of the most remarkable French agents in India" and who visited the Ahom kingdom in 1755, while recording the purpose of his visit wrote ". . . we could get a lot of gold, elephant tusks, pepper, lacquer, wood for construction and cotton balls, besides big cargo loads of those wools that are so renowned for their fine texture and beauty".[18] In 1787, a revenue officer of Sylhet, Lindsay, who was well acquainted with every article of commerce of Sylhet markets, wrote in his letter to John Shore, President, Board of

Revenue, that articles of trade brought by the Jayantiya traders to Syhlet "consisted of Assam clothes, iron, cotton and different fruits".[19] This indicates that the Assam cloth both silk and cotton, gold, aloe-wood, pepper were some of the chief articles traded at the frontier markets and these were brought by the Jayantiya traders to other parts of the kingdom. Again, during the late nineteenth century A.C. Allen while narrating the trade of Khasi and Jayantiya Hills, mentioned that among other articles "hand woven cotton and silk cloth were imported from the plains".[20]

The above study reveals that the Ahom rulers had maintained, in addition to the political relation, a relation related to the trade of the people of both the kingdoms. On the request of the Jayantiya ruler frontier markets were established by the Ahom government within their kingdom for the benefit of the Jayantiya traders. Over these markets the Ahom government had the full control, — all the administrative affairs were determined by the Ahom officials, and the Jayantiya traders had only the right to trade there by paying necessary tributes. The nature of establishment of the markets at Phulaguri, Salna and Sonapur shows that the Jayantiya king was responsible in the continuation of the commercial relations. Any violation of the existing norms and procedures in the continuation of political relations between them effected the commercial relations and the traders were not allowed to enter the market for trade.

NOTES AND REFERENCES

1. *Jayantia Buranji*, ed. by S.K. Bhuyan, Guwahati, 1964, p. 14; *Kachari Buranji*, ed. by S.K. Bhuyan, Guwahati, 1957, p. 21; *A History of Assam*, Sir E.A. Gait, Kolkata, 1967 (3rd revised edition), p. 108; *Ahom-Tribal Relations*, L. Devi, Guwahati, 1968, p. 109.
2. In the latter part of the sixteenth century, due to Koch invasion there was a setback in the political and diplomatic history of this region of the Brahmaputra valley. The Koch army, after subjugating the Ahom ruler Siu-kham Pha, invaded the Kachari kingdom. Being themselves in difficulties, the Ahom ruler could not come, to rescue the Kachari ruler, who was the *thapita-sanchita*, established and protectorate of the Ahom ruler. As a result, the Kachari king succumbed to the Koches and became a tributary of the Koch king Naranarayan. However, this situation soon changed, and the Ahom king got back his lost position. The Kachari king Yasanarayan, too, threw off the Koch suzerainty and became independent. Soon after when the Mughals invaded his territory, Yasanarayan repulsed them. Emboldened by this victory he invaded the Jayantiya kingdom and forced its ruler, Dhanmanik, to acknowledge the Kachari suzerainty by offering his daughter, Sandhyavati. In order to enforce the submission of Dhanmanik, the Kachari king took away Yasamanik, the Jayantiya heir apparent, as hostage to the Jayantiya capital. On the death of Dhanmanik, Yasamanik was

released from captivity and send to the capital, Jayantipur, after making him king subordinate to the Kachari king.

3. *Kachari Buranji*, p.21.
4. *Ahom-Buranji*, tr. and ed. by Rai Sahib Golap Chandra Barua, Kolkata, 1930, p. 36; *Jayantia Buranji*, pp. 14-17; *Kachari Buranji*, p. 22; *Deodhai Ahom Buranji*, ed. by S.K. Bhuyan, Guwahati, 1962, pp. 56-57.
5. *Jayantia Buranji*, p. 17.
6. *Ibid.*, pp. 17-18; *Ahom-Tribal Relations*, pp. 109-10.
7. *Ibid.*, p. 20.
8. The normal procedure, in diplomatic correspondence of the Ahoms with the subordinates was that the Ahom court would send five letters, one each by the king, three ministers and the frontier governor through whose province the envoys entered the Ahom kingdom, addressed to the subordinate ruler. In return, the subordinate ruler would send five letters addressed to each five separately.
9. *Jayantia Buranji*, p. 20.
10. *Ibid.*
11. *Ibid.*, p. 21.
12. The causes of sending army was that the Kachari king, Tamradhvaj, whose kingdom was invaded by the Ahom army in 1706, fled away from his capital and ultimately was captured by the Jayantiya king, who imprisoned him at his capital. Knowing this development Rudra Singha demanded immediate release of Tamradhvaj, but the Jayantiya king Ram Singha (1701-1708) refused to comply with the demand. Rudra Singha thereupon dispatched armies to Jayantiya capital to capture both the Kachari and Jayantiya kings.
13. *Tungkhungia Buranji*, ed. by S.K. Bhuyan, Guwahati, 1963, pp. 32-34.
14. *Jayantia Buranji*, p. 118.
15. *Ibid.*, pp. 119-37.
16. *Ibid.*, p. 127.
17. *Tarikh-e-Aasham*, Shehabuddin Talesh, tr. by Dr. Mazhar Asif, Guwahati, 2009, p. 53.
18. *The Adventures of Jean-Baptiste Chevalier in Eastern India (1752-1765)*, Guwahati, p. 23.
19. *The Sylhet District Records*, vol. II (1786-88), ed. by Walter K. Ferminger, Shillong, 1917, p. 205.
20. *Gazetteer of the Khasi and Jaintia Hill, Garo Hills*, Lushai Hills, B.C. Allen, Delhi, 1980, p. 92.

28

SITUATING THE PARTITION OF 1947 WITHIN THE FRAME-WORK OF POST-COLONIAL ASSAM

Moushumi D. Pathak

Studies on India's partition of 1947 so long have mainly focussed on Punjab and Bengal ignoring importantly the 'third' state affected by partition, i.e. Assam. Whatever little effort that has been attempted in this regard had made Sylhet, an erstwhile district of colonial Assam as the centre of their study. The impact of partition on Assam generally figures around Sylhet in their work. Again, partition historiography that previously emerged basically revolved around looking into the cause of the event taking little into account as to what partition had led to. It is only a matter of recent interest among historians and social scientists to introspect the afterlife or aftermath of partition in South Asia. In other words, they now look at how partition impacted on post-colonial history and politics (Bandhopadhyaya, 2004:464).

The Partition of 1947 divided the Indian sub-continent into India and Pakistan. It was basically a division on account of religion. The geographical redistribution of territorial boundaries on religious lines was primarily to fulfil the *divide etempera* policy of the colonialist. Partition was actualized by the Boundary Commission of Sir Cyril Radcliffe that divided both Punjab and Bengal thereby ceding in the process West Punjab and East Bengal to Pakistan. The colonial province of Assam handed over the district of Sylhet to East Pakistan, though it had been a part of Assam since 1874, by holding the Sylhet Referendum on July, 1947. However, the *thanas* of Patharkandi, Karimganj and Ratabari remained with India.

This chapter proposes to study the impact of Partition on the province of Assam and the consequences that the event had on the future politics of the State.

History of Partition teaches a lesson that the act of Partition should never merely mean the physical division of India, it had cut through the 'corporate living' of many thousands of people who had and still have, scores of cultural similarities. Political decisions based on communalism overpowered cultural and economic considerations to divide the people concerned into two distinct groups having contending passions (Pakrasi, 1971:1). The division that took place on communal basis was not only morally wrong, but also practically unfeasible. Most frontiers usually followed courses of rivers or mountain ranges. Indo-Pakistan frontiers did not follow any natural boundaries. They were drawn with the sole object of separating predominantly Muslim areas from the non-Muslim ones. But the communities had been so inextricably mixed up all over the sub-continent that despite the tortuously zigzagging lines, they failed in their object and did not satisfy either India or Pakistan (Singh, 1957:38). Moreover, so unevenly was distributed the religious population all over the sub-continent that division on religious grounds seemed to be entirely futile with the result of religious minorities sustaining themselves on either side of the border clinching inseparably to the 'land of their birth'. The genesis of Partition as propounded by the two-nation theory of the Muslim League and acquiesced in by Congress leaders proved to be a myth "with the 1991 Census earmarking the Muslim population in India to be 92.5 million" (Basu, 2002:163). The creation of Bangladesh in 1971, speaks of the futility of the creation of Pakistan in 1947 on religious lines with long expanse of territories between the two territories outdistancing them geographically.

The importance and economic irrationality of this unnatural geographical Partition also arose from the fact that West Punjab and Sindh were the most irrigated and fertile areas of undivided India. And again East Bengal accounted for almost the entire jute growing area and a substantially high proportion of the coarse paddy growing area of undivided India and naturally it had been the main source of supply of coarse paddy and raw jute. But, 98 per cent of the jute mills of undivided India were located at West Bengal in India (Prakash Shri, 2002:308). Rajani Palme Dutt, analyzing from a Marxist standpoint the British Imperialist rule and the resurgent national struggle for freedom, has rightly observed, "Partition is the time bomb planted by the British in their freedom gift to India" (Gokhale, 1948:15). Partition brought in problems relating to evacuee properties, compensation to be paid to refugees for the loss of their assets, provisions for the settlement of refugees, which thereby greatly strained the exchequer of India and the newly created state of Pakistan. (Vakil, 1950:8).

The deep-rooted impact of Partition on Assam was reflected through her political, social and economic condition. The Shukla Commission Report that was submitted to the Prime Minister of India on 7th March, 1997 (Shukla Commission 1997:www.planning commission.govt.in), enquiring into the infrastructure stated that "the North-East was uniquely disadvantaged by Partition which left its external perimeter with no more than 2 per cent contiguity with the rest of India. . . . No other part of the country barring Jammu and Kashmir has had to bear a comparable burden with severe market disruption, total isolation and loss of traditional communication infrastructure, all of which had pushed regional costs and prices well above national norms, transport subsidies notwithstanding". The ceding of East Bengal to Pakistan disrupted the traditional economic institutions in North-East India. It deprived the hill areas of the market for their agricultural products and handicrafts. It also meant an abnormal increase in the price of fish, a staple food and a decline in the price of jute. River communications as well as road links were disrupted. . . . Henceforth, the people of East Bengal needed passports to lawfully enter the Brahmaputra Valley and the tribals of Chittagong hill tracts to enter the Mizo hills; the people of Arunachal Pradesh were confronted by security forces near the borders of Tibet; the Nagas found themselves living in India as well as Burma; and the Mizos in India were separated from their kinsmen in Burma. All these groups had hitherto, prior to Partition, moved freely and, therefore, resented international frontiers that restricted their 'natural' movements (Singh, 1997:5). Historian David Ludden views the impact of Partition more emphatically, "Partition cut old routes of communication and mobility across new international borders more dramatically than almost anywhere in the world. The Bengal Assam railway track from Guwahati to Dhaka was torn up at the Cachar Sylhet border in 1965 which made communication between Dhaka and London easier than that between Dhaka and Guwahati" (Ludden, 2003:21). Moreover, 'tea' the most important means of subsistence for the economy of Assam was dependent on the foreign market through the sea-ports of Kolkata and Chittagong. But Partition robbed Assam of its easy accessibility to the port towns. With the emergence of East Pakistan, Chittagong came to be considered a foreign land and routes *via* East

Pakistan to Kolkata not only proved difficult, but were to be ultimately, totally snapped by December 1949 (Goswami, 1994:179).

Therefore, to look to the immediate impact of Partition in the post-colonial state of undivided Assam, we can put it in the words of B.G. Verghese that the Partition of 1947 caused the extreme isolation of the North-East. He described the region as South Asia's third landlocked state along with Bhutan and Nepal, except for the 22 km. long chicken-neck corridor at Siliguri (Verghese, 2001). The Census of 1951 observed, "Though Assam's loss in areas as a result of this Partition is negligible (it has lost only one-eighth of its areas), it has lost very nearly one-third of its entire present (1947) population, along with the vast paddy lands and the tea, lime and cement industries of Sylhet — the far reaching effects of this loss will continue to be felt by Assam as well as India for many years to come" (Vaghaiwala, 1951 Vol. XII, Part I-A:2-15). The redrawn political boundary of independent India thus isolating the region from the rest of the country had, therefore, "set its economy back by at least a quarter century" (Dass, 1989:61). The economy of the region had thus become too weak and frail to confront the post-Partition challenges of building up the new state. This has proved to be a source of conflict and tension in post-colonial Assam.

The Partition not only robbed the avenues of economic growth by way of segregation of communication lines and well developed markets in the plains of Bangladesh, but also added extra burden of population to the region. Assam being a neighbouring border state of East Pakistan was faced with an inflow of Partition-migrants reasonably as per the 'population transfer' scheme of Partition in the wake of the Sylhet referendum. The *Asamiyas* perceived the Partition of 1947 as an opportunity to attain their goal for territorial security and carving out a linguistically homogenous *Asamiya* province. Successfully 'dumping' off Sylhet into East Pakistan, the *Asamiya* post-colonial elite, ignored the idea of Assam being a shared *Asamiya* homeland or a multicultural society. In their bid to strive for linguistic nationalism, a section of the nationalists of the region not only sought for an introduction of the Official Language Act, 1960, but strove to impose the Assamese language beyond the spheres of the plains, i.e. the Brahmaputra Valley. This was resented in the hills and culturally 'different' Barak Valley (Dasgupta, 2001:41). It correspondingly was responsible for the rapid shrunk of the post-colonial territory of Assam following ethnic assertions by the Nagas, Mizos, and Khasis; all of whom consequently demanded their right to self-determination and independence.

It is, therefore, evident that Partition creating redefined space in the period of transition has also been the factor that brought in 'Partition' in every moment of crises in post-colonial Assam. Assam and the present day North-East became the hotbed of secessionism with the dislocation of the economy and a disruption in perceiving the society as multicultural. Partition rather than fulfilling the long cherished dream of attaining an Assamese homogenous territory has brought in assertions and consequent division to have thereby brought into existence of a shrunken geographical entity. As things stand in Assam today, Partition is still alive each hour and moment even till recently with the creation of a Bodo homeland, on 10th February, 2003 and further ethnic assertions. Partition as a mechanism to resolve longstanding issues failed in its attempt. It had rather propelled recurrent conflicts in post-Partition North-East.

Unsurprisingly, nothing, but nothing has been solved by Partition, all across the sub-continent, its legacy lives on in dismembered families, forced migrations, material and cultural dispossession, ethnic ghettoization and enclaves, communal riots, so-called illegal immigration, wars and the continued state of insecurity from low-intensity conflicts (Krishna, 1999:239).

REFERENCES

Bandhopadhyaya, Sekhar, *From Plassey to Partition: A History of Modern India*, Orient Longman, New Delhi, 2004.

Dasgupta, Anindita, "Migration, Identity and Conflict in the North-East: The Case of Assam", *Himalayan and Central Asian Studies*, 2001, Vol. 5 Nos. 3-4.

Goswami, P.C., *The Economic Development of Assam*, Kalyani Publishers, Ludhiana, 1994.

Gokhale, S.M., *India's Refugee Problems: Causes and Cures*, Prakash Publications, Baroda, 1948.

Krishna, Sankaran, *Post Colonial Insecurities: India, Sri Lanka and the Question of Nationhood*, University of Minnesota Press, Minneapolis, 1999.

Ludden, David, "Where is Assam? Using Geographical History to Locate Current Social Realities", *Ceniseas Papers-1*, Omeo Kumar Das Institute of Social Change and Development, Guwahati, 2003.

Pakrasi, Kanti B., *The Uprooted: A Sociological Study of the Refugees of West Bengal, India*, Editions Indian, Kolkata, 1971.

Prakash Shri, "Economic Irrationality of Partition", in S. Settar and Indira Baptista Gupta, ed., *The Pangs of Partition*, Vol. II: *The Human Dimension*, ICHR, New Delhi, 2002.

Singh, Khuswant, *Unending Trail*, Rajkamal Prakashan Pvt. Ltd., New Delhi, 1957.

Singh, B.P., *The Problem of Change: A Study of North-East India*, Oxford University Press, New Delhi, 1997.

Shukla, S.P., *Transforming the North-East*, 1997 (downloaded-www.planning commission.govt.in).

Vakil, C.N., *Economic Consequences of Divided India: A Study of the Economy of India and Pakistan*, Vora & Co., Mumbai, 1950.

Vaghaiwalla, R.B., *Census of India*, Vol. XII, Assam, Manipur and Tripura, Part-IA Report, Superintendent, Census Operations, Assam, Manipur and Tripura, 1951.

Verghese, B., *Unfinished Business in the North-East: Pointers Towards Restructuring, Reform, Reconciliation and Resurgence* in Seventh Kamal Kumari Memorial Lecture.

29

ORPHANAGES IN ASSAM AND MEGHALAYA
A Socio-Educational Study

Rosemary B. Choudhury

Introduction

Childhood is a formative period in which children gradually learn to grow under the loving care of parents, feeling emotionally and socially secure. But for children, who are deprived of parents the world is different. Such children, if they do not have suitable substitutes as parent figures, are compelled to internalize and become withdrawn.

A child's happiness largely depends on the contact he has with his near relatives especially his parents who love him and cater for his needs, but when a child has been deserted or literally rejected and realizes he will always be unwanted and uncared, a psychological imbalance is nurtured in him.

Gravity of the Problem of Orphan and Destitute Children

From early childhood to adolescence, experiences of parental love and family life serve as the building blocks of healthy personality traits. The experience of separation from parental figures at an early age creates a traumatic shock upon the child, this shock rouses anxiety in the child and produces aggression and despair. His emotional development is thus disturbed. The human child remains dependent for survival upon its mother for a long period during its infancy and childhood. The dependence is protected by parental love in a family situation. And when the child's biological dependence is replaced by cultural needs as he is growing into a social being, parental love and family life leads him to his goal.

Therefore, deprivation of family life and parental love is believed to distort the normal growth of human personality.

The problem of orphan children has grown so big at present and matters have become worse day-by-day, for the past several years the problem of orphans and destitute is being treated by the UNO as a problem common to all nation. The UNO has taken up the problem through its different branches such as UNESCO, UNICEF and WHO and has given it an international status.

In India for ages the problem of welfare of orphan children was tackled in a different way. The solution was in India's social structure itself, i.e. in the joint family system. People, here, lived in large family groups consisting of members belonging to three or four generations. In the event of emergencies in the family, grandmothers, aunts, older sisters and other such persons used to take up the role of the mother. Similarly, elderly male members used to take up the role of the father in such cases. Therefore, the problem of orphans was not acute in the Indian society several decades ago, as it is today, with the break of the joint family system.

The Changing Scenario: India, Assam and Meghalaya

The fast changing socio-economic scenario in the country in the last few decades has had far reaching consequences on socio-economic-medical-educational and psychological growth and development of the most marginalized, disadvantaged and vulnerable groups of our society. The process of modernization and urbanization are transforming society beyond recognition.

Individuals have become self-centered and have lost self-esteem and self-reliability. All these factors have caused a rift to the social and traditional fabric of the country. These factors on one hand have exposed the vulnerable groups to the increasing incidence of destitution, exploitation, deprivation and on the other hand to various forms of psychological and mental abuse, new form of social deviance, anti-social behaviour and a drift into cryogenic culture.

Causes of Orphanhood and Destitution

Factors such as death of parents, natural calamities, cyclone, tsunami, flood, drought, earthquake, terrorism, communal riots, insurgency, HIV/AIDS, maternal mortality creates severe disruption in the lives of children. Some children run away from home because of unbearable treatment, which includes physical, emotional and sexual abuse and mental torture.

Family breakdown, desertion, alcoholism, drug abuse, or criminal activities of family members also contribute to the problem.

Some children get lost or are deliberately abandoned by poor parents in a public place or near an orphanage in the hope that they will be picked up by a state agency or some voluntary organization. Illegitimacy is another contributory factor.

Initiatives and Intervention for Care and Protection of Orphan Children

The fact that children are entitled to rights has been acknowledged in various declarations and conventions from time to time. The Geneva Declaration of Right of the Child 1924 was the first convention adopted by the League of Nations to consider the rights of children. An independent Declaration of Rights of the Child was passed by the UN in 1959.

The central Social Welfare Board was set up with the object especially of assisting voluntary agencies in organizing welfare programmes for women and children. The major thrust in the Fifth Plan (1974-79) was on child welfare. During this period, child welfare was given highest priority. The Integrated Child Development Services (ICDS) was launched in 1975-76.

North-East India has a rich heritage of humanitarianism. Thousands of voluntary organizations and individuals are contributing to the national effort to lay the foundation of a healthier, more prosperous and productive generation.

Back in the States of Assam and Meghalaya arrangements with on going welfare programme for children have been made on the basis of orphanhood, destitution and abandonment. These include — NGOs and Religious people's contribution, SOS Children's Homes, CSWB and State Social Advising Boards, The State(s) Government Directorate of Social Welfare, UNICEF.

Terminology

Orphan

According to the Webster's dictionary orphan is a child who has lost both parents or a child who has been deprived of parental care and has not been adopted.

The distressed state of the orphans may be described by their position in the society of being classified into three categories:

1. Complete orphan — who is without any living parent, is not looked after by any other relation.
2. The maternal orphans — Children without mother.
3. Paternal orphans are without father.
4. Destitute and abandoned children.

Orphanages

An orphanage is an institution dedicated to caring for orphans, abandoned, destitute and neglected children. Generally, the word orphanage is used interchangeably with Children's Home. Largely seen as an inferior alternative to family-based childcare such as some forms of foster care, adoption and other family-based childcare, orphanages may be privately or publicly funded and many are run by religious organizations.

Today the term orphanage has given way to a softer language as 'Group Home', 'Children Home', or 'Rehabilitation Centre'.

Need and Justification of the Study

Child development has moved into the mainstream issues that concern the Government and the community alike. But it is heart breaking to see that there are a lot of children who loose their parents and come under the term of 'Disadvantaged Children' and 'Socially Handicapped' and, therefore, need institutionalization.

It is estimated that the number of orphaned and abandoned children is between 1 to 5 per cent of the total child population only a very few of such children are in the care of some kind of institution.

The study has been justified on the ground that in the States of Assam and Meghalaya very insignificant work has been done to explore in detail and depth the innumerable problems faced by orphan and destitute children, orphanages, the administrators, caretakers and teachers of these institutions. Moreover, problems of orphanages are also a social problem in the context of the changing social scenario after independence.

Objectives of the Study

The main objectives of the study are:

1. To identify and examine the major problems faced in the orphanages by the children, administrators and caretakers.
2. To study the Administrator's/Head's opinions and assessment of their Homes and Institutions.

3. To study the reciprocal relationship of the Caretakers and the orphan children.
4. To suggest measures within the present socio-cultural frameworks to improve the conditions of orphanages.

Variables

The variables in the study include:

Orphans
Sex — boys and girls
Institutions — Government, Non-governmental and Religious
Age 0-18 years
Area — Urban-rural, Hills and Plains.

Tools Used

The following tools were used for data collection:

- A self-constructed need-based questionnaire for Orphan and destitute Children, Administrators, Caretakers in Assam and Meghalaya.
- One Interview schedule for the Administrators/Heads of Children's Home/Orphanages in Assam and Meghalaya.

Methodology

In the light to the above discussion, the present study could be said to fall under the 'Descriptive Survey Method'. The objective of the present study is to investigate the socio-educational dimensions of the orphanages of Assam and Meghalaya, to examine the various services provided and the general functioning of the orphanages, the major problems faced by the administrators, caretakers and children.

The study also examines the impact of education on the moral and social development of orphan children. The study also wanted to see the societal impression towards orphans.

Sample

The sample for the present study have been confined to 100 + 100 children randomly selected from 10 Orphanages/Children's Homes living in Orphanages of Assam, and Meghalaya, with respect to the children's sex composition and their age division which was from 0-6, 7-12, 13-18.

Institutions in the study were governmental, non-governmental and religious.

Findings

The findings related to the different objectives of the study are summarized below:

Findings related to the problems of orphan children: The children's perception of their own needs

- The findings of the present study reveal that orphan/destitute/abandoned children do face certain problems regarding their various needs. The children of Assam and the children of Meghalaya faced the same problems, but in different degrees.
- In the orphanages of Assam and Meghalaya nearly 20 to 35 per cent children suffered from sickness, headache, bad sleep and physical handicap. In the case of Meghalaya the percentage seems slightly higher.
- As for the basic requirements of life, needs related to food, clothes and living conditions also gave satisfactory responses, revealed by the positive percentages of both States.
- In the area of social activities and relationships of the orphan children, it was found that the children of Assam were more selective in choosing friendship, as the percentage was lower than Meghalaya.
- Personal and psychological relationship was rather strained in some cases on account of prevalence of a sense of insecurity which was felt by around 18 per cent of children in both States. One fourth of the children experienced the feeling of running away from the Home. Anxiety, frustration, boredom and pseudo-superiority complex was felt by some children.
- Curricular and co-curricular activities and other programmes was found to be suited to the needs of the children in majority of the homes of both states. Though in some cases such as reading newspapers and magazines and writing articles for school magazines, etc. the inclination was less.
- Needs related to education seemed to be rather positive, that is more than 80 per cent children showed satisfaction with the teaching strategies in their scholastic life. Children of Meghalaya showed significantly more inclination in going to school and apprehending the teacher.
- Fifty per cent of the children in both states were afraid of examination. Nearly 58 per cent children needed constant reminding

to complete their work, 36 per cent children preferred, to play instead of studying in both states! But these problems at times are common with all children whether orphan or not.

- Need for vocational guidance was felt by many of the orphan/destitute children. They seemed to be rather uncertain about their future. Majority of the children needed more information regarding the selection of a particular vocation; they also showed a fair amount of anxiousness and uncertainty in respect of their future.

Findings related to the Administrators/Heads of the Children's Homes/orphanages of Assam and Meghalaya

- The marital status of the administrators of both the states were fifty-fifty which means 50 per cent of the administrators were married and 50 per cent unmarried, majority of the administrators were females.
- Findings about the administrator's assessment of their homes were that most of the homes in both states belonged to the homes (either by ownership or donated).
- Funding pattern in most of the homes of Assam and Meghalaya were a combination of Donations and Government Aid.
- Majority of the administrator's of both Assam and Meghalaya reported of having the necessary infrastructure.
- Medical Facilities seemed to be satisfactory in both the States of Assam and Meghalaya.
- All homes of Assam and Meghalaya provided special food on occasions and festivals in both States.
- Seventy two percentage homes had preparatory schools attached to them. Assam's percentage was more than Meghalaya. 67 per cent of homes in both States had arrangement for primary education for children in both states. Vocational education was available in only 33 per cent homes of both states.
- Facilities for games, sports, cultural programmes, excursion, teaching of art and craft, maintenance of community life was available in the homes.
- Attitude of the society in the opinion of the administrators of Assam and Meghalaya was found to be very helpful and cooperative.
- Rehabilitation facilities were prevalent in almost all the institutions. Majority of the administrators saw the future prospects of the orphan children in their homes as bright and successful.

- Adoption facilities were prevalent in only 34 per cent homes of both States.

Findings related to the caretaker's relationship with the Children: Problems faced by them (Children and Caretakers)

- It is worth noting that most of the caretakers' qualification was in the matriculate level: 55 per cent in Assam, 40 per cent in Meghalaya, their marital status was found to be mostly single. Percentage of female caretakers was greater than males, Meghalaya had more female caretakers.
- Reciprocal relationship between the children and caretakers of both States was found to be satisfactory. Though the children did face problems which were mostly emotional — caretakers dealt with these problems with advice, discussion and counselling sessions simultaneously.
- Treatment of sick children was mostly made in government hospitals and private nursing homes. All minor ailments of children were looked after by the caretakers and other staff members of the home.
- 71 per cent caretakers of the two States reported that there were library facilities, but only 26 per cent reported about the proper utilization of these facilities. Recreation facilities in the form of television, games and sports and indoor games were available in majority homes.
- Educational backup and support was found to be satisfactory. Extra coaching, residential teachers, and the caretakers were the main source of help in academic matters of children in the homes. Pass percentage of children was satisfactory.
- Special children who were physically and mentally challenged were managed by the combined effort of outside help (doctors and physiotherapy), personnel especially appointed for assisting these children and medicine. Homes in Assam had more of these children.
- Community life was seen to be maintained in both states. According to the caretakers, festivals and special days were celebrated with great pomp and enthusiasm.
- Visitors were allowed in all the homes of Assam and Meghalaya. The rules, regulations and timings for visitors differed from institution to institution.

Findings related to the interview cum information schedule for the Administrators/Heads of children's Homes/Orphanages

- It was found that, out of the 10 homes studied 6 were in the plains of Assam and 4 were in the Hilly areas of Meghalaya.
- The years of establishment ranged from 1915 to 2006.
- Around 34 per cent of the homes were situated in the urban areas near the main road. 66 per cent was situated in the semi rural and rural areas.
- Out of the 10 homes, 2 belonged to the SOS children's village, 1 was a Government home, 2 were run by NGOs, 2 belonged to the Missionaries of Charity (Catholic), 1 was run by the Silesian (Catholic) Fathers and Sisters, 1 belonged to Buddhist Missionary, 1 was run by Presbyterian Missionary and 1 home was run by a Private Trustee.
- The aims and objectives of all the homes were almost same that is providing shelter, security, food, clothing, education, medical care, recreation facilities, adoption (only in some) facilities, vocational education, guidance, counseling and rehabilitation facilities.

Suggestions

- The quality and quantity of food served could be improved. The children may also be involved in giving suggestions.
- There should be proper accommodation for children with decent bed linen, a bed for each child, lighting arrangements should be suitable.
- At least four pairs of clothes should be provided to every child in one year. Two pairs of shoes and slippers should also be given every year.
- Bathing and washing soap, oil, toothpaste, powder, etc. should be provided as and when necessary to ensure proper personal hygiene.
- Books, notebooks and stationery items should be provided in time and whenever required.
- Medical facilities need to be improved.
- Social activities, personal and psychological relationship's could be strengthened and given a right track. The bond between the caretaker and the children must be made special and strong.
- Children should be provided with enrichment programmes, such as adequate amount of recreational and cultural activities.

- Exposure of children to environment which encourage and facilitate better verbal interaction with adults and caretakers is very essential.
- A series of programmes that help in the full development and utilization of their innate capacities should be developed.
- Meditation and yoga are also very useful for all.
- Cultural activities that stimulate individual and group participation and encourages full involvement of their talents should be incorporated.
- The other helpers, caretakers, the residential teachers should also be given training in planning and administering such programmes for the inmates.
- The caretaker-children ratio and relationship should be made with a strong foundation.
- Educational and socio-educational needs are to be fulfilled with great care and caution.
- Superintendents, caretakers and the school staff need to develop an emphatic understanding of children's needs and problems.
- The homes and the schools should have well planned implementation of vocational and pre-vocational training programmes.
- The caretakers are to be made to understand that vocational training is one of the functions of institutional care.
- Experts of different vocations should be invited to the home to enlighten the children on different vocations.
- Caretakers should be oriented to present themselves in the image of parents, and give parental care to the children entrusted to them, as their own children.
- They are also expected to create and maintain a family-type of atmosphere in their homes through their caring pattern.
- The caretakers must be given some amount of training and orientation on the developmental needs of the children. They should be trained in the art of institutional management.
- There should be a way in which all the caretakers come together periodically to discuss their problems and difficulties and share their views regarding solution to the problems.
- Caretakers should posses a working knowledge of child psychology.
- Better remuneration and accommodation facilities, job security, increment in pay scale on the basis of educational qualification and training background should be made to raise the motivation of 'on the job' caretakers.
- One important factor is retaining the post of caretakers and maintaining continuity in the job.

- Guidance and counselling should form an essential feature of children's homes and orphanages.
- Keeping track of each child in homes is very essential. Cumulative record card of each child should be maintained.

Conclusion

With the suggestions given above the investigator concludes the report. It is hoped that the effort will be considered useful enough for further investigation into the problem and will be of benefit to the orphan, destitute and abandoned children of our society.

The problem of orphans is, however, not merely a problem of statistics and figures, figures will never help if they are not seen with compassion. Nor is it a phenomenon to be researched, investigated, studied, and kept in the shelves of libraries. But to psychologists and social workers they speak a lot more, since they realize that any number connected with such facts indicates more than a numerical problem. The fact of separation from parents throws these children into an emotional storm. The unavoidable circumstances which drive them into such plight perhaps have made us realize that it would be in fitness of things that we do not loose sight of the contradictions involved in the perception of children regarding their needs. These contradictions may be natural because orphan and destitute children living in Children's Homes and orphanages are not much vociferous in their revelations as expected of them. There is some sort of restraining force, which inhibit their exuberance and expression. Lack of parental protection and fear of authorities have made them cautious in giving expression to their thoughts.

If society is willing to see such children in the light of development and is prepared to listen to 'Their' voices and 'Other's speaking on their behalf then the first and most important step will be taken. . . .

30

TEA TROUBLE
Tea Garden Labour Strike in Assam from 1921 to 1939

Reeta Dutta Hazarika

Tea plants were found growing wildly all over the country to the south of the Brahmaputra in Upper Assam. Though tea was not commonly used in Assam as a beverage, the Singpho tribes who lived in the North-East of the Valley used tea as a regular drink making the same in Burmese method. This was first noticed in the 1815.[1]

Causes of Plantation Labour Strike

Tea plantation in Assam dates back to 1839.[2] Initially, the chief obstacle for the tea planters was non-availability of labour because Assam was very thinly populated at that time. Moreover, the Assamese people were unwilling to work in the tea gardens.[3] Therefore, the British tea planters had to get labourers from outside Assam. The first attempt to fill this need was by import of Chinese coolies. Later, labourers were primarily recruited from districts of Bengal, Madras, the United Provinces of Agra and Awadh and the Central Provinces.[4] From these places labourers were recruited by licensed contractors through unlicensed recruiters. A coolie was worth ₹ 80 to ₹ 150. During the time of departure from home, the coolies had no say as to which tea garden he will go to and it was very seldom that the coolies obtain any part of the price paid for them. The tea garden labourers had to live inside the plantations and housing was used as an effective means of enslavement by the plantation owners. The wages they received were among the lowest in the world.[5] The tea gardens are managed like a hierarchy: the managers live like gods, distant, unapproachable, and incomprehensible. Some even begin to believe that they are gods that they can do exactly what they like. *British writer Dan Jones, (1986) remarked on tea garden managers as follows:* "Managers have anything up to a dozen labourers as their personal, domestic servants. They are made to tie the managers shoe laces to remind them that they are under managerial control and that they are bound to do whatever they are asked". Therefore, Labour unrest was inevitable.

Tea garden labour strike in Assam started in an organized manner just after the Nagpur Session of Congress (1920). In the Session, a resolution was passed expressing sympathy with the labour class in their struggle for securing their legitimate rights. It also emphasized on the formation of labour unions.[6]

Besides, the Dibru-Sadia Railways strike and its success (50% enhancement of wages) had an important bearing on neighbouring areas. Many of the workers of the Dibru-Sadia Railways had their relations in the neighbouring tea gardens through which the railway line passed. Thus, the tea garden labourers of the neighbouring areas also followed the strike route for enhancement of wages.[7] In Assam during the period, 50 per cent tea garden labour strikes were for demanding wage increment and protesting against inhuman treatment and the other 50 per cent strikes were against the suppliers provisions — who demanded higher prices by creating artificial shortage of foods and day-to-day used commodities.[8]

Non-Cooperation Movement and Tea Garden Labour Strikes

Many of the tea garden labourers in Assam though prohibited from leaving tea gardens left the plantation upon hearing about Mahatma Gandhi's Non-Cooperation Movement (1921). Thousands of workers defied the authorities and chanted slogans of *Gandhi Raj Ki Jai.*[9]

According to Government reports, "tea garden labourer strike was one of the main events of Non-Cooperation Movement. Responding Gandhiji's Non-Cooperation call, on the 11th of April (1921)[10] labour strike began in Surma Valley. In the Chargola Valley in the Karimganj Subdivision of Sylhet the labourers of several gardens struck work and began leaving the gardens and crowding into Karimganj with the declared intention of making their way to their homes in the Central Provinces or United Provinces[11] and this led to the historic "Chargola Exodus". Thousands of tea labourers trekked to the nearest railway stations. The number of labourers at Chandpur station alone was four thousand on 19th May, 1921.[12]

Exciting Event of Chandpur

According to a Government report, in those days the journey from Orissa, Nagpur, etc. had to be performed through Chandpur. From Chandpur to Goalanda the journey was to be made by steamers. One ship came to Goalanda daily from Chandpur and the Government ordered that the labourers would have to travel with their own expenses. Hundreds of labourers assembled to go to Chandpur. But the ship was closed to them and as such the labourers moved here and there without food and shelter. In this dire distress many lost their lives.[13] The labourers had to live on public charity. The Congress and Khilafat workers worked hard during the period of strike when the matter became serious. Leader like Akhil Ch. Dutta started for Karimganj. Some thousands of rupees were collected to help the labourers. The Congress and the Khilafat workers lent every help towards the workers when many of them suffered from illness. Facilities for medical treatment were not there at all for the labourers and workers.[14] According to a Government report —

> "*Harmohan Nag of Chandpur gave timely help to these helpless people. On 20th May, 1920 at 10:30 P.M. the last train bound for Chandpur arrived. All the labourers were driven out from the platform including even the railway officers who were on duty. At 10 o'clock at the night, Mr. Kiran Chandra Day, Commissioner of Chattrangaon, Hon'ble Sushil Singha (Son of Lord Singha), S.D.O. of Chandpur, Fargusab tea planter and some jute merchants rushed to the railway platform with some Gurkha sepoys. One cannot imagine the inhuman police vandalism perpetrated on the sleeping labourers. After this occurrence the country witnessed the brewing tension and excitement which is beyond description*".[15]

Repercussion of Chargola Exodus

As protest of the atrocity committed by the Government, the Indian Railway officers and workers started a strike which continued for two years. All the officers of Sylhet district participated in that Railway strike. Many lost their jobs for taking part in the strike. "Chargola Exodus" led to the outbreak of a large number of strikes in the different districts in both Surma and Brahmaputra Valleys throughout the year. There were strikes on certain gardens in the South Sylhet Sub-division, but there the labourers had not left the gardens" *October, 1921.*[16] In the Brahmaputra Valley, the labourers of four gardens near Dibrugarh also struck work demanding a raise of wages without leaving the garden.[17] There was also a series of strikes and riots in the tea gardens in Darrang district. In Nowgong the same (considered) rates of wages were demanded as were demanded by the Chargola Valley coolies in Karimganj.[18] Tea garden labourers from all parts of the province attempted to boycott tea gardens, hats (bazaar). In connection with the "Chargola Exodus", the Assam Bengal Railway and the river streamer workers also started sympathetic strike which caused serious shortage of essential supplies to the province.[19]

In both the valleys, the number of meetings and other activities of volunteers increased during the period and the humiliation of Europeans and Government servants was common.[20] The labourers of the Helem Tea Garden in Tezpur struck work for non-sanction of leave on the Holi festival day. The matter led to the assault of the Manager by the labourers.[21] In Darrang district, European managers were assaulted on the Sonajuli and the Kacharigaon gardens and a number of Indian garden staff and labourers were injured in the incident. In the same district a riot occurred on the Dhendai-garden on 14th October, 1921 and the officiating Superintendent of Police, was knocked down and beaten by the labourers.[22] On the Arunabund Tea Garden, Cachar both the Manager and the Deputy Commissioner were assaulted. The Deputy Commissioner had come for investigation of the manager assault case and he was also hit on 5th of November, 1921.[23] In Chantak Tea Garden labour strike turned violent and they looted *Marwary* shops near the garden. The labourers created such a situation in the garden that the European manager and other employees left the garden and took shelter in other safe places.[24]

Hearing of the tea garden labour agitation, Gandhiji visited Assam in August 1921 with Maulana Muhammad Ali and Azad Subhani. They also visited Surma Valley while the labour strike continued in full swing along with the Khilafat Movement.[25] The local leaders were disappointed, as Gandhiji expressed disapproval of the tea garden labour strikes and *hartals* and censured them for lukwamness in what he regarded as the more important matters of boycott and the use of the spinning wheel.[26] Following the visit of Gandhiji there was repeated labour unrest in Darrang district. On two or three gardens labourers went on strike and demanded increased rates of pay which they said was ordered by Gandhiji. An incident took place on Ratna Tea Estate in Sylhet at the end of August, 1922, caused by the manager by ordering a woman out to work. The manager was confined in the office for four hours, one labourer threatening him with *dao*.[27] The manager of the Champabari garden in the Karimganj Sub-division of Sylhet was assaulted in his own compound on the night of the 19th February, 1922 by a number of tea garden labourers armed with *lathis*; their motive remained undetected.[28]

In Sibsagar district tea labourers of about fourteen gardens were on strike. Though the strike was unimportant, but the effect of the activities of volunteers on the tea garden labour force was extremely unsettling and leading to serious developments. The Government arranged for flag march by 400 to 500 Assam Rifles personnel throughout the Sibsagar district as a military demonstration.[29] But peace could not be restored in the garden. In a tea garden a special police Sub-Inspectors were injured by tea labourers. In another garden a survey party was assaulted, their records destroyed and instruments stolen.[30]

Short strikes which were all settled in a day or two also occurred on gardens in Lakhimpur, Sibsagar and Nowgong in the Brahmaputra valley.[31] There was a disturbance on the Belsiri tea garden in the Tezpur Sub-division on 10th November, 1921. The arrest of the ring leaders by the Deputy Commissioner nearly led to an attack by the labour force on the small guard of Assam Rifles. Similar disturbances were found in the Daha Garden in Sibsagar district and Jagacherra Garden in Sylhet 1921. At Tiphuk Tea Garden in Lakhimpur district, a large number of tea labourers were on strike for two days and broke all the windows in the factory.[32] According to Government report there was a small exodus of about 140 newly recruited Madrasi coolies from Tiphuk Garden. The coolies are looked after by the local swarajists in the Dibrugarh bazaar.[33] The coolies demanded to send back to their homes on the ground that (1) that they did not like the climate of the work and (2) that they feared head hunters.[34] On the Dayang Tea Garden in the Sibsagar district the manager, Mr. Whitten was killed in 1924. There had also been a riot on the Dhansree garden in the Balipara Frontier Tract in the course of which the manager was assaulted.[35] From the Lakwa tea garden in Sibsagar 400, Muttoch Tea Estates in Lakhimpur, 700 coolies were leaved the garden demanding higher pay. In Mirikajan Tea Estate Darrang where all the garden *Babus* were assaulted by the labourers.[36] A riot occurred on the Phulchera Tea Garden in Sylhet on 1st September 1924. The labourers protested against the ill behave of a women labourer at the time of her duty, which resulted rioting in the garden and attacked on the Assistant and General Manager, Shearer and Mr. Young, of the garden. They took refuge in an office where they were imprisoned for three hours and finally dispersed by the police from a neighbouring police station. The mob of the coolies broke the all glasses of the office windows.[37] The growing attitude of the tea labourers to fight with the authorities, compelled the garden owner and their staff to "carefully managed the labourers as the least thing might upset them". The result was that though the number of exodus from tea garden was decreased, but the number of strikes and demands were increased.

At Hautley Tea Estate, Golaghat Sub-division tea garden labourers some 1,500 came out for one day strike.[38] At Singiri Tea Estate in Darrang district, there was strike and riot where the European manager was badly beaten.[39] Similar incident was occurred on Loina Tea Estate, Lakhimpur district, in which the European manager, Mr. Arbuthnot was assaulted. He succumbed to his injuries the following day.[40] After the Chargola Exodus for a decade the labourers of Chargola region were comparatively quite. But on 16th January, 1931 there was a riot on the important Chargola Tea Estate in Sylhet district where a European Assistant Manager was knocked down and beaten. The riot arose while the labourers were being paid in consequence of one labour objecting to his pay cut, and the labourers pulled down the *kutcha* pay shed so as to use the bamboo as weapons. The following day the whole labour force of 3,000 persons remained absent from work and where in an exited mood shouting *Gandhi Maharaj Ki Jai.* The Additional Superintendent of Police managed to arrest all the ringleaders without further disturbance. In previous days such pay cut system was normally accepted by the coolies without a word of protest. But the change crept up. On the same day on Borbam Tea Estate in Lakhimpur district where 150 short term coolies left the tea garden, but were induced to returned by manager who made a slight reduction in their task of pruning.[41] It was very common at the period where the coolies pretend to left the tea garden if they were ill treated by their authorities or ignored their demand of hike wages. Labour trouble also continued in the tea garden in Sibsagar district where in a garden rioting took place and European Manager's hat was knocked off by a brick. Four men were arrested and released on bail of thinking that their arrest might lead to considerably violence.[42]

Table 8.1: Strikes of Tea Garden Labourers from 1930 to 1936

Sl.No.	*Year*	*No. of Tea Garden*	*No. of Labourer Participated in Strikes*	*Loss of Working Days*
1.	1930	3	1900	Not known
2.	1931	12	3200	Not known
3.	1932	8	3200	Not known
4.	1933	11	5500	Not known
5.	1934	8	4071	11,850
6.	1935	13	7091	20,360

It is found that within only in two years 32,210 man works was lost by the tea garden. Therefore, the Tea Garden owners tried to rescue this kind of lost from the labourers by pay cut process.[43]

During the first phase of 1931 an epidemic of strikes on tea gardens in Lakhimpur and Cachar indicated the elaborates plans which had been made by Communist agitators, reinforced from time to time by visit from persons like S.S. Batliwalan to take advantage of the heightened excitement due to the advent of the Congress to power. The most significant of them being those of Arunabam Tea Estate which began in early April 1939 and continued for 40 days, and of Alenpur Tea Estate, where in July 30, 1940, about 200 workers women struck work demanding higher wages and decreased in work-load, which soon secured the support of the entire labour force of the Garden.[44]

Formation of Labour Union

In 1920, the All-India Trade Union Congress was formed with Lala Lajpat Rai as president and Dewan Chaman Lal as secretary. In March, 1926 the Indian Trade Union Act was passed. It was after the enforcement of this Act that the process of unionizing the working class was started in Assam.[45] In December 1927, a two member delegation of the British Trade Union Congress Mr. Parcell and Mr. Hallsworth was visited Assam. They were "assisted by Amiya Kumar Das, editor of Assamiya newspaper" (at that time).[46] to get firsthand knowledge of the deplorable working condition in Assam tea gardens. Later All India Trade Union Congress sent one H.K. Sahu to organize tea garden laboureres in Assam. He was arrested and given a month's imprisonment.[47] This was followed by the formation of a labour union at Jorhat. The Upper Assam Tea Company Union (Dibrugarh), Makum (Assam) Tea Company Labour Union and (Margherita) Rajmai Tea Company Labour Union were formed and registered in 1939 under the Indian Trade Union Act, 1926.[48]

Conclusion

Initially, the tea garden labour strikes were peaceful. The laboureres tolerated the inhuman treatment of the European manager only because of fear. The labourer of tea gardens were brought from various places of India and they were entrusted to accept a type of slavery in the garden cut off from their relatives. They were even not allowed to contact with local Assamese people and neighbouring tea garden labourers. When the aggressive nationalists of Congress volunteers engaged themselves to organize the tea garden labourers, an attitude of disobedience against the European manager had been seen among the labourers. The result was that after the Non-Cooperation Movement incidents of attacking and assaulting on European Managers were increased. Among the incidents two European Managers of Doiyang and Loina tea garden were died and many European Managers and their employees injured in both the Brahmaputra and Surama Valley in Assam. Low wage, over work and inhuman treatment of tea-garden Managers had driven them to recourse to strike in the period. In the first phase of those strikes government tried to put off it by force mean. But later lenient policy was adopted when they found the local political leaders were supported the coolie strikes.

NOTES AND REFERENCES

1. Mann, Harold H., D.Sc., "The Early History of the Tea Industry in North-East India", *Bengal Economic Journal*, 1918. p. 6.
2. Gait, Edward, *A History of Assam*, 1926, Assam.
3. Mann, Harold H., D.Sc., "The Early History of the Tea Industry in North-East India", *Bengal Economic Journal*, 1918. p. 23.
4. Gunning, J.F., *Recruitment of Labour for Tea Gardens in Assam*, p. 3 https://archive.org/details/recruitmentoflab00grunrich).
5. *Ibid.*
6. Sarma, Golak Chandra, *Shramik Andolanar Dhara*, Dibrugarh, 1990, pp. 60.
7. *Home Political-Deposit*, File No 63 of June 1921. (State Archive Guwahati).
8. Kakati, Robin, *Gandhiji, Asom Aru Asomar Sah Majdur* (Assamese), Dibrugarh, 1989, p. 33.
9. Abstract of Intelligence, Assam police, File No. 18, year 1935, 1936 and 1938, (State Archive, Guwahati).
10. *Ibid.*
11. Home Poll., Confidential, File No. 63 Report for the Month of October, 1921 (State Archive, Guwahati).
12. Guha, Amalendu, *Planter — Raj to Swaraj, Freedom Struggle and Electoral Politics in Assam 1826-1947*, New Delhi, 1977, *op. cit.*, p. 130.
13. P.H.A., *Labour Strikes in Surma Valley Tea Estates (Gardens), Year 1934* (State Archives, Guwahati).
14. Abstract of Intelligence, Assam police, File No. 18, year 1935, 1936 and 1938, (State Archive, Guwahati).
15. P.H.A., *Labour Strikes in Surma Valley Tea Estates (Gardens), Year 1934* (State Archives, Guwahati).
16. Home Poll., 1921, Confidential, File No. 63 Report for the Month of June, 1921 (State Archives, Guwahati).
17. *Ibid.*
18. *Ibid.*
19. *Report on the Administration of Assam, for the year 1921-22*, Part II Report (State Archives, Guwahati).
20. Home Poll., File No. 18 Confidential, 1922, (State Archives, Guwahati).

21. Kakati, Robin, *Sah Majdur*, p. 59.
22. Home Poll., 1921, *Confidential*, File No. 63 Report for the Month of October, 1921 (State Archive, Guwahati).
23. *Ibid.*
24. Sarma, Golak Chandra, *Shramik Andolanar Dhara*, Dibrugarh, 1990, p. 60.
25. P. Strikes H.A., *Labour in Surma Valley Tea Estates (Gardens), Year 1934*, State Archives, Guwahati.
26. Home. Poll., 1921, *Confidential*, File No. 18, 16th September, 1921 (State Archive, Guwahati).
27. Home Poll., File No. 18, *Confidential*, 1922 (State Archive, Guwahati).
28. *Ibid.*
29. *Ibid.*
30. *Ibid.* and Home Poll, File No. 18, *Confidential*, 1922 (State Archive, Guwahati).
31. Home Poll., 1921, *Confidential*, File No. 64 Report for the Month of June, 1921 (State Archive, Guwahati).
32. P.H.A. File No. 85, *Fortnightly Report for 1930-1933*, N/A, New Delhi.
33. File No. 25 of 1924, NAI, *Fortnightly Reports on the political situation in India during the Month of July 1924* (State Archive, Guwahati).
34. *Fortnightly Reports for Assam for the Second Half of July 1924)*, NAI.
35. PHA/76/20, Confidential, *Fortnightly Reports for Assam for the Second Half of June 1924*, NAI.
36. *Fortnightly Reports for Assam for the Second Fortnight of August 1924*, NAI.
37. PHA/76/20,Confidential, *Fortnightly Reports 1920-25, Reports on the Internal Political Situation during the Month of September 1924*, SAG.
38. P.H.A. File No. 85, *Fortnightly Report for 1930-1933*, NAI.
39. P.H.A. File No. 18/XI of October 1930, SAG.
40. P.H.A. File No. 18/XI of November 1930, SAG.
41. Home Deptt. Poll. F. No. 13/31, SAG.
42. H.F.M. Records, File No. 127, *Fortnightly Report for 1937*, Home Poll. Deptt. File No. 18/6/37-Poll-1937, SAG.
43. Guha, Amalendu, *Planter-Raj to Swaraj, Freedom Struggle and Electoral Politics in Assam 1826-1947*, New Delhi, 1977, *op. cit.*, p. 189) also (Sarma, Golak Chandra, *Shramik Andolanar Dhara*, Dibrugarh, 1990, p. 72).
44. Barua, S.L., *Comprehensive History of Assam*, New Delhi, 1985, p, 557, *op. cit.*, *Guha*, p. 243.
45. *Nationalist Upsurge in Assam*, Arun Bhuyan, ed. Shrutidev Goswami, Article, "The Nationalist Upsurge: Its Impact on Peasants and Tea Garden Workers", Guwahati, 2000, p. 187.
46. Sarma, Golak Chandra, p. 72.
47. Guha, *op. cit.*, p. 188.
48. *Nationalist Upsurge in Assam*, Arun Bhuyan, ed. Shrutidev Goswami, Article, "The Nationalist Upsurge: Its Impact on Peasants and Tea Garden Workers", Guwahati, 2000, p. 187.

31

SOCIO-ECONOMIC CHANGE IN MEDIEVAL ASSAM

The Case of the Paik System

Banasree Phukan

Introduction

In Medieval times, the Brahmaputra Valley of Assam, located in the North-Eastern extremity of India, would bear witness to the Ahom kingdom spanning the period from 1228-1826 AD. The kingdom's origin is traced to a migrant group called the Tai-Ahoms, whose original number is estimated at 9000.[1] It stands unique amongst world histories for its astonishing uninterrupted duration of six centuries.[2] At its heart was a socio-economic foundation that would be known as the Paik system. The fate of the kingdom was linked to its foundation; the evolution, consolidation and eventual decay of the kingdom and the Paik system followed a similar timeline. This foundation continues to be re-visited time and again, not merely for academics, but also for a better grasp of contemporary issues that have festered for several decades, and that are linked partly to its legacy. Fortunately, long-term solutions now seem possible in the context of local histories and the broader idea of India.

Origin

The Paik system evolved in response to several basic challenges of its time and location, notably the need for arable land for wet rice cultivation, scarcity of manpower, absence of a monetary system, military needs, civic works and so forth. The Paik system unfolded as the Ahom state slowly evolved on the remnants of Kamarupa/Pragjyotishpura that had declined by the late twelfth Century AD.[3]

For the initial two and half centuries, the migrating Ahoms remained confined, and consolidate their presence around present day Sibsagar by befriending and absorbing many of their neighbours into their fold. They introduced wet rice cultivation which made surplus possible. Also, there was no money in the system, so a corvee system was devised to allot land in lieu of labour.[4]

Structure of the Paik System

Under the Paik system, every adult male, and possibly every female, in the age group of 15-50 years, was termed a *Paik*, and each *Paik* had to render compulsory state service, for 3-4 months, on rotation basis. State service included tending to community owned wet rice cultivation, civic works, and military service, as per exigencies and royal decree. Initially, a Paik came from the family as the unit. Four Paiks formed a *got*. The remaining Paiks of the *got* were bound to look after the fields and household duties of the Paiks on state service. In return, each Paik was allotted 2 *puras* or 2.66 acres of free land, in addition to land for his homestead. The Paik system was administered by the officials; *viz*., a Bora was in-charge of 20 *Paiks*, a Saikia of 100 and a Hazarika of 1,000, and so forth. In times of emergencies, upto 3 of 4 *Paiks* could be mobilized for state service. The extended nobility consisting of the landed aristocracy and the religious class did not pay tax.

The system ensured that production was never interrupted, and community cooperation maintained.[5] There was a provision for upward mobility of Paiks, including promotion to the rank of officers.[6] For example, Momai Tamuli Borbarua rose from a bondsman through the ranks to become the first Borbarua under Prataap Singha.

In the formative period, this corvee system offered a unique and ingenious solution to several issues. Firstly, it provided a pool of manpower from where a military force could be mobilized. The Ahoms did not have a standing army. Secondly, it provided manpower for public works. Public works of the Ahom period were labour intensive, and many have survived to this day.[7] Community effort and state intervention made it possible for land to be reclaimed for wet rice cultivation. Thirdly, setting aside the period for state service, each *Paik* had reasonable time to tend to his allotted free 2 *puras* land, and free land for homestead, and any additional uncultivated land that he could claim and keep for himself. Fourthly, it allowed even a non-monetary economy to emerge into a state, driven by surplus production.

It was in the period 1496-1516, whence, a seminal transformation took place. In the words of Guha, the nascent Ahoms ". . . leapt into Statehood".[8] Around this time, the need for a census was felt. Indeed, this was the case, and the first ever '*Piyal*', of adult males, is dated 1510. The state expanded between 1522 AD, when the Cutiya kingdom was annexed, and 1682, when the state's western extent was secured with the defeat of the Mughals. The kingdom was now approx. 500 miles long and 60 miles wide.[9] The population was now larger, more diverse, and spread out over a much larger area. In 1769-70, there were an estimated 80,000 Paiks serving in the khels.[10]

Challenges to the Paik System

Expansion brought in its wake newer challenges on several fronts. But the most serious were the gaps in the requirements of the state, and the aspirations of the populace. The Paik system was a legacy of upper Assam. The Paik system was a double edged sword. No doubt, it maintained agriculture, civic works, and the war machinery for territorial defence and also expansion. But it also sought to control the entire production machinery of the state. Lower Assam did not readily fit into it, influenced as it was, by the Mughal *Mansabdari* system. Also, the practice of wet rice cultivation was already prevalent.

The compulsory nature of the Paik system acted as a restraint, and left little room for growth of other independent, and important pursuits, notably trade and commerce, thereby precluding the overall growth of the economy. In fact, there is no record of minted money in Assam from the thirteenth-fifteenth centuries. The first minted money of Medieval Assam is dated 1543 AD. The absence of urban centres in upper Assam, in substantial measure due to lack of trade, was commented upon by the Mughal chronicler in 1662-63 AD.[11] In the later period, the contrast with upper Assam stood out in that in lower Assam, the economy was more advanced, with more money in the economy, and occupations more diverse.[12] Importantly, a mindset had come to prevail that, if possible, state service under the Paik system was to be avoided. Where possible, many opted for commutation of compulsory state service in lieu of tax, even though it came at great personal cost, and social implications, since medieval lower Assam lacked a strong army, and it changed hands several times between the Kochs, Mughals and the Ahoms. In any event, after a long four and a half centuries, the Paik system had reached a crossroad.

The Neo Vaishnavite movement of the fifteenth-sixteenth century AD could justifiably be credited with many things, notably its universal content and egalitarianism.[13] Its mass appeal also increased with time, an important factor being that religious functionaries, Monks and certain high castes were exempt from state service. Thus, *Satras* provided a sanctuary for thousands to join and claim exemption from compulsory state service. Although *Satras* were not an alternative to the state *per se*, they began to provide parallel pockets of development, and, also mitigated some of the emerging contradictions, by providing space that was not available within the Paik system. It may be noted that the Ahom practice of granting land, including land grants to *Satras*, totaled 3.16 per cent (tax-free), and 7.37 per cent (half rates), of the total settled area of Assam, as per British accounts of 1903-04.[14]

Contradiction was seen in the interplay of religious domains, Hinduisation of the Monarchy, and genesis of a feudal mindset. As the kingdom expanded and encompassed a larger Hindu populations, the monarchy took up Hinduism, abetted by the priestly class; the Tai god was equated with the Hindu god Lengdon Indra, conferring divine legitimacy. Ironically, the alternative Neo Vaishnavite philosophy of *Bhakti* to one god 'Eka Sarana Dharma', or the religion of supreme surrender to one, although at odds with Brahminical philosophy, actually ended up strengthening the monarchy, and contributed to a feudal mindset of a servile attitude to a superior being, which began to appeal to the common man.

There were many who tried to evade the state conducted census operations from time to time, even at great personal loss of their wet rice plots, homestead plots and dry rice fields claimed at personal effort that were customarily tax free. By welcoming such members, dubbed escapists by some authors, the *Satras* facilitated a colonizing effect and attracted settled cultivation in new areas. The burden of taxes and compulsory labour was so high that some actually preferred to be slaves or bondsmen (*golam, bandi*), or to seek escape by cloistering in *Satras*.[15]

In course of time, *Satras* would develop a well defined hierarchy, revenue collection and appropriation. It was not Feudal in the classical sense.[16] As with the egalitarian Paik system, it differed from a feudal set up in its absence of stratified social order. The element of slavery was not more that 10 per cent, and limited to those with land grants.

At the same time, by attracting the same pool of manpower, *Satras* began to undermine the Paik system. Revenue generation and manpower availability for the state was compromised: an untenable situation. This did not go unnoticed. Manpower shortage was further compounded by the practice of assigning Paiks (*Kanri Paiks*) for the personal service of the increasing number of state functionaries (nobles), at times reaching 30 per cent. Ahom policy towards the *Satras* was partly dictated by religious conflict between the Neo Vaishnavites and the Priestly class, but also by the need to enforce basic authority of the state, namely economic and political.[17]

The Ahom leadership seemed aware of the challenges, and attempts at redressal were made. An arrangement of Vassal states was brought into effect in Central and Lower Assam, some examples being Mayong, Darrang, Beltola and so forth. Here, the vassal states were allowed internal autonomy, and were obliged to provide Paiks or levies in the event of war. Land surveys and settlement were undertaken using experts brought from outside and using standardized measuring tools from 1682-1751. Paiks in lower Assam (Koch-Hajo area) were allowed to keep a greater amount of land compared to those in upper Assam. At the same time, frontier governors (e.g. Sadiya Khowa Gohain), and also donees with land grants became more autonomous.

The original Paik system underwent subsequent changes to incorporate the concept of payment in lieu of labour. More numbers of Paiks were allowed to pay tax in cash in lieu of state service. But this could only be allowed to the extent that the requirements of the state coffers were met. Disputes and defaults mounted regarding the taxes payable, and the state felt compelled to enforce the Paik system. In hindsight, it seems that in the changed circumstances, coercive power of the state was inappropriate.

In the seventeenth Century, the Ahom kingdom took many features of its mature form. The Paik system was reorganized under the *khel* or guilds system, based on occupation, replacing the kinship based *phoid* system. Khels were envisaged as self sufficient units, and designed to provide specific services to the state such as boat making, revenue collecting, provision supplying, fighting, etc. But cultivation was a priority, and all occupational groups practised agriculture.

Newer groups emerged; the *apaikan chamua* was the gentry that were freed from the khels and paid only money-tax. The *paikan chamua* consisted of artisans, the literati and skilled people that did non-manual work and rendered service as tax. The *kanri paik* rendered manual labour. Lower in the rung were the licchous, *bandi-beti*, serfs, bondsmen. Later addition of several occupational groups based on caste, such as *Baniyas* (Goldsmiths), *Sutars* (carpenters), *tanti* (weavers), *kamars*

(Potters), *Candalas, kaivartas, dhobas* (washermen), as also no caste specific occupations like ploughmen, boatmen, could not be readily accommodated within the provision of inter khel transfer of the Paik/ Khel system, testifying to economic contradictions that could not be reconciled.[18]

Remedial measures were neither adequate nor timely enough, beyond even the reach of one of Ahom period's ablest monarch, Rudra Singha (1696-1714). 1682-1769 was a period of relative peace, and it offered a window of opportunity, to accommodate the changing workforce and their mindset, skills, aspirations. In hindsight, the opportunity could not be capitalized. A testimony to the extent of grassroots discontent has been recorded in the long march of 4000 Paiks from Darrang to the Ahom capital in 1770.[19] Such discontent, abetted by indiscrete provocations unbecoming of the leadership, would eventually culminate in the internal rebellion of 1769.[20] The subsequent period, from 1769-1826, would witness unremitting conflicts, including external aggression. The armed wing of the state had been weakened by insufficient numbers, loss of discipline, and perhaps most significantly, change in thinking. In 1826 the Ahom kingdom passed into the hands of the British, and the Paik system was quickly abolished thereafter.

Conclusion

When medieval Assam is revisited today, it is clear that the *Paik* system was the very foundation of the Ahom kingdom (1228-1826 AD), at least for the first 450 years or so. Its functionality and resilience of the Paik system were most evident during the period of Ahom-Mughal conflicts, when it enabled the state to successfully thwart formidable challenges to its very existence. The importance of historical events such as these has only belatedly been acknowledged in contemporary Indian History.

It allowed the state to come into being and endure, in the process bringing diverse groups into one body polity, a point of special importance when seen in the light of numerous ethnic identity movements, at times separatist, that dot Assam today. As noted in the early colonial period, there must have been something intrinsically good.

Ironically, and tragically, the Paik system failed to adapt during the most peaceful period in Medieval Assam. With its foundation weakened, the time had passed for a state overwhelmingly dependent on a corvee for meeting its needs; its eventual downfall, a fairly violent one, after six long centuries, decreed by its inability to respond to the winds of change.

NOTES AND REFERENCES

1. Padmeshwar Gogoi, *The Tai and the Tai Kingdoms*, Guwahati, 1968.
2. Lord William Bentinck, "Governor General of India (1828-1832)", quoted in W.H. Macnaughten, *Beng Pol Cons*, 1831, Nos. 2 and 3.
3. Buranji 3000 pots for 3 mouths each.
4. John M'Cosh, *Topography of Assam*, 1837.
5. Edward Gait, *A History of Assam*, 1926, Reprint 1992, Guwahati,
6. Surendra Kumar Goswami, *A History of Revenue Administration in Assam (1228-1826)*, Guwahati, 1986.
7. B.C. Handique (Ed.), *Changrung Phukanar Buranji*, 1961.
8. Guha, Amalendu (December 1983), "The Ahom Political System: An Enquiry into the State Formation Process in Medieval Assam (1228-1714)", *Social Scientist*, 11 (12): 3-34.
9. William Robinson, *A Descriptive Account of Assam*, 1841.
10. Gunabhiram Barua, *Assam Bandhu Journal*, Kolkata, 1885, Vol. 1, No. 1.
11. Sehabuddin Talesh, *Tarikh e-Asham*, Complete English Translated from Original Persian document (1662-1663), Guwahati, 2009.
12. Kirtana Ghosa of Sankardeva, Uresa Varnana.
13. Maheshwar Neog, *Sankardev and His Times Early History of the Vaishnava Faith and Movement in Assam*, Guwahati, 1998.
14. *Imperial Gazeteer of East Bengal and Assam*, p. 103 as quoted by S.K. Goswami 1986, p. 213.
15. Maheshwar Neog, *Cultural Heritage of Assam*, Omsons Publications, New Delhi, 2004.
16. Amalendu Guha, "The Ahom Political System" in Surajit Sinha (Ed.), *Tribal Politics and State Systems in Pre-Colonial Eastern and North-Eastern India*, K.P. Bagchi, Kolkata, 1987. N.N. Acharya (Ed.), *North-East as Viewed by Foreigners*, Guwahati, 1985. H.K. Barpujari (Ed.), *The Comprehensive History of Assam*, Guwahati, 1990.
17. Dhrubajyoti Bora, *Itihas Chinta*, Jyoti Prakashan, Guwahati, 1988.
18. Kirtana Ghosa of Sankardeva, Uresa Varnana.
19. Amalendu Guha, *Medieval and Early Colonial Assam*, Kolkata, 1991.
20. Sanjeev Kakoty, *Science, Technology and Social Formation in Medieval Assam*, Cambridge University Press, New Delhi, 2012.

32

CUSTOMARY LAW IN THE NORTH-EAST
Status of Women

Debajani Choudhury Kar

Tribes and Customary Laws

In any society, customs play an important role in the pattern of behaviour it displays in its various facets. Customs are traditions that get built up in an organized society over a period of time. In the primitive age, and even in the middle age, there was no coded law as such among peoples of various denominations. By and large, the society used to follow their religious edicts and scriptures. Even then, customs and traditions formed the bedrock of social behaviour even among relatively advanced communities. A hill tribe or a plains tribe, a comparatively small body of people having many genetic traits in common, however, has always been slightly less advanced in education, economic activities, etc. owing to its somewhat isolated existence. The tribes in North-East India, as we know them, were much less acquainted with even broader religious scriptures of the plains people of the same region, because they had over the ages remained more or less confined in their respective pockets with hardly any communication with the outside world. They generally believed in the power of Nature and developed their own faiths based on animism. Their social growth was, therefore, dependent on various customs that they practised and got imbibed with through a process of trial and error. Their traditions, therefore, virtually took the force of law in their day-to-day life. Thus, each and every tribal group or community came to have their respective social mores, which can be called 'customary law'. With their own genius, each of the tribes also created a system of justice delivery for any breach of their customary law by any member of the group, a male or a female.

The North-East region is a vast area with criss-crossing mountains, rivers and valleys and is an abode of scores of tribal groups, most of them living within their ill-defined territorial boundaries. Essentially, most of the tribes belong to Tibeto-Chinese and Mongoloid stock having come to their present day habitations on migration from their original homeland — mainly Tibet and China — during the centuries preceding and following the birth of Christ. Unknown and unrecorded in history, they settled down in their habitats as we find them now. It is very difficult to assess now the *raison d'etre* of their migration to their present locations in the North-East, including the compulsions for their moving out from their original homeland in the first place. Their ancestors must have had undergone severe privation in the process of the migrations over the centuries. However, the geographical location of the tribes and their neighbourhood determined a great deal their behaviour pattern and customs. In the pre-British days these tribes in Arunachal Pradesh, Nagaland, Manipur, Mizoram, Tripura, Meghalaya and Assam lived in their own way absolutely without any interference from the ruling dynasties of the kingdoms of Assam and Bengal.

The British annexed virtually the whole of North-East with the Treaty of Yandaboo in 1826 without really establishing their authority in the hills and the various tribal groups living there. They, however, proceeded to take direct control of the hills sandwiching the valleys at various points of time in the middle and later parts of the eighteenth century. However, they did not interfere with the customary laws of the tribes and allowed them to live with their traditions by only having political control over them.

The North-East India is home to more than 300 ethnic tribes, who have distinct identity shaped by the geographical, historical and political factors. Of India's 80 million tribal communities, around 12 per cent live in this region. They are unevenly distributed over the region and there is a wide diversity among them.

Table 32.1: Tribal Population in the North-East — State-wise

State	*Total Population*	*Tribal Population*	*Percentage (%) of Tribal Population*
Arunachal Pradesh	10,97,968	7,05,158	64.2
Assam	2,66,55,528	33,08,570	12.4
Manipur	21,66,788	7,41,141	34.2
Meghalaya	23,18,822	19,92,862	85.9
Mizoram	8,88,573	8,39,310	94.5
Nagaland	19,99,036	17,74,026	89.1
Sikkim	5,40,851	1,11,405	20.6
Tripura	31,99,203	9,93,426	31.1

Source: Census of India, 2001.

The North-East is a huge panorama. Among the Nagas inhabiting the Naga Hills, there are at least thirty sub-tribes, the most prominent among them being Sema, Angami, Lotha, Kanyak, Tankhul, *et al.* The present Arunachal Pradesh has 25 tribes and more than a hundred sub-tribes living in its mountains and (their) narrow valleys, notable among them being Adis, Nyishis, Mishmis, Hill Miris, Singphos, *et al.*, Meghalaya has three main tribes namely Khasis, Garos and Jaintiyas. The Mizos are divided into numerous sub-tribes, which include the Lushais, the Raltes, the Hmars, the Khiangtes, the Paites, and the Pawis. In the Assam plains, a good number of tribes live and they include the Bodos, the Rabhas, the Tiwas, the Karbis, the Kukis, the Dimasas, the Hmars and so on. Similarly, Tripura also has a few tribes like the Jamatias, the Hrangkhals, etc.

It is pertinent to note that the customary laws of the tribes got a great deal influenced by Hinduism and its branch, Vaishnavism, and later by the introduction of Christianity by Baptist, Presbytarian and other missionaries during the British rule. As a matter of fact, with western education being inculcated by the missionaries in the hills, the tribal mores got modified a great deal and thereby the customary laws practised by them also changed over the years. Christianity has brought about a significant emancipation of the tribal women. While earlier women were restricted from attending schools, it is the missionaries who opened schools and encouraged girls to attend them.

Customary Law in Practice

General perception about the tribal societies is that women generally enjoy respectable status compared to their counterparts in non-tribal communities. Yet, recent studies have revealed that customary laws do not always protect the interests of women in the present context and all is not well for women in some tribal societies of the North-East. This was mentioned by Dr. Biloris Lyndem, Chairperson State Commission for Women, Meghalaya.[1]

Matrilineal system prevails in Meghalaya. There are tribes like the Khasis, the Jaintias, the Garos and the Lalungs of Meghalaya who follow the matrilineal system. Women in Meghalaya have property rights. Youngest daughter gets entire property. But all decision-making authority lies with her maternal uncle — which is nothing, but a reversion to the authority of men.

Arunachal Pradesh in the North-East bordering China and Myanmar still practices some age old customary laws. After the death of the wife, marrying sister-in-law without her consent by using force is allowed in

Arunachal Pradesh. Primitive practices like polygamy, child marriage and forced marriage are much in vogue in some parts of the State till today. The traditional customary law allowing the keeping of many wives if the person is financially well off is also in practice. A woman has no right to inherit her husband's property. As it is, in a male dominated society, women have no power of decision-making. Social activists want induction and codification of just laws as women are exploited even today in the name of traditional, but unjust practices like polygamy and child marriage.[2]

In Mizoram, a man simply has to say, "I *mak* (divorce) you" and the wife has to go. An archaic tribal system in a remote area near the Burmese border allows a man to divorce his wife instantly, grab her savings and property and marry another woman the same day. After divorce or separation, women live in a desperate condition, as they don't have any property right. Polygamy is very much in practice there. About divorce and inheritance, women have no say and are deprived of their rights. Over 90 per cent of marriages are unofficial and unrecorded. Many women are dumped by their husbands with a simple "diktat" (get out). For these damsels in distress, alimony is a far cry. A divorcee is sometimes forced to get into prostitution to earn her living.[3] In Kuki community wife cannot inherit husband's property if she does not have any male child.[4]

Mizo women in Mizoram are extremely discriminated against with regard to the inheritance of property as they are never given rights over the landed property. If there is no male child in the family, the family property including ancestral home should go to the nephew of the husband. The women in Mizo society are excluded from all decision-making bodies in both social organizations and church life. They get no representation in the church administration in spite of playing a crucial role in the evangelical work.

Dimasa women only get a share in their mothers' property. Mothers' property is a few silver ornaments that she has had and clothes that the mother has sewn herself. If there is more than one sister, these things get divided among them. In case there is no son in a family, the girl gets a small portion from her father's property, and rest is decided by the village head. There are tribes in Manipur with customary inheritance practices that go to great lengths to keep land out of the hands of women. In case a family has no male child, it has to adopt one, else property goes to the nearest relative with a son or to the clan leader to decide on the heir. Practices are of similar patriarchal nature among most tribes in other states in the region — except in Meghalaya.

The general perception about Naga women enjoying equal status with men and being much better off than the women in the rest of the country seems to be a misleading notion as the reality of the status of women in the State remains grim with Naga Women having no right to inheritance of property and access to land resources. Over 50 years of statehood had passed and there has been no woman in the Nagaland Legislative Assembly. It indicates that unless women sit at the government level, promotion of women's status will never be achieved.

Article 371(A) has been the biggest stumbling block to the empowerment of women, although it guarantees protection of Naga rights and culture. Due to the unwritten customary laws, discriminatory customary practices, and partisan interpretations by the village judiciary comprising only male members, it is very difficult for women to get fair judgments in their cases. Naga customary law has unfair gender bias.

Tribal communities of Tripura are governed by unmodified customary laws. Tribal women enjoy freedom of movement without veil or *purda.* Before marriage, young boys and girls are permitted to stay together to understand their compatibility in possible marital life. The widows and divorcees are allowed to remarry. The system of bride price is there for giving marriage of girls. Girl child is really not unwanted as the economic participation of the tribal women is higher than that of their male counterparts. Cultivation is the main source of their income. Patriarchal system and male domination is there in this tribal society. Paternal property goes to the son, not to the daughter. Tribal women are discriminated against in regard to inheritance, which shows the unequal social status of tribal women. Unequal payment for equal work is certainly a discriminatory attitude towards tribal women. Women do not have the right to participate in decision-making in matters relating to her family or community. They are not permitted to take part in any religious rituals. Most of the tribal women are illiterate.

Property relations differ among Sikkimese ethnic groups. Bhutias and Lepcha households follow a patriarchal family system, with the adult male (father) being the head of the household. Bhutias are generally polyandrous (one common wife shared by all brothers), a practice still in widespread existence today (Lama, 1994). Marriages are not arranged. Lepchas are polygamous, and marriages are not arranged — Lepchas are free to choose their partners. There was apparently a tradition of polyandry among the Lepchas at one time (Kotturan, 1983). Among both Lepchas and Bhutias, all property, either moveable or immovable, belongs to the father, or male head of household. Women have no legal right to family property. However, women and girls are given gifts and assets including livestock, utensils, ornaments, land (if the household is wealthy) and other goods, which may be taken with them after marriage.

As both Bhutias and Lepchas are scheduled tribes, they are not subject to the Hindu Marriage Act of 1955, which was extended to Sikkim in 1989. Custody of children and of household property is determined by customary law, which relies on elders to resolve custody issues. Child marriage and the dowry system are unknown in Bhutia and Lepcha households (Lama, 1994). Bhutia and Lepcha daughters have no rights of inheritance to their fathers' properties, even when there are no sons. Bhutia and Lepcha women who marry outside their ethnic group forfeit their rights to any personal property.

The Dimasa society in Dima Hasao district of Assam is patrilineal. The property rights are vested in a male member and the sons can only inherit the paternal property. There are three types of property in the society; firstly, the paternal property which consists of land, weapons, money, house, cattle, etc.; secondly, the mother's property consisting of jewellery, clothes, looms and accessories; and lastly, the common property mainly consisting of cooking utensils, brass metal, etc. According to customary law, the paternal property (including land) is solely inherited by the sons, the maternal property by the daughters only and the common property is inherited by the sons and daughters equally. The sons can never inherit the maternal property even if there is no daughter in the family, in which case the property will pass to the nearest female relative. Similarly, the daughter cannot inherit paternal property. The widow of a deceased husband can be guardian of the younger members of the family, but she cannot have any claim over the property of the dead husband. She can remain as guardian of the family although her eldest son is regarded as the actual head of the family. She is, though, entitled to be maintained by the inheritor if she stays in her husband's house without re-marrying.

Among the Karbis, inheritance is patrilineal. All the sons inherit the father's land, but the eldest gets a larger share. The rest get equal shares from the remaining portion. However, the widow can inherit her husband's property in rare circumstances except in the case of remarriage according to customary law. However, Karbi women play important roles in the family especially in religious activities. After marriage, the women retain her surname, partly maintaining her individual identity unlike in other parts of India. They are involved in economic activities like cultivation, cutting, weeding, clearing jungles for jhum or collecting fruits, tubers, etc. But they are not allowed to attend the village court or partake food along with men in religious and community feasts. Among the settled agricultural groups, whether Hinduised or not, women are forbidden to work the plough. This custom effectively means that they are not to participate in an important event of the agricultural cycle, but perform other tasks such as planting, hoeing and weeding that are back-breaking and involve bending in wet fields for long periods. They are not allowed to inherit landed property.

Among the Lalungs, inheritance is matrilineal. The youngest daughter inherits the property of the mother. She remains in the original family house and the husband comes to live in her house. This system appears to be very similar to that of the Khasis and this is perhaps due to their location being adjacent to the Khasi Hills.

Conclusion

The above survey of the conventions the tribal communities in the North-East follow indicates a lot of common things among them. The scores of other communities which are offshoots of larger groups like Bodos, Kacharis, Khasis, Garos, Karbis, Nagas, Mizos, Kukis, Mismis, Nyishys, Singphos, Misings, Lepchas and so on, also follow the same or similar practices in their social and cultural life. These conventions have metamorphosed into their customary laws owing to long usage. The Constitution of India has recognized the customary laws of some of the major tribes as constitutionally and legally valid. Thus, the state is not expected to ordinarily interfere with the customary laws in respect of the communities concerned. The basic philosophy behind the retention of the customary laws was that the tribes concerned have unique cultures of their own, which need be preserved and protected.

A look at many of the practices mentioned above makes it amply clear that they are mostly discriminatory, inequitable and violative of many basic human rights. Even as the rest of the country makes definitive progress in legal and social practices, a handful of people in a remote part of the country are kept away isolated and debarred from enjoying natural liberty and progress like their brethren in other parts of the country. In the name of preservation of culture, they are kept frozen in time in a near primitive state.

The customary practices of the North-East tribes have two salient features namely, one, deprivation of women from their legitimate marital and inheritance rights; two, arbitrary powers of adjudication vested in a handful of village elders. These are a negation of modern day constitutional and legal rights, which no modern society can and should put up with. A comparison can be drawn of the said state of affairs with that perpetrated by *Khap Panchayats* in Haryana. It is unbearable to think that while a woman in the plains can acquire education, enjoy equal marital rights with her man and have absolutely equal property rights on her family property under the law of the land, a woman in a tribal community will remain deprived of all the three above.

Customary law disallows participation of women in decision-making, whether in family or in the community or even in religious matters. This is a total denial of natural justice to women in such societies and under these circumstances, their empowerment is unthinkable. Citizenship of the country confers on all citizens equal rights regardless of caste, community and creed. Why, therefore, should a dark cocoon be created and kept only for a section of India's citizens?

NOTES

1. *The Times of India*, 9 March, 2005.
2. *The Sentinel*, 4 December, 2005.
3. *The Sentinel*, 11 October, 2005.
4. *The Telegraph*, 12 April, 2002.

REFERENCES

Dr. Debajani Choudhury, *Response of the State to Domestic Violence on Married Women with Special Reference to Guwahati City* (Doctoral Thesis).

Kusaum and P.M. Bakshi, *Customary Law and Justice in the Tribal Areas of Meghalaya.*

Law Research Institute, *Guwahati High Court — A Study of Administration of Justice Among the Tribes and Races of North-Eastern Region.*

Neishoning Koireng, *Unwritten Customary Law in North-East India.*

Priyadarshini M. Gangte, *Customary Laws of Meitei and Mizo Societies in Manipur.*

The Constitution of India.

Walter Fernandez, Melvin Pereira and Vizalenu Khasto, *Customary Law in North-East India: Impact on Women.*

33

UNIVERSALIZATION OF ELEMENTARY EDUCATION IN ASSAM

Still a Dream

Tasrina Hussain

Education is one of the major life processes of human individuals and primary education is the initial step of knowledge, which has now been considered as the "education of the masses".

Elementary Education constitutes a very important part of the entire structure of education because at this stage, the child starts going to formal institution and the education which he receives there provide the foundation of this physical, mental, emotional, intellectual and social development. It is also the basis of sound secondary and higher education. Primary education has been given highest priority to secure social justice and democracy and also for raising the competence of the average worker and for increasing national productivity. Elementary education is of utmost importance for spreading mass-literacy, which is a basic need for economic development, modernization of the society and effective functioning of democratic institution. In fact, today, primary education has been considered as a basic requisite in a democracy because success of democracy demands that its every citizen must have knowledge in three Rs' which is necessary for understanding the significance of his vote as well as his rights and obligations. So, to achieve the cherished dream of successful democracy in India, the principle of free and compulsory primary education to all children within the age group of 6-14 years was declared through Article 45 of the Constitution of India in 1950.

If we trace the history of primary education in Assam, we find that the need and importance of primary education was felt long before the British came to the state. During the Ahom rule, though there was no organized system of primary education, the priestly class had taken the charge through their study of Astrology and religious books.

Assam came under the British rule in 1826 and at that time the state had the indigenous system of education including the Pathsalas, Maktabs and Tols. Apart from these there were also the *Satras* for the Vaishnavas.

The recommendation of a grant of ₹ 1.00 to every ten boys attending a school of Wood's Despatch of 1854 greatly helped in the development of primary education in Assam.

But the Hunter Commission of 1882 recommended the transfer of primary schools to the local authorities and introduced the system of payment by result in giving grant to the schools which adversely affected the growth of primary education in the State. Lord Curzon's policy on primary education helped to increase the number of primary schools in the state. Gokhale's attempt and the Government of India's Resolution of 1913 led to further expansion of primary education in Assam. After the Government of India Act of 1919, the Government of Assam also made legislative provisions prior to Independence as well as after the Independence to make primary education compulsory in the state. These acts include (1) Assam Primary Education Act of 1926(2) Assam Primary Education Act of 1947(3) Assam Basic Education Act of 1954, (4) Assam Elementary Education Act of 1962 (5) Assam Panchayati Raj Act, 1972 and its modification in 1986.

All these Acts were aimed at enforcing compulsion for removal of illeteracy, but the effects of the Acts were not successful. Complete removal of illeteracy in the state has not been made possible through legislation. A study of them gives a discouraging picture. Census Report of 2011 shows that the percentage of literacy in Assam is 73.2 per cent which is 0.84 per cent lower than the all India literacy rate of 74.04 per cent. This shows that even after about 63 years of independence, universal literacy in Assam is far from satisfaction. The goal of universalization of elementary education continues to be elusive. The participation of girls, scheduled caste and scheduled tribe children remain a challenge. These group of children comprise a large proportion of drop out. Low levels of learning achievement in many school, particularly in the rural areas is a matter of concern. Despite tremendous improvement in access at primary level, there is still a big gap between enrollment and attendance, specially in the rural areas. There is also sharp difference between male and female literacy ratio in the State. According to 2011 Census male literacy rate of Assam is 78.8 per cent with a female literacy rate of 67.3 per cent which is 1.84 per cent higher than the national average. According to

1991 and 2001 Census also the female literacy rate of Assam was significantly higher than the All India average which can be seen from Table 33.1.

Table 33.1: Literacy Rate of India and Assam

Year		*Male (%)*	*Female (%)*	*Total (%)*
1991	India	63.01	39.12	52.11
	Assam	62.39	43.70	53.43
2001	India	75.85	54.16	65.38
	Assam	71.93	56.03	64.28
2011	India	82.14	65.46	74.04
	Assam	78.80	67.30	73.20

While recognizing that female literacy level in Assam is better than in some parts of the country, it needs to be emphasized that there are large pockets with very low female literacy rates. There are still 457 villages with less than 10 per cent female literacy rate in Assam.

Over the years, the number of primary schools have increased by 2.70 times. As per National Survey, the total child population in the age group of 6-10 years in the state is 31.75 lakhs out of which 29.72 lakhs are enrolled in the primary level. There are 5811 nos. of Government and provincialized L.P. School in the tribal sub-plan areas of Assam and also 1433 nos. of middle schools in the same area. As per Tribal Sub-plan document of the Department of Welfare of Plains Tribals and Backward Classes (WPT & BC) Government of Assam, the State has enrolled 7.80 lakh tribal students in the elementary schools and these 6.10 lakhs are in the age group of 6-10 years and 1.70 lakhs are in the age group of 11-13 years. Enrollment escalation is not the only criterion for educational Improvement of the children in the primary stage. At this stage retention is a very serious problem. This is more applicable in case of scheduled tribe, tea garden and Char areas students of Assam. Due to their comparative backwardness and geographical aloofness coupled with poverty and subsistance economy, the people of these backward communities are not getting adequate attention.

According to a report published by CAG, about 1,18,603 (2.02%) Children in the age group of 6-14 years in Assam are still out of school at the end of the 11th Five Year Plan. The target for achieving the goal of universal elementary education was 2005, but even at the end of March, 2011, 1.25 lakh out of 58.86 lakh children remained uneducated. Although there is remarkable increase in the enrollment in the primary school of Assam after launching *Sarva Siksha Abhiyan*, but the high drop-out rate has proved that we are yet to achieve the target. The target of universal retention by 2010 was also not achieved due to the dropout rate of 8.3 per cent in lower primary schools and 15.2 per cent in upper primary schools as of March, 2011. According to the Chief Minister's Vision for Women and Children, 2016, the total drop-out at the lower primary level in Assam is 12.8 per cent of which 11.9 per cent are girls and in the upper primary level it is 15.2 per cent of which 14.3 per cent are girls. The CAG report again pointed out that this dismal picture was due to inadequate infrastructural facilities in school, shortage of new schools as per norms, inadequacy in training of teachers, poor management of mid-day meal scheme, absence of an effective mechanism of tracking and enrollment of out of school children, uneven deployment of teachers, high pupil teacher ratio and irregular supply of free text books. The CAG observed that the Education Department was yet to convert 33.26 per cent school buildings into *pucca* structures while 8.69 per cent schools were not provided with drinking water facility and 40.18 per cent schools had no girls toilet. About 90.60 per cent schools were not supplied with electricity and 18.26 per cent lower primary schools have one teacher to teach five classes in a single room. All these factors make the parents also indifferent towards the education of their wards.

National experience with the pursuit of Universalization of Elementary Education (UEE) had established that UEE is contextual. The contextuality varies widely across the country. Even in State like Kerala where participation is near universal, much requires to be done in respect of quality, facilities and achievement. In other states participation and demand aspect need more attention.

Planning of UEE has hitherto been mainly at the national and State level. Barring some States and Union Territories, these entities are too large and heterogeneous for effective planning. They cannot provide contextuality. Ideally the planning should be from below right from the village upwards, but given the objective conditions, a beginning has to be made with district as the unit of planning. The district plans are to be prepared through as intensive process of interaction with the local bodies, teachers and NGO's so that it is owned by all who are to be associated in implementation and it reflects the ground level realities.

The strategies for UEE have so far emphasized mainly access in terms of construction of classroom and appointment of teachers. This has been inadequate and needs a holistic planning and management approach which goes beyond implementation of a disjointed set of individual scheme, perceives the task of UEE in its totality, integrates all the measures needed to achieve UEE. This planning should try to incorporate the more difficult aspect of access, particularly access to girls, disadvantaged groups and out of school children. It should also try to improve school effectiveness and strengthen the alternatives to schooling particularly the non-formal education system and toning up teacher competence, training and motivation. Stress should also be given on learning competence and achievement and improved teaching learning materials. Such efforts will definitely help to fulfill the cherished dream of Universalization of Elementary Education in Assam.

REFERENCES

Aggarwal J.C., *Land Mark in the History of Modern Indian Education.*

Aggarwal, Dr. Sunita, *Development of Education in India.*

An Assessment of Trends in Access and Retention, NIEPA.

Basu, B.D., *History of Education in India.*

Borua, Jatin, *Bharatar Shiksha Itihasor Adhyayan.*

Kohli, V.K., *Current Problems of Indian Education.*

Mukerji, S.N., *Education in India: Today and Tomorrow.*

Progress Report of 15th Joint Review Mission, Ministry Human Resource Development, Government of India.

34

USE OF TOBACCO AND ORAL CANCER

Mrinmoyee Baruah

Cancer, the word conjures up deep fear of a silent killer that strikes without warning. Also the word cancer evokes such depression that it has become a metaphor for grief and despair. Over 20 million people are estimated to be living with cancer the world over Ten million new cases of cancer are diagnosed every year, and a large majority of them lives in developing countries. Every year about 10,00,000 new cancer cases are diagnosed in India resulting in over 5,80,000 cancer related deaths every year. By year 2020 the incidence of new cases is expected to be 15 lakh.

Cancer is the disease of the smallest units in the body of the cells. There are different types of cells in the body and different types of cancer can arise from the different types of cells. However, unlike normal cells, the cancer cells are abnormal and multiply "out of control".

Cancer is a disease related to "lifestyle". Tobacco habit in any form, alcohol, exposure to toxic chemicals and dietary habits leading to obesity are known risk factors which are controllable. It is estimated that by lifestyle modifications such as (healthy diet, exercise, etc.) almost one third of cancers can be prevented. Reduction in smoking in USA has resulted in decline in deaths from lung cancer. The government and people at large need to take preventive measures seriously to reduce the burden of cancer. Other active preventive measures include vaccination against Hepatitis B and HPV (a type of virus known to cause carcinoma cervix).

Cancer in the head and neck region is one of the most common cancer in India. This is largely because of the unique habit of chewing tobacco. The combination of smoking or chewing tobacco and excessive drinking creates a much higher risk of oral and throat cancer. Excessive exposure to ultra violet rays also can cause damage. Leaving tobacco in the oral cavity for hours, which is often practiced by people, results in damage to the lining of the oral cavity. Cancer of the cheek, jaw, tongue, voice box are some of the common cancers occurring in the head and neck region.

Scenario in the North-East

The recent times have witnessed an increase in the incidence of cancer in the North-East. Two decades ago, six million new cases of cancer were diagnosed each year and four million deaths were reported annually due to the disease world wide. Over all cancer incidence is higher in the North-East compared to the incidence rates available from the other parts of the country. Not only the same trend prevails in the North-East India, but certain types of cancer are relatively very high in the region compared to the national figures.

The incidence of stomach cancer is very high in *Mizoram* and is comparable to that of Japan, the highest in the world. The incidence of cancer in Mizoram state is high because some people of Mizoram are in the habit of consuming water filtrate of tobacco which is even sold in the open market by the local name "Tuibur". Popular habit of consuming smoked meat, higher drinking habits, high level of cigarette smoking, etc.

In *Manipur*, the incidence of lung cancer is very high both in males and females. This is owing to the habit of tobacco use in the form of smoking, hookah, etc. (a pastime in the past) and smoke filled housing environment as prevalent before electricity was available in Manipur. In Assam, oesophageal cancer, hypopharyngeal cancer and oral cancer are very common mainly due to the habit of consumption of betel nuts (Areca nut) and perhaps higher use of alkaline food.

In *Nagaland*, nasopharyngeal and stomach cancers are very high mainly because of high consumption of smoked meat, fish and alcohol besides other factors.

The trend in *Meghalaya* is very near to that of Assam and is high on oesophageal cancer and hypopharyngeal cancer because of the similar habit of betel-nut chewing.

In *Assam* as per three Population Based Cancer Registries (PBCRs), among males cancer of the esophagus is the leading site in Dibrugarh and Kamrup urban district and the fourth leading site in Silchar town. Seven of the ter leading sites of cancer, are anatomical sites associated with use of tobacco. In North-East India, Assam occupies the top most spot in the list of head and neck cancer patients followed by Meghalaya, Nagaland, Arunachal Pradesh, Manipur, Mizoram and Tripura.

Stomach cancer is also common in *Arunachal Pradesh* and in *Sikkim* because of similar habits as in Mizoram (Except use of tuibur).

Head and neck cancers are related to consumption of tobacco in various forms, lime and raw tobacco with betel leaf, betel nut and smoking habit. In India the habit of tobacco consumption is not only a habit today. It has become a tradition and religion for the people in India. In North-East India, chewing of raw betel nut, betel leaf with lime and raw tobacco is practiced very widely mainly in the states of Assam and Meghalaya. Betel nut has been recognized as a major cancer causing agent by the National Cancer Institute, USA. Urbanization of the society is leading women also to pick up the habit of tobacco like men. Following the Western culture, adults, many teenagers and school going students are seen to be adopting the habit of tobacco at young ages. Alcohol also contributes towards causing the cancer in head and neck region. If alcohol is consumed with tobacco its ability to cause cancer becomes double. It clearly indicates that the common people in North-East India are still unaware of cancer. In tribal belts all over India and particularly in the North-East, people prefer to go to a cancer hospital or centre after rural or traditional treatments are done. Lack of cancer awareness is also a reason due to which people cannot reach to the knowledge of cancer. Illiteracy is also a common cause and poverty makes the treatment incomplete.

Scientists have identified over 5,300 different chemicals in tobacco smoke. The International Agency for Research into Cancer (IARC), stated that there are more than 70 chemicals in tobacco smoke that have been found to cause cancer in studies involving people or in the laboratory. Many other thousands of chemicals are toxic and harmful to the health, including carbon monoxide, hydrogen cyanide and ammonia. Chemicals found in tobacco smoke can damage DNA. For, e.g. studies have shown that benzo (A) pyrene damages gene called p53 that normally protects our cells from cancer. The cocktail of chemicals in tobacco smoke is even more dangerous as a mix. Toxic metals found in tobacco smoke, like cadmium, arsenic and lead, stop our cells from repairing DNA damage. This worsens the effects of chemicals like benzo (A) pyrene that damage DNA and makes it even more likely that damage cells will eventually turn cancerous.

The harmful effects of nicotine were published in a report by the Royal College of Physicians They compared nicotine to other supposedly "harder" drugs such as heroine and cocaine. The study found out how these drugs cause addiction. The report concluded that nicotine is a highly addictive substance, particularly when people are exposed to it through using tobacco, and that tobacco dependence is at least as serious as addiction to harder drugs.

Indian studies have also recognized tobacco use as a major health hazard in India. Tobacco is used for smoking as well as in smokeless form in India. Smoking of tobacco is mainly in the form of *bidi*, followed by cigarette, *hukah, chilums*, etc. The habit of smokeless tobacco is also very common. Information on prevalence of tobacco use in India is available from surveys carried out in general community. As per various surveys carried out the prevalence of tobacco use among men varied between 43 per cent and 63 per cent in urban areas and between 32 per cent and 74 per cent in rural areas. Among women it varied between 2 per cent and 16 per cent in urban areas and between 20 per cent and 50 per cent in rural areas.

Economic Considerations of Tobacco in India

The Ministry of Health and Family Welfare in India constituted an expert committee to undertake a comparative study on the economics of tobacco use inter-alia examining the tax revenue and foreign exchange earnings, employment and consumer expenditure on the one hand and the cost of tertiary level medical care facilities for treatment of tobacco related diseases on the other hand with a view to making an economic study of the impact of tobacco consumption in 1999. The committee noted that information on costs due to tobacco related cancers, coronary artery disease and chronic obstructive lung diseases are available through a study of the Indian Council of Medical Research. The total costs incurred for these three diseases in 1999 was ₹ 27,761 crore.

Major Efforts for Tobacco Control in India

Recognizing the health hazards of tobacco, the Government of India promulgated laws stating the prohibition of smoking in public places and near educational institutions. Cabinet Secretariat by an administrative order in 1990, prohibited smoking in certain places such as near hospitals and educational institutions and also discouraged sale of these products near to these institutions which may create social nuisance.

The problem of tobacco control in India is complex, in view of the varied nature of its use and association of a large number of sectors like health, agriculture, finance, mass media, labour, education, industry, welfare, etc. The situation necessitates multi sectoral approach, wherein different sectors (government as well as non-government) identify themselves as contributor to a radical social change leading to tobacco control.

In view of the deep rooted nature, the eradication of tobacco habit would require concerted action resulting into a social change. Community education regarding tobacco and its health hazards would necessarily be an integral component of such an action plan. Anti-tobacco education needs to be targeted at decision makers, professionals and the general public, especially the youth.

The NGOs working for eradicating such a social menace should take appropriate steps to carry out awareness and screening camps in the remote areas, make people aware and along with the government should initiate concrete steps to control the use of tobacco. Coverage of entire country for anti tobacco education is a formidable job and cannot be achieved without active support from non-governmental organizations and mass media. They, however, need support from the health departments for availability of reliable and impartial information on the subject.

The establishment of tobacco control cell in the Department of Health, New Delhi is also note worthy. The activities initiated through this cell includes educational programmes through mass media and schools, motivate the farmers to cultivate alternate crops, advocacy workshops for non-health sectors and establishment of tobacco cessation clinics.

The awareness regarding the health hazards of tobacco use seems to have increased during recent times. The indication to this effect comes from the discussions on comprehensive legislation in the parliament, litigations by the NGOs and their demand for stricter legislation for tobacco control. This indicates that social environment is conducive for major activities for tobacco control. Decision makers in different Ministries/Departments at the centre are aware of the problem, but logistic aspects are still major impediments. Research has been initiated on various economic and employment related aspects and efforts are on to work towards a major reduction on tobacco use in the country.

REFERENCES

Cancer — Facts that all should Know by Dr. Rajesh Mistry, Cancer Surgeon, Kokilaben Dhirubhai Ambani Hospital, Mumbai.

Cancer: Need for Total Care by Dr. Tapan Kr. Saikia, Head of Medical Oncology and Research Director, Prince Aly Khan Hospital, Mumbai.

ICMR: Cancer Research in ICMR. http//www.icmr.nic.in.2000.

Tobacco Control in India — Search for Strategies by A.K. Prabhakar and K. Chaudhury.

Total Management of Cancer: A Handbook published by Cancer Patients Aid Association, Mumbai.

35

ASSAM PRADESHIK MAHILA SAMITY AND WOMEN'S EMPOWERMENT IN ASSAM

Kashmiree Gogoi Baruah

The Assam Pradeshik Mahila Samity is the oldest non-political voluntary women's organization of Assam. It was initially formed with the motive of working for the welfare of women and children. Its history is one of continual progress from small beginning to greater and wider fields of welfare works affecting primarily women and children and also society in general. The depressed condition of women in society was the main factor which lay behind the formation of this voluntary organization. A section of society felt that many social customs and institutions came in the way of progress and they also realized that women suffered from various social injustices which needed immediate redress. This realization led to the creation of a particular platform for agitation for the redressal of women's disabilities. The teaching and works of social workers like Raja Ram Mohun Roy, Mahatma Gandhi, Swami Vivekananda, Vinoba Bhave also inspired them to render services for the welfare of the down trodden. The struggle for freedom led by Mahatma Gandhi, encouraged women of Assam to form organizations for their emancipation.

In the beginning of nineteenth century, a series of women's organizations were formed in different parts of India. But these women organizations had no branch in Assam and, therefore, no direct influence of these organizations has been seen on Assamese women. The women's movement in Assam started during India's freedom movement. The emergence of Mahatma Gandhi in Indian Politics and his call to women to involve themselves in social and political activities inspired the Assamese women. In 1921 Mahatma Gandhi visited Assam and he encouraged Assamese women to get involved with the activities other than household chores. Gandhi's call gave a momentum to the organization of women in Assam and inspired them to participate in social and political affairs of the country. This new spirit contributed to the formation of Assam Mahila Samity which later known as Assam Pradeshik Mahila Samity. Chandraprova Saikiani was the beaconing light behind the women's organizations in the state. It was under her aegis that the Assam Mahila Samity was formed in 1926 in Dhubri. Persons like Benudhar Rajkhowa, Nagendra Narayan Choudhury and others also helped in forming the state level women organization — Assam Mahila Samity. Since, its inception to present day, the Samity has been working for the empowerment of women and has taken an active part in condemning evil social customs and practices which denied equal status to women.

Empowerment of women means providing them with equal opportunities in all spheres of life. In fact, empowerment is a process which helps women to realize their identity, create large scale awareness with the active participation of women themselves. The Assam Pradeshik Mahila Samity felt that empowerment of women was a tool to bring about changes in socio-economic condition of women. The Samity undertook all such activities which were directed to change gender biases and to create social change by educating women, by fostering awareness among them about their rights and duties. The status of women reflects the real picture of a society. Jawaharlal Nehru once remarked "To awaken the people it is the women who must be awakened. Once she is on the move the family moves, the village moves, the nation moves". The Assam Pradeshik Mahila Samity (APMS) and its branches were very much aware of this and they initiated several measures for the well being of women. Poverty, lack of education and continuous discrimination were identified as the major barriers to the development of women resulting in huge cost to society at large. Till 1926 there was no effective organization in Assam, which protected the interests of women or extended real concrete help to them. Even the government did not pay much attention to the problems of uplifting the status of women in society. Hence, APMS considered women welfare services as the best way to mitigate the various problems of women.

The APMS was actually the path finder for various voluntary organizations in Assam and for the first time with greater concern, various welfare activities for women were taken under its aegis. Recognizing the fact that lack of education and illiteracy were crucial factors in the continued subordination of women, the Samity paid interest to the expansion of women's education. In fact, education is the first and formost aspect in empowerment of women. Women have to be educated first to make them aware of their rights and previleges. Lack of education implies lack of awareness about their social status, injustice, women violence, etc. At the initiative of the Samity, the first girl's school was established at Tihu in Kamrup district in 1928. The chief aim behind the establishment of this school was to educate the girl child. Moreover, to fulfill its educational objectives, the Samity decided to award scholarships to intelligent, but economically backward girls. In fulfillment of this object, the Samity and its branches collected funds for giving financial aid to girls for persuing their studies. In some places, the Samity constituted women's welfare associations to help the village women. Under the Assam Mahila Samity, these associations used to invite eminent social workers and reformers to speak on women's issues so as to create an awareness among women. Articles written by the members on women's education, social reforms, rights and responsibilities of women and on other related matters were read and discussed at these meetings.

Narayani Handique, mother of Krishna Kanta Handique, worked for women's empowerment under the Samity. She prescribed over the third session of Assam Mahila Samity at Golaghat in 1929. There she emphasized on the importance of female education. She observed that female education and its expansion were the best instruments for creating consciousness among women. In the beginning of the twentieth century, the British government introduced a new educational policy in India. During this time, demands for a changed educational system were raised in Assam as well. At the initiative of Manik Chandra Baruah, Cotton College was established in 1901. But till then women's education was still not a universally accepted concept. Moreover, the doors of Cotton College were closed for girls. Thus during that time few Assamese girls, who aspired to get the taste of higher education, has to travel all the way to Calcutta and get admission in colleges there. Assam Mahila Samity constantly pressed the authority to open the Cotton College to the girl students. Chandraprova Saikiani, Rajabala Das and other leading workers of the Samity played laudable roles in this regard. At last in 1934 Cotton College was opened for girls students. In this way, the Samity had worked in the field of imparting education among the Assamese women and greatiy helped them in taking the path of progress and advancement even before the independence.

In the largely patriarchal society of Assam, the status of Assamese women has not been very satisfactory. Although, in the post independence period, constitutional provisions have been incorporated to remove gender inequalities, the position of women is still not satisfactory. Taking advantages of their various disadvantages of illiteracy, ignorance and poverty, illegalities and exploitation are being committed on them in an unmitigated manner. Development is impossible until the women folk are intimately involved in the welfare and development projects. It is true that there are laws to ensure security and protection of the women, but due to the loopholes in these laws, exploitation and atrocities on them are continuing unabated.

Lack of security, social justice and economic prosperity are the chief obstacles to the Indian women in achieving adequate dignity in a primarily male dominated society. The women get very little opportunity to work in a dignified position, leading to the loss of their self confidence. Women face certain challenges and obstacles in their working place that man do not. Often they face gender discrimination not only in working place, but also at home. In fact, most of the problems that beset women are rooted in the social perspective of the position of women. Traditionally, men are seen as the bread winner and women as the house keepers, child bearers and rearers. This continues to put obstacles before the women.

From its very inception the Assam Mahila Samity has been working in ensuring women's socio-economic status and self confidence. Realizing that government welfare schemes alone are not enough to bring all round development of the women and there must be an overall awareness among them about their needs, aspirations and goals, the Samity has endeavoured to instill this sense of awareness among the women through its relentless fights against social evils by ensuring women's education. Since the nineteenth century there has been opposition to child marriage and to the consummation of marriage of pre-puberty girls. But there was no popular movement or organization in Assam against the social evil. Assam Mahila Samity was the first women's organization to raise its voice against child marriage. The Assam Mahila Samity and its branches organized campaigns against child marriage and worked towards the implementation of the child Marriage Restraint Act which was passed in India in 1929. When information about prospective marriages of minor girls with elderly grooms was received, the Samity issued notices to concerned families to prevent them. If the families ignored such notices, the workers of the Mahila Samity used to go personally and prevented such marriages from taking place.

A major problem faced by women in Assam is lack of economic independence. Economic independence is most important for a woman.

It creates confidence and provides her social security. So economic empowerment is a must for women which enables women to participate in and benefit from growth processes. In the traditional Assamese society, women engaged in household duties and there was no scope for gainful and wage earning activities for them. In tribal villages and in cultivating castes and communities, women worked in the field particularly in transplantation, weeding and harvesting paddy. Though these economic activities contributed towards family's earning, they did not contribute to her economic self sufficiency, which increases self confidence and moral courage besides ensuring social security. In fact, without economic freedom, social and political freedom become meaningless. The Samity has been working untiringly to ensure financial self sufficiency among the women through various welfare schemes. To create economic independence, the Samity paid attention to the promotion of spinning and weaving which have been the traditional skills of Assamese women since ages. Even today, many of the households in the villages have a loom on which the women folk weave cloths in their spare time. It is an additional source of income for some households. The Samity and its district branches actively encouraged weaving and spinning as a socio-economic activity for women. The Samity opened many spinning and weaving centres in different places of the state. To facilitate a proper market for the products of women weavers, the Samity opened 'weavers' stores in different places. Under the instruction of the Samity, some district Mahila Samities organized spinning and weaving competitions among young girls and women to encourage them in spinning and weaving skill. Exhibitions were also organized by the Samities where women of different ages participated to demonstrate their skill in spinning and weaving. With a view towards providing financial freedom to women, the Assam Pradeshik Mahila Samity also started a weaver's body, *Sipini Sangha* and arranged training in Cottage industry such as bamboo and cane works, Jute products, Carpet weaving and embroidery. After receiving training, many women started making articles such as bamboo baskets and flower vases, bags with plastic pearls and thread, handkerchiefs and table cloths at home. Thereby they paved the way for self sustenance for women. A resolution on financial empowerment of women was adopted in the 50th session of Assam Pradeshik Mahila Samity held in Tezpur in October in 1975. Since a majority of women live in the villages and since they depend on cottage industry for their survival, the Samity laid stress on the revival of cottage industry. The Samity called upon the concerned departments to provide materials required for *Khadi, Endi, Muga, Jute* items and to extend all possible help in this regard to the Assamese women weavers. The district and primary committees were also asked to do the needful in this regard.

Since its inception, the Assam Pradeshik Mahila Samity has been relentlessly striving to ensure social upliftment of the women. Women were barred from entering the Madhab Mandir at Hajo. The Samity objected to this discrimination and in 1947 a delegation led by Chandraprova Saikiani threw ajar the Haigrib Madhab Mandir for all people irrespective caste, creed or sex. Such activities of the Samity generated considerable awareness among women and helped them to strengthen their own identity.

Comprehensive well being of the women can never be achieved without equality and social justice. In consideration of this, demands were raised in the 50th session of the Samity held in Tezpur in 1975, to ensure proportionate representation of women in the Public Service Commission, *Mahakuma Parisad* and other government and semi-government organizations. The Samity also considered the aspect of creating political awareness among the women, because it was felt that women's interests would be better secured only if they have enough representations in the administration and in the legislature. The Samity tried, albeit, unsuccessfully, to send an Assamese woman representative to the council formed immediately after the independence to initiate the process of administration. After the formal adoption of the constitution in 1950, India became a sovereign nation. In that year, the Samity demanded an Assamese woman representative in the Rajya Sabha. Chandraprova Saikiani, an active worker of the Samity sent telegrams to Prime Minister Jawaharlal Nehru, reiterating the Samity demand for electing women representatives. The then Assam Chief Minister, Bishnu Ram Medhi, social worker Bhubaneswar Baruah and other extended their moral support to this demand of the Samity. Consequent upon these concerted efforts, Puspalata Das got elected to the Rajya Sabha on that occasion. Subsequently, Rani Manjula Devi and Begam Mafida Ahmed were elected to the Lok Sabha while Bedabati Borgohain got elected to the Rajya Sabha. Usha Borthakur, first elected as a Legislative Assembly Member, was later elected to the Rajya Sabha. Padma Kumari Gohain, Lily Sengupta, Kamal Kumari Baruah were also elected as members of the Legislative Assembly. The local branches of the Samity played active roles in this matter.

Very often the feeling of insecurity and lack of confidence keep women bogged down. In the Indian joint family system, women were part of the greater household. Economically, emotionally and socially they depended on their parents, husbands or relatives. Quite often a married woman suffered from mental or physical harassment in her husband's home, but was unable to leave because she had no place to go. There were also instances of young girls lured into the flesh trade by undesirable elements of society. To create a sense of social security, the Samity decided to provide shelter to needy women of all categories. The Samity established an Ashram known as *Anath Kalyan Kendra* in Guwahati for homeless women. The female inmates of the Ashram were trained in weaving and sewing. Such training helped several inmates to become self sufficient in life and subsequently helped them in providing higher education to their children. The Assam Pradeshik Mahila Samity felt that proper counseling and guidance could solve many problems of women. Even today majority of the Assamese women are usually unaware of rules and regulations and ways of availing legal assistance. If a woman wants to take a legal action against her husband or in laws or other relatives for their unpleasant behaviour, she can not do so due to lack of knowledge or money. Hence, the Samity decided to provide legal aid to needy women. The Samity started its 'women's Legal Aid Cell' on 14th November, 1989. Since, its inception the Legal Aid Cell has been solving many cases of women like maintenance cases, separation, custody of child, dowry, etc. By starting such a branch, the Assam Pradeshik Mahila Samity makes women aware of their rights, makes them competent enough to fight for their rights and to get their rights.

Health is an important and ideal way to ensure women's empowerment. Health can not be given to anybody or distributed. It is to be actively acquired or won. Positive health depends on nutrition, safe drinking water, sanitation and on medical facilities. From the very beginning, the Samity has been providing health related services for women. These were primarily in the form of camps organized either for certain specific diseases or general checkup camps. Their duration ranged from one-two days and the services of a doctor or a team of doctors were made available. The Samity had organized seminars relating to preventive and curative health related topics.

Thus, the Assam Pradeshik Mahila Samity was the first state-wide women's voluntary organization which took the policy of women's empowerment in an organized way. The Samity took all necessary measures to equip women with all necessary skills required to help them to grow and provided larger space for women to bring all-round development to them. After Independence, Government of India has been trying to empower women in all possible ways. Our Constitution also empowers the state to ensure women's rights, equality and previleges. But government policies and Constitutional provisions are not enough to bring all round development of women. Each and every Indian should voice against the existing evil practices and discrimination in regard to women's rights, privileges, gender equality and so on. Moreover, women should themselves realize the importance of change their behaviour and surroundings. Since, its inception in 1926 to present day, the Assam Pradeshik Mahila Samity has been untiringly striving to ensure dignity, self dependence among women besides actively protesting against the illegalities and exploitations heaped on them. Its contributions in generating social, economic and political awareness among women in Assamese society commendable.

REFERENCES

Debola Hazarika and Runu Barua (ed.), *Smark Grantha*, APMS, 1985.
Dipti Sharma, *Mukti Jujat Loitpuria Nari*, 1995.
G.R. Madan, *Indian Social Problems*, 1991.
Hiranmoyee Devi, *Mukti Sanggrami Chandraprova*, 2002.
Sadiniya Asomiya, 22 July, 1928.

36

SOCIO-ECONOMIC STATUS OF SCHEDULED TRIBES OF NORTH-EAST INDIA
Problems and Prospects

Faraz Ali Ahmed

Introduction

The North-Eastern region comprises of three plain States and four hill States. All the four hill States are predominated by tribal. In other three States also a significant proportion of the total population is tribals. The tribal groups of this region can be broadly categorized into two divisions, *viz.* tribal living in the hills and the plain tribals. The tribals in hills remained isolated till the advent of the British. The tribals in the plains have been living with other non-tribal groups since time immemorial. There are 16 major tribes in Nagaland, 16 in Arunachal Pradesh, 4 in Meghalaya, 7 in Assam, 9 in Manipur, 3 in Mizoram and 6 in Tripura.

The tribal communities represent an important social category of Indian social structure. The tribals are said to be the original inhabitants of India. India is a country of multiracial stock. Different types of groups occupy different parts of India, having their own cultural characteristics and levels of development. A number of groups are still in primitive stage and they are very often referred to as tribals, adivasis, and so on. The tribal population of India, according to the 1991 census was 67.76 million. This was almost equal to the population of the United Kingdom. The tribals formed 8.08 per cent of the countries total population (*The Hindustan Times*, July 1, 1995). At present India has the second largest tribal population in the world, next only to Africa on the basis of 50 per cent of the Scheduled Tribes population, areas have been identified in the country. In such areas more than 65 per cent of their total population lives. It means that the tribal people are the dominant groups in some areas. In Nagaland, Meghalaya, Arunachal Pradesh, and Mizoram majority of the population belongs to Scheduled Tribes.

Table 36.1: Distribution of Tribal Population in North-East States (1991 Census)

Predominantly Tribal State	*Percentage*
Assam	12.82
Arunachal Pradesh	63.16
Mizoram	94.75
Meghalaya	85.53
Manipur	34.41
Nagaland	87.70
Tripura	30.95

The term 'tribe' is not easy to define. In fact, there is no satisfactory definition for the same. To ordinary man the word 'tribe' implies simple folk living in hills and forests, to people who are a little better informed. Definition formulated by Dr. D.N. Majumdar is found to be acceptable one. According to him a tribe is "a collection of families bearing a common name, members of which occupy the same territory, speak the same language and observe certain taboos regarding marriage, profession or occupation and have developed a well assessed system of reciprocity and mutuality of obligation". In the words of Gillin and Gillin a tribe is a group of local communities, which lives in a common area, speaks a common dialect and follows a common culture". Gandhiji called tribes a "Girijans".

Problems of the Scheduled Tribes of North-East States

The tribes who constitute 8.8 per cent of the total population of India are distributed in various states of the country and are facing many problems. The major problems of tribals are as follows:

1. The tribals possess small and uneconomical land holdings because of which their crop yield is less and hence, they remain chronically indebted.
2. Literacy rate among tribals is very low while in 1961 it was 18.53 per cent, in 1991 it increased to 29.60 per cent which compared to general literacy rate of 52.21 per cent in the country is very low because while the growth of literacy rate in the past three decades in the country was 28.21 per cent among STs it was only 11.7 per cent. (*The Hindustan Times*, July 11, 1995) through tribal literacy

rate in Mizoram is 82.71 per cent and between 57 per cent and 61 per cent in Nagaland and Sikkim.

3. A good portion of the land in tribal areas has been legally transferred to non-tribals. In fact, the tribals had earlier enjoyed considerable freedom to use the forest and hunt the animals. Forest not only provide them materials to build their houses, but also give them fuel, herbal medicines for curing deseases, fruits, etc. Their religion makes them believe that many of their spirits live in trees and forest. The tribals have reacted sharply to restrictions imposed by the government on their traditional rights.
4. About 90 per cent of the tribals are engaged in cultivation and most of them are landless and practice shifting cultivation. Though the tribals argue in favour of Jhum or shifting cultivation, it creates ecological imbalances in the region due to massive cutting down of trees and burning of forest. They need to be helped in adopting new methods of cultivation.
5. Extensive areas in the North-East are still having poor connectivity. Rail connectivity is still a dream in majority areas in the region including Assam. Due to poor connectivity the region is still lagging behind many other states in the country.
6. Most of the development schemes, special assistance reservation, etc. given in the name of tribals go to the tribal elite only. Poor people get less access of it. In many cases the poor people are deprived of by the elite in all segments of development
7. Banking facilities in the tribal areas of North-East are so inadequate that the tribals have to depend mainly on the moneylenders. Being miserably bogged down in indebtedness the tribals, therefore, demand that Agricultural Indebtedness Relief Act should be enacted so that they may get back their mortgaged land.
8. The burning insurgency problems in the North-East retards development. Due to insurgency there is low FDI flow in the region, which causes slow industrial development. The insurgency groups especially PLA in Manipur, NSCN in Nagaland, DHD in Karbi-Anglong and North Cacher Hills of Assam and NDFB in Boro areas are creating havoc in the region. Besides the presence of ULFA in Assam is creating panic in the region.

Measures for the Upliftment of Scheduled Tribes

Independent India has been paying due attention to the problems of the scheduled tribes and attempts are being made to deal effectively with those problems.

Constitutional Safeguards

The Constitution of India has made various provisions to safeguard the interests of the tribals.

1. Article 15 of the Constitution provides equal rights and opportunities to all the citizens of India including the tribals without any discrimination.
2. Reservation in employment is made for the tribals under Article 16(4), 320(4) and 335.
3. Article 338 empowers the President of India to appoint a Commissioner to look after the tribal welfare activities.
4. Article 164 empowers the State government to appoint a separate Minister to look into the welfare of the tribals.

Economic Programmes and Facilities

Majority of the tribals are extremely poor and economically backward. Various economic programmes and projects have been undertaken to improve their economic position. The Government spent ₹ 30 crore, ₹ 80 crore, ₹ 101 crore, ₹ 172 crore and ₹ 257 crore on tribal welfare activities during the 1st, 2nd, 3rd, 4th and 5th Five Years Plans respectively. Integrated Tribal Development Projects (ITDPs) evolved for the tribal development during the 5th Plan (1974-79) covered today 19 States/Union Territories and 374 lakh tribal population. The amount allotted for the tribal sub-plans in the 5th plan was ₹ 1,100 crore, in the 6th Plan (1980-85) it was ₹ 5,535 crore and in the 7th Plan (1985-90) it was ₹ 10,500 crore.

Table 36.2: State-wise Poverty Estimate (% Below Poverty Line) of NE State

States	*2004-2005*	*2011-2012*	*Decrease*
Assam	34.4	32.0	2.4
Arunachal Pradesh	31.1	34.7	–3.6
Manipur	38.0	36.9	1.1
Meghalaya	16.1	11.9	4.2
Mizoram	15.3	20.4	–5.1
Nagaland	9.0	18.9	–9.9
Sikkim	31.1	8.2	22.9
Tripura	40.6	14.1	26.5
All India	37.2	21.9	15.3

Note: An negative sign before the number in column four (decrease) indicate an increase in percentage of population below the poverty line.

Source: Review of Expert Group to Review the Methodology for Estimation of Poverty (2009), Planning Commission, Government of India.

The tribals are persuaded to give up their system of shifting cultivation and to settle permanently in a place of their selection by making agriculture their occupation. Thousands of tribals in Assam and Tripura have been made to settle down permanently for agriculture.

Educational Facilities

Measures to provide educational facilities to the S.T. have been taken by the Government. Schools are established in some tribal areas. In the First Five Year Plan itself about four thousand schools were opened in the tribal areas. The students belonging to S.T. are getting various concessions such as free tuition, stipends, scholarship, free supply of text books and other equipments. For the S.T. 20 per cent of the seats are reserved in the technical education and relaxation is made in respect of the age limit and qualifying marks.

Table 36.3: Percentage of Literacy to Total Population of NE States

States	*1991*	*2001*	*2011*
Assam	52.89	63.25	73.18
Arunachal Pradesh	41.59	54.34	66.95
Meghalaya	49.10	62.56	75.48
Manipur	59.89	70.53	79.85
Mizoram	82.26	88.80	91.58
Nagaland	61.65	66.59	80.11
Tripura	60.44	73.19	87.75

Source: Census of India 2011.

Medical Facilities

Various medical facilities have been provided for the tribals in the north-east regions. In some places, hospitals are established and in many places mobile hospitals facilities have been provided. Many preventive and curative measures to combat the diseases like malaria, leprosy, forest fever, money fever, typhoid, small pox, skin diseases, etc. are undertaken. Medical camps are organized in the tribal areas to enable the tribals to realize the importance of modern medical facilities.

Two basic indicators used in analyzing health status are infant mortality rate and the life expectancy at birth. The Infant Mortality Rate (IMR), measured in terms of death per thousands of children below six years, is considered to be a sensitive indicator of not only the health status of the population, but also the level of human development in the context of education, economic conditions, nutrition, etc. poverty, malnutrition, decline in breast-feeding and inadequacy or lack of sanitation are all associated with high infant mortality.

Table 36.4 State-wise Infant Mortality Rate in North-East

States	*1991*	*2001*	*2011*
Assam	92	78	55
Arunachal Pradesh	91	44	32
Meghalaya	80	52	52
Mizoram	53	43	34
Manipur	28	25	11
Nagaland	51	NA	21
Sikkim	83	52	26
Tripura	82	49	26
All India	77	71	44

Source: Office of the Registrar General of India, Ministry of Home Affairs.

Research Work into the Problems of the Tribals

Tribal Research Institute, which undertake intensive studies of tribal art, culture and customs and problems have been set up in many States of India. The research work done in this field has thrown light on the tribal life and problems. The research institutes are engaged in providing planning inputs to the State Governments, conducting research and evaluation, Studies, collection of data, conduct of the training, seminars and workshop. Some of these Institutions are also having museums exhibiting tribal artifacts.

Special Central Assistance

Special Central Assistance is given to states to supplement their efforts in tribal developments. This assistance is basically meant for family oriented income generating schemes in the sectors of agriculture, horticulture, minor irrigation, soil conservation, animal husbandry, forests, education, village and small scale industries and for minimum needs programme.

Conclusion

It can be concluded from the above discussion that the traditional concept of "backward" of tribal is not justified. In the eastern region tribals are emerging as one of forward communities. It will be accurate to say that at present only the "poor" are backward all over the countries. But not on caste and community wise. Over the years a huge amount of money has been flowing in the name of tribal development. They have been given special provision on job reservation, seat in educational institutions, scholarships, etc. Though the Central and the State Governments have taken much interest in the tribal welfare programmes, projects and schemes, much remains to be done. The progress achieved in this field is far from satisfactory. The welfare programmes have not been effective due to the inadequacies in the administrative machinery, lack of sensitive trained management, lack of general preparedness for large investments deficiency in the accounting systems, procedural delays and lack of proper monitoring and evaluation. S.C. Dube is of the opinion that in the absence of "Strong Political Will" and "Bureaucratic Commitment" all our plans and projects are bound to become failure.

REFERENCES

Ahuja Ram, *Social Problems in India*, 2009.
Bhushan Vidya, and Sachdeva, D.R., *An Introductory to Sociology*, 2001.
Bordoloi, B.N., *Constraints of Tribal Development in North-East India*, 1990.
Das, G.N., *Tribal Development in North-East India*, 2008.
National Sample Survey 1991, 2009, 2011, Government of India.
Shankar, Rao C.N., *Primary Principles of Sociology*, 1990.
Shankar, Rao C.N., *Sociology of Indian Society*, 2008.

37

SOCIO-ECONOMIC ANALYSIS OF THE ELDERLY POPULATION OF GUWAHATI CITY

Indrani Kalita Choudhury

Population ageing is the process whereby older individuals account for a proportionally larger share of the total population. Starting first in the more developed countries, it has now become apparent in much of the developing world and will affect virtually all countries over the medium-term. It is a matter of pride for the whole human race to have delayed death through spectacular medical progress. But additional life will bring little cheer if it is burdened with sickness and suffering. The phenomenon of population ageing is becoming a major concern for the policy makers all over the world since the last two decades. Ageing of population is affected due to downward trends in fertility and mortality, i.e. due to low birth rates coupled with long life expectancies. It is turning out to be a major population issue, more so in developing countries because of the deteriorating conditions of the elderly.

Ageing as is commonly perceived, is accompanied by decreasing body energy and resources, along with physical infirmities due to decaying and weakening of one's bodily organs. Aspects like physical impairment or incapacity to work or the psychological frame depend upon economic condition, social status, environment, health and medical services, education, etc. Thus ageing not only shows individual variation, but also varies from society to society and even among different classes within the same society.

India is a land where age and wisdom are traditionally respected. But improved longevity is challenging age old assumptions. In India, the size of the elderly population, i.e. persons above the age of 60 years is fast growing. As per the data of 2011 Census, 7.5 per cent of the total population was 60 years and above, with males accounting 7.1 per cent and females 7.8 per cent respectively. The United Nations defines a country as 'ageing' where the proportion of people over 60 reaches 7 per cent. India has already exceeded this and is likely to reach 12.6 per cent by 2025. Moreover, United Nations Organization has declared October 1 as the International Day for elder persons. Ageing poses mounting pressures on various socio-economic fronts including pension outlays, health care expenditures, psychological problems, etc. In view of the increasing need for intervention in area of old age welfare, Ministry of Social Justice and Empowerment, Government of India adopted 'National Policy on Older Persons' in January, 1999. The policy provides broad guidelines to State Governments for taking action for welfare of older persons in a proactive manner by devising their own policies and plans of action. The policy defines 'senior citizen' as a person who is 60 years old or above.

The present chapter is focused on the social and economic analysis of the problems of the elderly population living within the municipal limits of Guwahati city. The city because of its geographical location acts as a connecting link for the north-eastern states with the rest of India. With its growing importance as a link city, Guwahati is responding to the needs of urbanization and modernization. With a population of just 0.2 million in 1971, Guwahati is a million plus city today. However, the city appears to be in a state of transition. It is the younger generation who is rapidly changing, whereas the old social morals and values are still adhered to by their predecessors. Changes have occurred in all spheres of life starting at the very household level. The role of the family in taking care of the elderly people has diminished largely. The study is addressed to the following objectives:

- To examine the health conditions of the elderly people.
- To examine the pattern of living of the elderly people.
- To find out the economic contributions of the elderly people and participation in paid work.

This chapter aims to bring into focus the social and economic aspects of the problems of the ageing population in Guwahati. The respondents have been selected on the basis of their age taking 60 as the cut-off age. A total of 100 respondents have been selected including both male and female respondents. The sample has been randomly selected so that people of different communities and income level can be covered.

Sampling unit is the elderly people. The study is based on available secondary data and data collected through primary survey. The census remains a very important source of data. The study based on micro-level primary data attempts to assess the importance of socio-economic variables like health, living pattern, and engagement in work in the elderly life situations, which have received little attention in the existing literature. Besides the detailed personal information on the individual socio-economic characteristics of the elderly respondents, data is also collected on the kind of facilities available to them. The emphasis is on the living arrangements of the respondents. Socio-demographic factors such as sex, place of residence, personal income, health care, marital status, occupation status and leisure time activity are considered as response variables for the analysis.

Health Status of the Elderly People

The subjective feeling of the elderly respondents about their health is an important issue in studies analyzing the health situation of the elderly. To many elderly persons, ill health in old age is, but a natural phenomenon. In some cases, however, it is affected by the financial condition of the family. The study reveals that 16 per cent of the total elderly respondents consider themselves unhealthy whereas a majority of them consider themselves fairly all right. Detailed information on the kind of ailments from which the elderly persons reported to be suffering are recorded during the survey. The types of ailments are degenerative (rheumatism, etc.), lifestyle (blood pressure, diabetes, gastroenterology, etc.), waterborne, respiratory and others. Based on the above observations made on the health conditions of Guwahati's elderly population, it can be concluded that some definite health intervention measures are necessary to cater to specific diseases associated with old age. This calls for the establishment of special geriatric wards within public sector health facilities through identity cards for the poor elderly.

Economic Activities of the Elderly Persons

The economic status of the respondents is categorized into two namely, Above Poverty Line (APL) and Below Poverty Line (BPL). 35 per cent of the total respondents belong to BPL while 65 per cent belong to Above Poverty Line (APL).

Since 1981, the Census of India defined work as participation in any economically productive activity. Such participation may be physical or mental in nature. It also includes unpaid work on farm or in family enterprises. The same definition is followed during the sample survey for the present study. The main objective is to find out if and how the elderly people contribute to their family income by participating in productive activities.

It is observed from the survey that elderly persons of lower income households engage themselves in income-generating work to supplement family income. Such work ranges from casual work to daily labour and even private work for those with a minimum level of education. A few others are still actively engaged in business in tandem with their son(s). One of the prime requirements for engagement in work by the elderly persons is their physical fitness. Hence, it may be inferred that elderly persons are more likely to work when they belong to lower income households and more of elderly males work compared to elderly females.

The work participation rate of elderly female has always remained lower than that of elderly male. Participation of older women in labour force indicates deterioration in the support structure and economic conditions of the elderly women.

Health status, engagement in any income-generating work and management of financial matters in the household are important indicators of the socio-economic aspects of the elderly persons. The probable factors which affect these indicators are their age, sex, social status (i.e., caste), economic status and whether their spouse is alive or not. The health condition of elderly persons is inversely related to their economic status. Generally, higher income level is favourable to health due to better nutritional status and availability of medical treatment facilities. But sometimes it may so happen that lifestyle ailments like high blood pressure, diabetes, heart-trouble, etc. are associated with a higher economic status of the household.

Living Arrangements of the Elderly Respondents

The pattern of living of the elderly people is reflected in their living conditions and living arrangements within the household. It influences their living conditions positively and enhances the quality of their life. Living conditions are described in terms of the type of facilities available to a person within the household. These facilities are the type of housing, toilet facilities, sources of drinking water, sources of fuel and lighting, etc. Availability of a separate room is an important component of the condition and status of the elderly in the household. Field survey shows that of the total respondents 28 per cent of them do not have a separate room. They mostly belong to the lower economic status (BPL) and those staying in rented houses.

With growing urbanization and modernization, the joint family system of the household is giving way and nuclearization of families is the current trend. As a result, there is a noticeable change in the living arrangements of the elderly persons in Guwahati as found in the survey. 50 per cent of the elderly respondents live with spouse and children which includes married sons, married daughters, and unmarried children. The study reveals that when elderly persons do not have their spouses, 31 per cent of all elderly respondents live with their children. Again, the percentage of female elderly widows living with only children is more (22%) as compared to that of males. This may explain the fact that at higher ages the number of females exceeds males and hence, more of widows than widowers. 6 per cent of the elderly persons were found to stay alone. Usually, children stay away from their parents on account of their occupational demands or the current trend of nuclear families. 5 per cent of the elderly persons, all of them females, responded living with relatives or neighbours.

Traditionally elders are accorded a higher status in the household hierarchy in Assam and this still remains the norm. A majority (79.62%) of elderly respondents reported that they are the head of their households. However, considerable gap exists in the female and male headship ratio, calculated as the ratio of number of head of the household to population in the group. The female headship ratio (0.35) is much lower than the male headship ratio (0.80). One of the prime reasons for it may be economic independence of the elderly males as compared to the elderly females.

There is gender variation in the management of financial matters in the household. Widows take up such responsibility only after the death of the head of the household, who are generally the males. Besides, there is a negative relationship between income level and management of financial matters. Elderly persons who do not have any regular source of income (current income, savings, pension, etc.) are likely to lose the authority of taking up such responsibility in favour of some other member of the household, usually the earning son(s).

Summary and Findings

A major challenge for policy-makers is to avoid viewing the elderly as a 'problem'. The concerns of older persons must be mainstreamed into overall development agendas and poverty-reduction programmes. The goal is to have a society for all ages. The aim of this study is to identify and understand the nature of the problems of the elderly population of Guwahati city and co-relate them with the socio-economic background of the respondents.

On the basis of the above analysis, the following findings emerge from the study:

- Co-residence with spouse, children and kin has been observed to be the main form of living arrangement among the elderly persons of Guwahati city. This has a positive impact on the physical and mental health of the co-resident elderly persons.
- A regular means of subsistence ensures the possibility of the elderly persons being the head of the household. Health of the elderly persons is primarily affected by the economic status of the household, which in turn determine their nutritional status and availability of medical treatment facilities. Lifestyle ailments may adversely affect the health of the elderly persons of higher income groups.
- For majority of the elderly persons, the inducement to participate in income earning activities is low level of household income. Hence, there is negative relationship between income level and work participation of the aged people.
- A large number of needy elderly persons have not benefitted from the government sponsored social security measures such as National Old Age Pension Scheme, Annapurna Scheme, etc. Limited coverage, selection of ineligible beneficiaries, small amount of benefit, etc. are some of the problems which call for remedial actions.

When asked what the respondents think are the serious problems of the elderly, the answers received were varied in nature. The most common problem appears to be declining health. The next important aspect ailing the elderly is that of loneliness, i.e., how to creatively utilize their time. This is more evident in case of widows, widowers and unmarried. Financial insecurity and security of life and property are also reported to be other problems of the elderly population. Moreover, those living below the poverty line expressed financial insecurity to be their problem leading to malnutrition and inadequate medical treatment facilities. Another important problem of elderly Guwahatians is that of movement. Bad condition of roads, improper lighting of the streets, increasing number of vehicles on the road, etc. create hurdles in moving out of their homes. The importance of the protection of the constitutional rights of the elderly in India is guaranteed under the 'Parents and Senior Citizens (Welfare and Maintenance) Act, 2006' which had received the assent of the President on Dec. 29, 2007. Under this act, the Government is bound to create various amenities to ensure dignified living conditions for the elderly.

There is an emerging need to pay greater attention to ageing-related issues and to promote holistic policies and programmes for dealing with the ageing society. The dazzling progress of science and technology has extended life longer, but victory will be incomplete if it has no positive effects on ageing. The duty of the present world, hence, lies in finding whether the improvements in mortality are only adding years to life or adding life to years.

Suggestions

A few suggestions are made to make the lives of elderly in Guwahati a little happier and comfortable, in the light of the above findings and conclusions:

- Health needs of the elderly persons should be assessed and addressed. For instance, health insurance system needs to be designed so as to take care of the treatment costs in old age.
- Co-residence is an important factor in the general well-being of elderly persons reflected in lower morbidity rate and higher income entitlement. So, policies should be devised to assist the households in continuing co-residential living arrangements. In this respect, voluntary organizations can also play a significant role.
- Economic valuation of the work done by the elderly people needs to be done. Besides, adequate policies should be formulated to integrate the increasing number of elderly persons to the economy.

It has been observed that life in Guwahati have changed over the years. The advent of television, expansion of education, communication revolution providing easy access to world-wide events and changes have influenced the life of people. As a result, attitudes towards old cultural traditions and values are also changing, which is having a detrimental effect on the elderly section of the society.

When asked what the respondents think are the serious problems of the elderly, the answers received were varied in nature. The most common problem appears to be declining health. The next important aspect ailing the elderly is that of loneliness, i.e., how to creatively utilize their time. This is more evident in case of widows, widowers and unmarried. Financial insecurity and security of life and property are also reported to be other problems of the elderly population. Moreover, those living below the poverty line expressed financial insecurity to be their problem leading to malnutrition and inadequate medical treatment facilities. Another important problem of elderly Guwahatians is that of movement. Bad condition of roads, improper lighting of the streets, increasing number of vehicles on the road, etc. create hurdles in moving out of their homes.

There is an emerging need to pay greater attention to ageing-related issues and to promote holistic policies and programmes for dealing with the ageing society. The dazzling progress of science and technology has extended life longer, but victory will be incomplete if it has no positive effects on ageing. The 'elderly population' constitute a precious reservoir of human resources as they are gifted with the knowledge of various sorts, varied experiences and deep insights. The duty of the present world, hence, lies in finding whether the improvements in mortality are only adding years to life or adding life to years.

REFERENCES

Alam, Moneer, "Ageing, Old Age Income Security and Reforms — An Exploration of Indian Situation", *Economic and Political Weekly*, 2004, Vol. 39, No. 33, pp. 3731-3732.

Bhende, Asha A. and Kanitkar, Tara, *Principles of Population Studies*, Himalaya Publishing House, 1994.

Chattopadhyay, Aparajita, *A Comprehensive Look at Ageing*, Book review of "Growing Old in India: Voices Reveal, Statistics" by Ashish Bose, Mala Kapoor Shankardass, B.R. Publishing Corp, New Delhi, *Economic and Political Weekly*, 2004, Vol. 39, No. 40, Oct. 02-08, pp. 1-2.

Deka, Amal K. and Nath, Dilip C., "Socio-Demographic Correlates Explaining the Longevity of Graying Population in a Traditional Society", *International Journal of Pure and Applied Sciences and Technology*, 6(1), 2011, pp. 21-34.

Dandekar, K., *The Elderly in India*, New Delhi, Sage Publications, 1996.

International Labour Office, *World Labour Report 2000: Income Security and Social Protection in a Changing World*, Geneva, 2000.

Prakash, Dr. Indira Jai, *Ageing in India*, Prepared for WHO, Geneva, 1999, pp. 11-13.

Sarma, Chandana, *Social and Psychological Aspects of the Problems of the Elderly Population — A Case Study of Guwahati City*, OKD Institute of Social Change and Development, 2000, pp. 3, 48.

Status Paper, *The Aged in India: Policies and Programmes* presented by Ministry of Social Welfare, Government of India in the World Assembly of Ageing, Vienna, July 26-August 6, 1982 as reprinted in *Ageing in India*, Eds. M.L. Sharma and T.M. Dak, New Delhi, Ajanta Publications, 1982.

Sujaya, C.P., "Some Comments on National Policy on Older Persons", *Economic and Political Weekly*, Oct. 30, 1999, pp. 73-74.

World Bank, *Averting the Old Age Crisis: Policies to Protect the Old and Promote Growth*, Oxford University Press, Oxford, 1994.

38

DEVELOPMENT, DISPLACEMENT AND SOCIAL MOVEMENT IN NORTH-EAST INDIA

Devajyoti Gogoi

Introduction

This chapter is an attempt to critically examine the various perspectives pertaining to development and its relevant effects of displacement leading to the occurrence of social movement with special reference to North-East India. In order to achieve rapid economic development Countries of the world have been undertaking development projects to improve the quality of life of its people through planned development. Such projects include dams, power, mining, industrial and allied infrastructures, transport network, urban development, commercial forestry and other projects. Some of these projects have brought adverse effects in the form of displacement of people from their original place of habitation due to large-scale land acquisition. Development-induced displacement in the countries have brought severe economic, social and environmental problems to the displaced people. Magnitude of people displaced and severity of the problems due to multipurpose dam projects is too high as compared to other projects in the countries. They also lead to submergence of high quality of land, destruction of the watershed, disturb the delicate ecological balance and distort the surrounding environment, loss of wildlife and precious irreplaceable flora, etc. and most notorious problems of flooding, water-logging and salinity. The experience of North-East India of various projects initiated across the region especially the post-independence period suggests that the long drawn out process of displacement has caused widespread traumatic psychological and socio-cultural consequences. These include the dismantling of traditional production systems, desecration of ancestral sacred zones, graves and places of worship, scattering of kinship groups, disruptions of family system and informal social network and thereby creating impoverishment such as landlessness, joblessness, homelessness, marginalization, food insecurity, increased morbidity and mortality, loss of access to common property and social disarticulation.

Due to these displacement the authorities of development have to face tremendous resistance from the displaced population. Civil society itself has emerged as a social movement in recent years, while it has always been part of larger social movements in society.

Finally, in conclusion various ideas have been put forward to minimize the problem or mitigate its consequences.

Methodology

The present chapter is based on the secondary data collected from the secondary source, i.e. published literature of the subject concern. Moreover, classification and tabulation of data have been prepared by applying various mathematical and statistical methods.

The Concept of Development

Traditionally, the concept and process of development was usually explained in economic terms. That means, by the term Development we mean Economic development. It is the term that generally refers to the sustained, concerted effort of policy-makers and community to promote the standard of living and economic health in a specific area. Such effort can involve multiple areas including development of human capital, critical infrastructure, regional competitiveness, environmental sustainability, social inclusion, health, safety, literacy, and other initiatives. Economic development differs from economic growth. Development means quantitative and qualitative improvement of the economy, i.e., growth of GDP as well as high standard of living of the people. Therefore, Development is chiefly a matter of capital, technology and education and the appropriate policy and planning mechanism to successfully combine these element. Whereas, economic development is a policy intervention endeavour with aims of economic and social well-being of people, economic growth is a phenomenon of market productivity and rise in GDP. Consequently, as economist Amartya Sen points out: "economic growth is one aspect of the process of economic development. However, in the past few decades there has been a change in this approach.

Presently the tendency across the globe is to view development with social and human orientation besides the economic and political orientations. With the turn of the century the issues, such as the realities of globalization, paradigm shift in development strategy emergence of society actor as development practitioner, resurgence of grass root assertion for development and the emergence of new social movement and so on have provided several new and alternative conceptual empirical dimension to the concept and process of development.

Projects of Development

In order to achieve rapid economic development Countries of the world have been undertaking development projects to improve the quality of life of its people through planned development. Such projects include dams, power, mining, industrial and allied infrastructures, transport network, urban development, commercial forestry and other projects.

Consequence of Development

Displacement

In order to achieve rapid economic development Countries of the world have been undertaking development projects to improve the quality of life of its people through planned development. Such projects include dams, power, mining, industrial and allied infrastructures, transport network, urban development and other projects. Some of these projects have brought adverse effects in the form of displacement of people from their original place of habitation due to large-scale land acquisition. Development-induced displacement in the countries have brought severe economic, social and environmental problems to the displaced people. Development-induced displacement is the forcing of communities and individuals out of their homes, often also their homelands, for the purposes of economic development. It is a subset of forced migration. It has been historically associated with the construction of dams for hydroelectric power and irrigation purposes, but also appears due to many other activities, such as mining and the creation of military installations, airports, industrial plants, weapon testing grounds, railways, road developments, urbanization, conservation projects, forestry, etc. Development-induced displacement is a social problem affecting multiple levels of human organization, from tribal and village communities to well-developed urban areas.

Development-induced displacement or the forced migration in the name of development is affecting more and more people as countries move from developing to developed nations. The people that face such migration are often helpless, suppressed by the power and laws of nations. Michael Cernea, a sociologist, who has researched development-induced displacement and resettlement for the World Bank, has identified eight interlinked potential risks intrinsic to displacement.

1. *Landlessness:* Expropriation of land removes the main foundation upon which people's productive systems, commercial activities, and livelihoods are constructed.
2. *Joblessness:* The risk of losing wage employment is very high both in urban and rural displacements for those employed in enterprises, services or agriculture. Yet creating new jobs is difficult and requires substantial investment.
3. *Homelessness:* Loss of shelter tends to be only temporary for many people being resettled; but, for some, homelessness or a worsening in their housing standards remains a lingering condition. In a broader cultural sense, loss of a family's individual home and the loss of a group's cultural space tend to result in alienation and status deprivation.
4. *Marginalization:* Marginalization occurs when families lose economic power and spiral on a "downward mobility" path. Many individuals cannot use their earlier-acquired skills at the new location; human capital is lost or rendered inactive or obsolete. Economic marginalization is often accompanied by social and psychological marginalization.
5. *Food Insecurity:* Forced uprooting increases the risk that people will fall into temporary or chronic undernourishment, defined as calorie-protein intake levels below the minimum necessary for normal growth and work.
6. *Increased Morbidity and Mortality:* Displacement-induced social stress and psychological trauma, the use of unsafe water supply and improvised sewage systems, increase vulnerability to epidemics and chronic diarrhea, dysentery, or particularly parasitic and vector-borne diseases such as malaria and schistosomiasis.
7. *Loss of Access to Common Property:* For poor people, loss of access to the common property assets that belonged to relocated communities (pastures, forest lands, water bodies, burial grounds,

quarries and so on) result in significant deterioration in income and livelihood levels.

8. *Social Disintegration:* Displacement causes a profound unraveling of existing patterns of social organization. This unraveling occurs at many levels. When people are forcibly moved, production systems, life-sustaining informal networks, trade linkages, etc. are dismantled.

Others have suggested the addition of other risks such as the loss of access to public services, loss of access to schooling for school-age children, and the loss of civil rights or abuse of human rights, such as loss of property without fair compensation, or violence from security forces or risks of communal violence in resettlement areas. Displaced people often internalize a sense of helplessness and powerlessness because of their encounter with the powerful external world, although there are also several examples of active resistance movements against development-induced displacement. In every category, particularly among marginalized groups, women are the worst hit and pay the highest price of development. A study carried out by the national commission for women in India (NCW) on the impact of displacement on women reveals that violence against women is increased. An increase in alcoholism due to displacement has led to a marked rise in domestic violence in India. In the Lincoln Park Community of Chicago, Illinois, where Jose (Cha-Cha) Jimenez founded the human rights Latino organization: Young Lords, Mayor Richard J. Daley displaced tens of thousands Puerto Ricans and the poor. This displacement helped to proliferate growing street gangs. Today these gangs enterprises with murder for hire, arson for profit and drug sales as its prime motivation. Displacement has made men feel helpless or insecure and turned women and children into scapegoats. Displacement also leads to deterioration in health and high mortality rates as services in those selected areas are the first to be cut. The nutrition and health of women, which is worse than that of men even under normal circumstances, is bound to go down in the event of an overall worsening in health caused by displacement.

Scope of the Displacement Caused by Development Projects

While an estimated 25 million people are displaced world-wide by conflict, the number of people uprooted by development projects is thought to be much higher. In 1994, a study of all World Bank-assisted development projects from 1986-1993 that entailed population displacement found that just over half were in the transportation, water supply and urban infrastructure sectors. Extrapolating from World Bank data to derive estimates of global figures, the study concluded that, in the early 1990s, the construction of 300 high dams (above 15 metres) each year had displaced four million people. Urban and transportation infrastructure projects accounted for six million more displaced each year. According to the World Bank's latest review of resettlement and development, between 90 and 100 million people have been involuntarily resettled over the past decade. In India alone some 23 million have been displaced since 1950. Hydroelectric dam projects, each year, lead to the involuntary relocation of between 1.2 and 2.1 million people. In Africa, dams on the Volta (Ghana), Aswan (Egypt). Zambezi (Zambia and Zimbabwe) and Bandama (Côte d'lvoire) rivers have caused the forcible relocation of hundreds of thousands of people, mainly farmers and herders, but also towns people. In China. water conservancy projects since the 1950s have created over 10 million displacees. But it is not just dams that create displacement. Unknown additional relocation continues as a result of forestry, mining and parks development. The scale of the phenomenon is enormous, the consequences for those displaced can be devastating and the expected advantages to the nation which are used to justify the displacement are not always realized. In Orissa, more than lakhs of families are displaced by projects mostly related to Large Industries, Large Dams and hydro-electric projects, and Mining projects. 20 thousand families displaced by Hirakud Dam Project are still not rehabilitated as per promise.

Among the north-eastern states, development induced IDPs are more visible in Assam. The oil sector in Assam also contributed towards the problem of displacement. New oil townships are established in various places of upper and lower Assam displacing the inhabitants of those areas. Two paper Mills of Assam at Jagiroad and Cachar have also forced people out of their homes besides destroying the greenery. The Jagiroad paper mill has mostly displaced the people belonging to Tiwa tribes. On the other hand, the Cachar Paper Mill in Barak Valley of Assam has reduced the bamboo forest in the neighbouring area. Moreover, urban expansion of Guwahati city has displaced the tribal mostly belonging to Karbis and Bodos. Urban expansion is pushing these people out of the city to the periphery. In 1973, when Assam's capital was shifted from Shillong to Guwahati once again the tribals had to sacrifice. An estimated 1,00,000 population were displaced at that time. Again educational institutions like Guwahati University and IIT, Guwahati have also displaced the original inhabitants of the outskirts of the city without proper rehabilitation. The Pagladiya Dam Project is to be constructed in Nalbari District of Lower Assam. The project is going to irrigate 54,125 hectares of land, protect 40,000 hectares of land from flood and erosion, and generate only 3 MW of electricity. But it would displace almost 1,05,000 population most of whom are tribal people. The rehabilitation and resettlement package offered by the government is also not acceptable to the people of the area. Besides many of them do not posses proper ownership documents and, therefore, will not get any compensation. Hence, the people have started their movement under the banner called "Pagladia Bandh Prakalpar Ksatigrastha Alekar Sangram Samiti" against the implementation of the project. The Central Government as well as the Brahmaputra Board, which is the implementing agency of the project, is making all efforts to construct the dam there. But till now the resistance of the people have been quite successful and the authority has failed to do even the ground survey because of the massive resistance of the people. For the construction of the fourth bridge over the mighty Brahmaputra 'the Bogibeel Bridge', already more than 2,000 *bighas* of land have been occupied. According to an estimate, almost 500 families having ownership documents of these lands are not compensated yet. It is to be mentioned that the land has been taken for keeping stones and other materials required for the construction of the bridge.

The 2,000 MW Lower Subansiri project to be constructed on the border areas of Assam and Arunachal is already facing lot of opposition from the people as well as from the governments of both the sectors. The project was planned by National Hydro Electric Power Corporation (NHPC), a government run public sector unit and it is very keen to construct the dam as it has obtained environmental clearance for the projects. The proposed height of the dam is 116 meters and it will submerge 3,436 hectares of land. At the same time more than 1 Lakh tribals of Arunachal Pradesh will be adversely affected by the dam, out of which about 15,000 faces the threat of physical displacement. Besides it will affect the rich bio-diversity of the region as 42 hectares of land belonging to Tulley Valley reserve forest will also be submerged, where many rare animal species can be found. The NHPC has already constructed their office on an elephant corridor. As a result of this the elephants have started attacking and destroying the neighbouring villages. The indigenous people of Arunachal are also worried over the threats posed by these projects to their habitats and unique cultural heritage. They further fear that the project would also lead to influx of outsiders creating social problems. Again, the project is going to submerge a vast tract of cultivable land in Arunachal Pradesh impoverishing a large number of indigenous people, while people of other states will get the benefit. However, in a significant development, the Ministry of Power has decided to drop plans for the construction of Upper Subansiri Dam in Arunachal Pradesh following directions by the Ministry of Environment and Forest on the basis of Indian Board of Wildlife.

The Dumbar Dam of the Gumti Hydel Project in South Tripura district, aims at generating 8.60 MW of power, has displaced a total of 5,845 tribal families — between 35,000 to 40,000 people in all. The Gumti Hydel Project has mainly displaced the people belonging to Reang community. Although a rehabilitation scheme was taken up for the permanent rehabilitation of the affected families and payment of compensation in terms of acquisition of their land was also undertaken by the State government, but it is experienced that most of the affected population dispersed in different localities of Tripura State and they are not in a position to response during the course of rehabilitation activities. Another point to be mentioned here is that the affected Reang communities are mostly jhumias and they are having no land records even of their homestead land. Therefore, it is virtually impossible for them to get resettlement without land document. Likewise, Tipaimukh Multi Purpose Project is also going to displace over 15,000 people. It would mainly attack two tribal communities — Zeliangrong Nagas and the Hmar. It is to be mentioned here that the tribal people have very close relationship with the nature. Moreover, they are attached to the mother earth and have a very well knit web of community life. The construction of such projects disturbs their community life and breaks their relationship with the nature. Besides, in the North-East such displacement due to development creates the problem of space further creating ethnic conflicts among them.

Tuli Paper Mill of Nagaland has also displaced hundreds of tribal families and affected the rich bio-diversity and environment. The Loktak Hydel Project in Manipur displaced around 20,000 people as their villages went under water. In Arunachal Pradesh more than 20,000 would be displaced by the Siang Project. It is difficult to estimate the number of IDPs caused by environmental degradation, i.e. flood, riverbank erosion, and landslide, etc. However, some reasonable conclusions can be drawn about the enormity of the problem. As a result of continuous environmental degradation; flood and river-bank erosion in the plains, and landslide in the hills have become endemic. This has caused innumerable deaths, destruction and population displacement.

Studies on the social impact of development projects suggest that indigenous people and ethnic minorities are disproportionately affected. Coming from politically marginalized and disadvantaged strata of society, these groups often end up neglected and impoverished. In India, the Adivasi or tribal people, although only representing eight per cent of the total population, make up 40-50 per cent of the displaced. In Nepal, indigenous groups displaced by a dam on the Kaligandaki river have lost their land and livelihood and have reportedly been inadequately compensated. The livelihood of an estimated 35,000 indigenous Ibaloi people is threatened by the construction of the San Roque Dam in the Philippines. Mon, Karen and Tavoyans in Burma are probably among the worst off, displaced by large infrastructure projects and subject to forced labour and abuses by the military.

2. *Social Movement*

The most important consequence of development-induced displacement is the rise of social movement against the development projects. By the term social movement we mean a collective identity of various groups, namely, women, environmentalists, students, peasants, workers, etc., who are organized on the basis of common identity and interests. Therefore, a social movement is a collective actor constituted by individuals who understand themselves to have a common interest, and at least some significant part of their social existence, a common identity. However, participation in social movements may not always be for the quest of an identity; rather, it may be for the gratification of political and material interests.

Displaced people often internalize a sense of helplessness and powerlessness because of their encounter with the powerful external world, which compels them to go for active resistance movements against development-induced displacement. There are several examples of resistance against internally displaced people, but we name a few especially in the context of North-East India.

Even before Independence, there were instances of anti-dam struggles such as the one led by Senapati Bapat in opposition to the Mulshi Hydroelectric Project in the Western Ghats. The first large river valley project in India, Hirakud, resulted in widespread protests in 1946 after the initial notifications. People also launched a struggle against the Rihand Project in 1963-64. However, such early protests could not be sustained, partly because of their failure to attract larger alliances, under the overwhelming influence of the nationalist rhetoric of nation-building that accompanied the construction of large dams in India. The success of the mobilization against the Silent Valley Project, resulting in the decision to shelve the project in 1983, led to a new phase in the history of resistance to big dams in India. Other notable early struggles against big dams were local movements opposed to the Suvarnarekha, Koel Karo and Srisailam Projects. The most celebrated protest movement against big dams so far has centred around the mega Sardar Sarovar Project on the river Narmada. A number of protest groups gathered under the leadership of activist Medha Patkar and in 1988, local resistance organizations federated into a common platform known as the *Narmada Bachao Andolan* (Save the Narmada Movement). The construction of these Dams displaces many poor and underprivileged communities destroying their self-sufficient, environmentally sound economy, culture and becoming homeless. The Narmada Bachao Andolan is one of the most important people's movement fighting for the rights of these poor tribal people who are being robbed of their homes, livelihoods and ways of living in the name of national interest. Apart from Narmada Bachao Andolan, other organizations actively involved with the regular anti mega dam stirs are *Kisak Mukti Sangram Samiti* (KMSS), National Alliance for People's Movement and All Assam Students' Union (AASU). Akhil Gogoi, an RTI activist and general secretary of KMSS has become extremely popular for his aggressive leadership to the movement, particularly against the Subansiri Dam Project. Since mid-2009, Gogoi has been leading a state-wide movement against construction of big dams in the ecologically sensitive regions of Assam and Arunachal Pradesh. In particular, his organization KMSS demands immediate halt to the ongoing construction of the dam of Lower Subansiri, a mega hydroelectric power project under NHPC with an estimated capacity of 2,000 MW. He minces no words when he says that such disregard of the voices and plights of the common people, putting their lives and livelihoods at risk is tantamount to 'neo-colonialism'. Those opposing the mega dams like the lower Subansiri Hydroelectric Power Project, point that because of high seismic activity, and because of several recent instances of earthquakes, the dams can easily give away and cause devastating floods. History only corroborates this apprehension.

A significant development has been the revival of struggles by people displaced by dams completed years ago, such as on the Bargi (completed 1990), Koyna (1964), Tawa (1975) and Mahi-Kadana (1978). By ensuring that these voices are heard, these movements have succeeded in compelling governments, both Central and State, and powerful funding agencies like the World Bank, to rethink their policies on displacement and rehabilitation. Opponents of big dams have argued that big dams are part of a development strategy that intrinsically impoverishes and disempowers the poor. The opponents to big dams in India have also challenged the dominant orthodoxy that development, especially state-induced development, by necessity entails the human costs of displacement or involuntary resettlement. Another important issue in the debate around big dams in India is the question of whether the state should retain the power to compulsorily acquire private land for development projects without the consent of the owner or owners of such land.

Conclusion

As in the growing economic development is inevitable to fulfil the ever increasing demand of modern societies, but it must be ensure that development cannot be used as an argument to disguise discrimination or any other human rights violation by stressing that development-related displacement is permissible. Therefore, measure must be taken to minimize the cost of the project in the form of the displacement along with functioning of the development projects. Various ideas, therefore, have been put forward to minimize the problem or mitigate its consequences.

Displacement creating development is going to continue because developing societies, particularly those with a rapidly expanding population, have to balance benefits of safe water supplies, irrigation, effective transport systems, or urban growth with the costs and pains of resettlement. But rehabilitation and the re-establishment of livelihoods must follow displacement. Inadequate and ill-conceived planning and defective implementation of projects have been most marked where people's basic entitlements have been disregarded from the very inception of a project right through to its completion.

To avoid conflict, and make the most of the gains of development, it is essential that donor organizations and donor governments, managing authorities (which will increasingly mean private companies and consortia) and developing world governments recognize the need for development initiatives that increase employment, reduce poverty and promote social integration. A top priority of national government should be to find non-displacing alternatives to displacement-inducing and environmentally damaging projects. If displacement is unavoidable, action should be taken to ensure that affected people are not only fully compensated and able to purchase replacement land and other assets, but, at the very least, that they should be able to regain their earlier living standard. This means that adequate financial resources must be built into the project budget, with flexibility in the management of that budget to ensure that money finds its way, in time, to those who need it.

Affected people, including potential host communities, should be informed and participate fully in the determination of their future. At the very least, national governments should incorporate the emerging international standards into national policies and domestic legislation for mitigating the negative impacts of involuntary displacement The policy and legal framework must go beyond 'eminent domain' and protect the social, economic and cultural rights of people displaced and affected by development projects.

REFERENCES

A Status Report on the *IDP Situation in North-East India*, presented by Monirul Hussain, August 2006.

Cernea, Michael. "Bridging the Research Divide: Studying Development Oustees", in Tim Allen (ed.), *In Search of Cool Ground: War, Flight and Homecoming in North-East Africa*, London: United Nations Research Institute for Social Development, Africa World Press and James Currey, 1996.

Cernea, Michael, "Risks, Safeguards and Reconstruction", in Michael Cernea and Christopher McDowell, eds., *Risks and Reconstruction: Experiences of Resettlers and Refugees*, World Bank, Washington, DC, 2000.

Cernea, Michael, "Why Economic Analysis is Essential to Resettlement: A Sociologist's View", in Michael Cernea (ed.), *The Economics of Involuntary Resettlement: Questions and Challenges*, Washington, DC: World Bank, 1999.

Downing, Theodore E., *Avoiding New Poverty: Mining-Induced Displacement and Resettlement*, International Institute for Environment and Development, 2002.

Muggah, Robert, "Through the Developmentalist's Looking Glass: Conflict-Induced Displacement and Involuntary Resettlement in Colombia", *Journal of Refugee Studies*, 2000, 13(2): 133-164.

United Nations, *Guiding Principles on Internal Displacement*, New York: Office for the Coordinator of Humanitarian Affairs, 1999.

World Bank Environment Department, *Resettlement and Development: The Bankwide Review of Projects Involving Involuntary Resettlement, 1986-1993*, Washington, DC: World Bank, 1994.

World Commission on Dams, *Dams and Development: A New Framework for Decision-Making*, London and Sterling, Virginia: Earthscan, 2000.

39

INFLUENCE OF GANDHISM IN THE SOCIO-POLITICAL AND ECONOMIC HISTORY OF ASSAM

Nurul Islam

Mohandas Karamchand Gandhi as we call Gandhiji and the father of the nation, spearheaded the Indian struggle for Independence against the British rule in India and had been the greatest Political and Spiritual leader of modern India. He had a Political, Economical and Social philosophy of life, which together later on has been termed as Gandhism. Gandhi was such an influential personality in Indian society that during his time almost every Indians were influenced by his ideals. Particularly, non-violence policy has been recognized by one and all. His philosophy has opened up to the world a new dimension of the Indian attitude towards life, society and spirituality. His entire life and work represent the perfect synthesis of religiousness and society. Religion, the source of all his entire Social and Political attitude is not creedal. Gandhi says: "I do not believe that the Spiritual Law operates in a field of its own. On the contrary, it express itself only the ordinary activities of life. It thus affects the Economic, the Social and Political fields" (Mahatma Gandhi, *Young India*, 3 September, 1925).[1]

In fact all the modalities that have been supported by Gandhi for bringing about social change actually spinning from our ancient spiritual tradition. According to him the concepts of non-violence (*Ahimsa*) and *Satyagraha* (Adherence to Truth) emanate from some inner power. The ultimate goal according to Gandhi is to attain self-realization. But it cannot be achieved without Service to Society. It is necessarily connected with *Sarvodaya* "The greatest good of all". Such *Sarvodaya* in its turn requires Social and Political stability.

The scope of Gandhi's thought and ideas are very comprehensive. Gandhi has not excluded any aspects of human life from his area of discussion. But yet basic characteristics of Gandhiji's thought and ideas are God, Truth, *Ahimsa* (non-violence), *Satyagraha* (Adherence to Truth), Politics, Religion, Education, Economic and Social concepts. These ideas and thoughts of Gandhi has permanent validity and relevance in the present age of Science and Technology. Gandhi use the term God, Truth and *Ahimsa* in a synonymous way. Gandhi himself says "I have nothing new to teach the world. Truth and non-violence are as old as hills. All I have done is to try experiments in both on as vast a scales are I could. In doing so, I have sometimes erred learnt by my errors. Life and its problems have thus became to me so many experiments in the practice of truth and non-violence. In fact, it was in the course of my pursuit of truth that I discovered non-violence" (D.M. Dutta, *The Philosophy of Mahatma Gandhi*, p. 77).[2]

Gandhi advised to the peoples of India to use the same ideal in the field of politics, economics, society and also in the individual life. Gandhi's influences in the socio-political and economic history in Assam had a tremendous effects. Gandhi came to Assam on four occasions. All of his visit was purposive and effective. His first visit was in the year 1921 in connection with the non-cooperation movement. His second visit took place in 1926. It was during the 1sat session of the Congress held in Assam. In 1934, Gandhiji came to Assam for the third time. It was exclusively for the *Harijan* work and his fourth and last visit was 1946. During this period he gave *Darsana* to multidinous people (Kakati Satish Chandra, *Discovery of Assam*, pp. 2, 3.).[3]

Influence of Gandhi's Ideals in Socio-Political and Economic History of Assam

Political Influences

Gandhi came to Assam for the 1st time in the year 1921 in connection with non-cooperation movement. That was a historic year in Indian modern history when he called upon his countryman and women to fight for Independence through the cult of non-violence and truth. In Assam thousands of volunteers took part in the freedom struggle under the leadership of Gandhi. Even literary and cultural personality like Ambikagiri Rai Choudhary, Jyoti Prasad Agarwala, Bishnu Ram Medhi, etc. participated very actively in the freedom movement.

Gandhi in his first visit to Assam was accompanied by late Maulana Mohammad Ali and Maulana Azad Sobhani. He stayed in the Guwahati residence of Late Deshbhakta Tarun Ram Phukan who was at that time Gandhi's virtual lieutenant in this region in participating non-cooperation and other movement initiated by Gandhi. He addressed at Guwahati, a crowed of over 10,000 people. The largest ever seen in a public meeting in Assam till then (Kakati Satish Chandra, *Discovery of Assam*, pp. 1, 2).[4]

As like as other provinces in Assam too, popular response to the regressive measure was massive. Many people of Assam such as — Maniram Dewan, Pioli Boruah, Bahadur Gauburha, Farmud Ali, Mohendra Mohan Choudhury, Bijoy Chandra Bhagawati, Haldhar Bhuyan, Moti Ram Borah, Purna Chandra Sarmah, Pitambar Goswami, Bimala Prasad Chaliha, Kamakhya Prashad Tripathi, Jyoti Prasad Agarwala, Prafulla Goswami, Mohadeva Sharma, Lakheswar Baruah, Rajendra Nath Baruah, Beliram Das, Jinaram Das, Purnanada Chetia, Fakurruddin Ali Ahmed and other so other so many persons took active part in freedom movement selflessly. They were also tortured by the Britisher for their active participation in the movement. Even women were also not in distance from it. Chandra Prova Saikia, Puspalata Das, Gunneswari, etc. are arrested by the British for celebrating the Independence Day at 26 January, 1946. In Quit India movement most of the Assamese people were involved actively. Young generation and student union were also not far from the Quit India movement. In 1942 so many people of Assam such as — Mohammad Taibullah, Debeshwar Sarmah, Bishnu Ram Medhi, Fakurruddin Ali Ahmed, Harekrishna Das, Lila Boruah, etc. are arrested by the British Government. Gopinath Bordoli and Siddhi Nath Sarmah were arrested at Dhubri when they were returning from the Nikhil Bharat Congress Committee meeting in Bombay. Even the commandments of Assam Pradesh Congress Committee was hidden by the British, so that, it could not be spread among the people of Assam. The first revolution against the British rule as began in 1828 by Gomdhar Konwar, the son of Ahom king Fena Konwar. In 1930 Pioli Phukan openly revolted against British Government. To control the movement so many people of Assam were hanged and some other was sentenced long imprisonment. Yet the Assamese people never retreated from the movement. Thus, in the freedom movement both Assamese men and women were influenced by Gandhi is elementary. Therefore, they took active part in the freedom movement and even did not care for their life also. In that time, the jails in Assam were immediately filled up with more then 4,000 political prisoners and many also died. Moreover, the 41st annual session of Congress was held at Pandu, at the foot of Kamakhya Hill in December 1926 in Assam due to mass support to Gandhi. There was an recognition of the Central role played by Gandhi's leadership. It was a tremendous morale booster for the people of Assam. Gandhi's participation was an additional incentive. Moreover, majority of the Students also played their active role only because of Gandhi's influences. Assamese young student leaders like Omeo Kumar Das and Hemchandra Boruah appealed to the students to get involved in the movement (*Dainik Agradu*, dated 31 August 2014, p. 10, by Nripen Nath Borthakur).[5]

Social Influences

Gandhi's influences were very much in the social life of Assam. He came in 1934 for *Harijan* upliftment and raise fund for the welfare of *Harijan* of Assam. A *Harijan* leader of Assam told Gandhiji at Guwahati "The untouchability in Assam is much less than in other part of the country, e.g. in respect of water, temple entry, touch of caste Hindus, etc. (Kakati, Satish Chandra, *Discovery of Assam*, p. 2).[6] At that time Gandhi stayed at Sarania Ashram Guwahati (Now in Ulubari) to give *darsana* to people of Assam. Therefore, many people of Assam including freedom fighters, writers, novelists felt themselves as disciple of Gandhi till today.

Assamese writers including novelists could not escape from the great influence of Gandhism, which was a spirit of that age. A group of Assamese novelists like Daibachandra Talukdar, Dandinath Kalita, Jogesh Das, etc. wrote soem social reformation novels based on Gandhi's philosophy of life and Indian freedom struggle movement. They were volunteers themselves during the freedom struggle. They showed in their novels social reformation programmes like stopping opium eating and untouchability. Communalism also continued side-by-side under the influence of Gandhism. For that reason it can be said that Assam is a State where the diseases like untouchability, communalism, hatred, etc. are very less in comparism to other States in respect of castes, creeds and rituals.

In that time opium consumption in Assam had became a cause of great concern because addiction to the drug had reached immense proportion and was consumed irrespective of the price demanded. Gandhi's fervent appeal to the congress workers to make Assam free from opium had a stirring effect. "Even women like Chandraprova Saikia and others went to the village of Assam and made aware the villagers on women education, child marriage, etc. Moreover, they took the responsibility to spread Gandhi's principles of truth and philosophy all over Assam (*Dainik Agradut*, dated 31 August 2014, p. 10, by Nripen Nath Borthakur).[7]

Economic Influences

Gandhi gives his own theory regarding the condition of Indian Economy. He was a believer of simple living and high thinking. Gandhi's economics, specially gives importance on the welfare of the poorest class of the society. According to Gandhi, the economic basis of society must be a moral one, society must be based on love and trust.

Gandhi was in favour of small industries. He thought that each and every individual should give importance on crafts like: carpentry, poultry, spinning, weaving or any other similar handicraft. By actually doing manual work while learning, the individual will develop interest in his work and will be able to give out his best (*Harijan*, 31st July, 1937).[8]

The non-cooperation movement had a tremendous impacts on Assam. In this movement by the influence of Gandhi, people of Assam boycott foreign goods and gives importance on their own crafts. The concept of *Khadi* was received with equal enthusiasm in Assam where the tradition of spinning and weaving was already strongly entrenched. Gandhi requested the people of Assam to popularize small industries. Of course, after getting the influence of Gandhi, Assamese people gives importance on the small industries. It is because of Gandhi, Assam became one of the developed state in case of small industries. Majority of small industries like spinning, weaving, poultry or any other similar handicraft also formed even today in most of the houses in rural Assam. In support of Gandhi's small industries, people of Assam started doing cooperative farming and people began to show more interest in doing agricultural work.

Thus, Assamese people gives importance on the small industries or on bread labour as taking up spinning and weaving propagating the use of *Khadi* and *Charkha* and boycotting the foreign goods. Moreover, the home industries are still flourishing in Assam and there is a good prospect for spinning and weaving in future. Obviously, Mahatmaji's visit to Assam were few and far between. All the same, Assam was dear to him. In the time of distress and calamity, it was he who toned up the moral of the people here as elsewhere; it was he again who watched and helped in shaping the destiny of Assam. During the Second World War when Assam turned into one of the Principal operational bases, Gandhi sent messages to the Assamese people as to how the people including women folk, should resist the state of rape, debauchery, murder, molestation and all the views which gushed out of war conditions, regardless of whichever quarters perpetrated them on the innocent people (*Discovery of Assam*, p. 3).[9]

How devoutly Assam responded to the call of Gandhiji through all the stages of the freedom struggle is illustrated by a remark of the last Viceroy of India, Lord Mountbatten, made at a public meeting at Guwahati in 1947. Lord Mountbatten said: "Assam is one of the provinces where Gandhiji's ideals followed." Thus from the view of Lord Mountbatten it can be said that Gandhi as such a influential person in Assam that whose ideology is followed by many of the Assamese people. Even today Gandhi has remained a factor motivating the people of the state to move ahead in the path of peace, prosperity and harmony.

NOTES AND REFERENCES

1. Baruah, S.L., *A Comprehensive History of Assam*, Munshiram Manoharlal Publishers Pvt. Ltd., New Delhi.
2. Deka, Dr. Umesh, *Post Was Assamese Novel*, Published by Chandra Prakash, Guwahati, 1989 and 2008.
3. Gupta, Krishna Roy Chandra, *Essays in Social and Political Philosophy*, Indian Council of Philosophical Research, New Delhi in associate with Allied Publishers New Delhi, Bombay, Calcutta, Madras, Lucknow, Bangalore, Hyderabad, Ahmedabad, 1989.
4. Goswami, Priyan, *The History of Assam*, Orient Blakswan Private Limited, New Delhi.
5. Kakati, Satish Chandra, *Discovery of Assam*, Arunchandra Guha 21, Patuatola Lane, Calcutta, 1964.
6. Lal, Kumar Basant, *Contemporary Indian Philosophy*, Motilal Banarsidas Publishers Pvt. Ltd., Delhi, 1973.
7. Prashad, M., *Social Philosophy of Mahatma Gandhi*, Visva Vidyalaya Prakashan, Gorakhpur, 1958.
8. Sharma, Satendra Nath, *Asomya Upanashar Bhumika*, Published by Arunudai Press, Guwahati, 1965.
9. Sarma, Govinda Prasad, *Upanash Aru Asomiya Upanash*, Published by Sri Ajoy Kumar Dutta, Students Stores, College Hostel Road, Guwahati, 1995.
10. www.Google.com.in

SECTION IV

Traditional Practices and Culture

40

TRADITIONAL FOOD HABITS OF ASSAMESE PEOPLE

Sunil Kr. Saikia

Assam is the oldest and largest states (in terms of population) in the North-Eastern Region of India. The North-Eastern Region (NER) of India, on the other hand, comprises of eight states, *viz.* Arunachal Pradesh, Assam, Manipur, Meghalaya, Mizoram, Nagaland, Sikkim and Tripura, with about 8 per cent of the country's geographical area and about 4 per cent of the population of the country. The Region is home for rich cultures, nature-friendly traditional technologies and enduring social institutions. The region is home of more than 150 tribes and sub-tribes, along with host of non-tribal, most of whom are traditional inhabitants of the region. The State of Assam is also inhabited by a large number of tribal and non-tribal groups. The major tribal groups in Assam are the *Bodos, Rabhas, Mishing, Deoris, Tiwas, Karbi, Hojai, Sonowal Kacharis, Mech*, etc. are the Plains tribes and the *Dimasa Kacharis* of the Hills tribe. Similarly, the non-tribal communities are the *Tai Ahoms, Koch-Rajbangshis, the Kalitas, Chutias, Morans, Mataks, Chaodangs, Brahmins, Nath-Jugi, Muslim*, etc. During British regime, quite a large number of people from Bangladesh (the then known as East Pakistan), Bihar, U.P., Andhra Pradesh (as *Tea labourers* and later known as *Tea Tribes*), Rajasthan, Punjab, West Bengal, etc. were also migrated or brought to Assam for business purpose, searching for skilled jobs and also as ordinary workers, etc. and a few of them have been settled in the state. All communities in Assam in due course are known as '*Akhamiya*' or '*Ahkhomiya*' or Assamese is the lingua-franca of Assam.

The State of Assam is presently spread over a geographical area of 78.44 thousand sq.km. As per the Census of India, 2011, the population of Assam is 3,11,69,272, out of which 1,59,54,927 are male and

1,52,14,345 are female. The State has 27 districts, out of which four districts are under the Bodoland Territorial Council (BTC). Topography of the major part of the State is plain except two districts namely Karbi-Anglong and Dima Hasao. Altitude of the State ranges between 50 mt to 1650 mt from MSL. The State falls within Agro-climatic zone II. Based upon agro-climatic characteristics, the State has been sub-divided into eight major sub-zones primarily based upon rainfall, temperature and soil moisture regimes. In the State, 85.92 per cent of the total population is rural. Agriculture is the mainstay of the major part of the population. Agricultural workers account for 54.44 per cent of the total workers of the State.

The State of Assam has a very rich culinary heritage. The traditional cuisine of Assam is full of exotic and mild flavour some dishes that appeal to people with liking for all tastes. So, much is the variety of food in Assam that it seems experiment and innovation is an additional ingredient of every Assam delicacy. The cooking styles and flavours of each and every community in the State is unique and differs from each other with considerable influence of Thai, Burmese (Myanmar), Bhutan, Tibetan, Bengali, Nepali, and Chinese cuisines.

Rice is the staple diet in the entire State and also in the region and is eaten in various forms throughout the day. The people of the State generally **take non-vegetarian diets (90-95% of people)** and prefer less oily and less spicy food. Along with rice, other supplementary food includes lentils, fish curry, meat curry with plenty of vegetables, leafy vegetables, wild herbs, leafs, roots, barks, etc. and also various types of traditional chatnis, pickles, salads, ambals, etc. The **fish curry** is generally prepared with variety of vegetables, leafy vegetables and also poured with lemon concentrate or other sour vegetables like "*oou-tenga*" (deliers-indica), "*thekera-tenga*" (gambouse), "*amora-tenga*" (hog-plum), "*konbilahi-tenga*" (cherry tomato or small size local tomato), etc. In some other sour curry preparations, it is prepared from varieties of leafy vegetables like '*paleng*' (spinach/spinacia oleracea), '*lie*' (lai/wild mustard), '*lafa*' (lafa), etc. or green vegetables like — '*jika*' (cornered gourd), '*jati-lou*' (ball-gourd), '*kumura*' (white gourd melon), etc., but while preparing such kind of curries (at the time of boiling such curries), '*neemu-rokh*' (lemon concentrate) or '*thekera*' (gambouse), or '*teteli* (tamarind) or tomatoes are put or mixed with such curries. Sometimes such fish curries are prepared with some of the non-soured vegetables mentioned above and also without putting any lemon concentrate. Similarly, other popular fish curries preparations are fish in "*horiah* *bota*" (mustard gravy) or fish pieces covered with mustard powder and cooked in banana leaves, fish head cooked with '*kochu-sak*' (a typical wild green leafy vegetables/Egyptian arum) or with rice and spices or *mug dal*. In most of the fish curry preparations, potatoes, turmeric, ginger, onion, garlic, etc. are also used, depending on the type of preparations. However, the use of mustard oil and other spices are very minimal in Assamese society.

The **meat curry is prepared with** ginger, garlic, cardamom, cinnamon, onions and also with vegetables like green papaya, white gourd, etc. Authentic traditional Assamese cuisine is simple, yet very delicious. Very little oil and spices is used. Generally, mustard oil is used for cooking and occasionally, butter or ghee is used. Almost all Assamese people are non-vegetarian. Fish is very popular in non-vegetarian dishes. It is difficult to find anyone who does not eat fish and meat and eggs. Meat, particularly goat meat ('*Patha*' or '*Khasi manxo*'), '*Hanh*' (duck), '*Rajhanh*' (goose), '*Paro*' (pigeon), '*Pahu*' (deer) and '*Kancho*' (turtle meat are popular among the Assamese society) (now deer meat and turtle meat are legally prohibited). However, Chicken is taboo in orthodox families and there are some, who even not eat any meat. Traditional Assamese food is cooked in earthenware (in Assamese language it is called as "*Chowka*") on a wood fire, giving it its unique flavour and taste. Assamese traditional cuisine is a mixture of different indigenous as well as external influences with a lot of regional variations.

Another popular Assamese preparation is called "***Khaar***" or "***Kshar***" (***alkali***) or "***Kola-Khar***" which is prepared with vegetables or dal. "*Khar*" is a traditionally prepared alkali, prepared from the barks of "*Bhimkol*", a local variety of banana barks, burned in firewood and than make it powder). Assamese people believe that '*Khar*' is supposed to have the power of curing all stomach troubles and also some other physical ailments. Another typical vegetable preparation from banana tree is called "***Posola***", which is prepared from the barks of the banana tree, particularly the interior parts of the banana tree. Fried or roasted banana flower/spadix of banana (locally known as '*kol-phul*' or '*koldil*') is also another delicacy in Assam.

Like '*khar*' or '*posala*' mentioned above, Assamese people are also **fond of taking 'tita' (mild bitter taste) items**, prepared from variety of herbs, leafy vegetables, vegetables and from wild flowers, etc. Such preparations are either gravy or dry fry. Some of the vegetables, herbs, wild flowers are '*tita-kerela*' (bitter gourd), '*bet-gaaz*' (calamus rotong or tender cane tree), '*hukuta-tita*' (corchorus olitorious), '*sewali phool*' (nyctauthes arbor trists), '*titamora sak*', '*durub phool*' (laucas linifolia), '*kalmou*' (bitter watercress) '*bo'k-phool*' (sesbania grandiflora), '*bahak tita*' (justicia adhatoda), '*mahaneem*' (neem), '*meethi*' (fenugreek), '*bhekuri-teeta*' (solanum indicum), etc. However, local people do not take '*khar*' (alkai) and '*tita*' (bitter taste preparations) together in the same meal.

Another vegetarian or non-vegetarian mashed items called "*pitika*" or "*hona-pitika*" is also very popular in Assam. Some of the such mashed items ("*pitikas*" or "*hona-pitikas*") are — Boiled or roasted potatoes with herbal spices (*dhania*-pat), onion, raw mustard oil, salt, etc. Boiled or roasted potatoes with boiled eggs, Boiled veg, banana ('*pura-kol*') with or without potatoes, roasted banana flower with or without eggs ('*koldil-pura/pitika*'), Boiled pumpkin ('*rangalao-pitika*'), Roots of Egyptian arun ('*kachu-pitika*'), Boiled or roasted brinjal with or without potatoes or eggs, herbs, etc. Some people also like to have deep fat fry of the above items or deep fry with grinded paste of rice flour ('*pithaguri*') or dal paste.

Leafy vegetables are boiled or fried is also a popular dish in Assam. Some of such important leafy vegetables which are boiled or fried are —"*dhetia*" (boerhavia diffusia), "*horiah-sak*" (mustard green vegetables), "*lie*", "*jilmil*" (chemopodium album), "*khutura*" (amoramtus spinoons), "*puroi*" (besella rubra), "*ponougewa*" (boerheavia diffuse), "*mahabringaraj*" (eclipta enecta), "*malbhug-sak*" (portulaca quadrifide), "*paleng*" (spinach), "*brahmi*" (siphononthus indica) "*morisa*", "*dherua* or *morisha*", etc. On the other hand, soups and koftas are not very popular in Assamese society except boiled vegetables, vegetables stew, etc. In Assamese dishes, another popular item is known as **"*Paita-bhat*"** or one/two days fermented rice (boiled rice is pouring in filtered water for 1-2 days), which is generally taken (eaten) with raw salt, raw mustard oil, fresh onion, raw ginger, chilly, etc. or with mashed potatoes.

In addition to the food habits mentioned above, **different castes or communities in Assam have also have some traditional food habits of its own.** For example the **Ahom community** are non-vegetarian people and they usually take boiled rice with meat, fish and also eggs. They are very much fond of '*tenga*' (sour) dishes made from sour fruits or green leaves like '*teteli*' (tamarind), '*jalfai*' (olive), '*bogori*', '*kordoi*', '*thekera*' and also green vegetables like '*suka sak*', '*paleng sak*', '*dhekia sak*', '*bamboo shoots*', etc. **Bodos community** on the other hand, prepare meat or fish is mostly by boiling, baking, drying or smoking and mixed with vegetables, ginger, onion, garlic, '*panak*' (a local leaf), etc. They grinde the dried fish and put into the bamboo seige. This process is known as "*Nakham*". Similarly, **Deori community** prefer pork as one of their favourite choice and it is accepted as the sacred in the religious ceremony. Boiled food is still popular among the **Mishing communities**. Along with rice, boiled edible leaves (e.g. '*dermi*', '*ombe*', '*pakkam*', '*takuk*', etc.), meat ('*adin*') and fish ('*ango*') are some of the popular food items of the villagers. Dried meat and fish are also very popular. Other favourate dishes of Mishings are '*purang*' rice, fish '*namchring*', chicken curry with '*pithaguri*' (grinding of rice), etc.

The general Assamese people, apart from taking two main meals (as lunch and dinner), also take **breakfast (known a '*jalpan*') and snacks ('*pithas*')** in the morning and afternoon. The main menu or food items in the breakfast generally are — "*chira*", "*akhoi*", "*muri*", "*hurum*" (all are different varieties of local corns), "*komal chawul*" (a type of rice without boiling), "*korai guri*", "*sandoh*", "*pithaguri*", etc. (all are different varieties of rice flour or rice grindings in baked/toast form or without baked or toasted form) mix with hot or cold milk or '*doi*' (curd/yogurt), '*hor*' (thick cream of hot milk), '*cream*' (thick milk), '*gur*' (jiggery/ unrefined sugarcane sugar) and ripe banana. Occasionally local people also prepare such breakfast by putting the rice or rice flour with small quantity of water or into a fresh bamboo tube/seize and burn it in the fire or hot ash. Such type of breakfast items are known as "*chunga-chawal*", "*chunga-pitha*", "*bhat-pitha*", etc. and it is mixed with milk or curd, *gur*, etc. Similarly, different types of "*pithas*" or traditional cakes are prepared from the rice flour (grinding of rice) and mixed with '*gur*' (jaggery), '*til*' (sesame seeds powder) or '*narikal guri*' (desiccated coconut powder), etc. and baked or fried in mustard oil. The name of some of the popular Assamese '*pithas*' are (all mentioned in Assamese names) — "*til pitha*", "*gheela pitha*", "*narikal pitha*", "*tekeli mukhot dia pitha*", "*pani pitha*", "*haneki pitha*", "*paat pitha*", "*bhaja pitha*", "*sunga pitha*", "*anguli diya pitha*", "*chitow pitha*", "*gokul pitha*", "*kolpitha*", etc. Tea is always served with the breakfast.

After consuming the main food or breakfast or even tea and snacks, there is a system of taking some mouth freshener — called **"*tamul-pan*", i.e. betel nut and leaf.** Such betel-nut and leaf ("*tamul-pan*") is also offered to all the guests visiting any Assamese family. In Assam the local people like to take the betel nut, leaf, lime and tobacco together. However, very few people take Pan and supari, Sweet pan or Zarda pan.

In conclusion we can say that versatility of Assamese cuisine is very wide. There are hundreds of fish preparations, curry preparation or *pitha*

(Assamese snacks) preparations. Similarly, each Assamese community has its own unique lentil and herb dishes. Taste of wide range of *khar* (alkali), *posola, pitika, chutneys* varies from community to community. Many families still have their closely guarded recipes. Now some of the enterprising youth of the state have been set up some hotels, restaurants, dhabas, where they are serving typical Assamese traditional food. Some of the popular such restaurants in Guwahati are, "Paradise", "Akhol", "Kharika", "Majulir Ehaj", "*Juti Logai Khaun*", "Highway Dhaba", "Dichang", "Spring Valley", "Brahmaputra Resort", "Alfreshco", etc. In Kaziranga, Jorhat, Sibsagar, Tezpur, Margherita, etc. such type of traditional Assamese foods are also available. More local youth should come forward in this area.

41

THE MARRIAGE CEREMONY OF THE AHOM
Continuity and Change

Sikhamoni Konwar

Introduction

Marriage is a very old institution current among the human society, sociologists terms marriage "a social institution complete by itself".[1] As social institutions represents the social structure and machinery through which human society organizes, directs and executes the multifarious activities required to satisfy human needs.[2] Thus marriage is socially sanctioned union between man and woman and considered a sacred institution in all times and climes and is performed with pomp and gaiety. Every human society is marked by its own unique and distinctive marriage rites and rituals, and customs. As such Chak-long is the customary marriage ceremony of the Ahom of Assam. The Ahom are one of the most predominant extreme western most of the Tai groups, who had migrated to the Brahmaputra Valley in the early thirteenth Century and founded a new kingdom which was sustained for as long as Six hundred years under a single dynasty (1228-1826 AD). Originally, the Tai speaking people come from Mong Mao that bordered the south western region of China and Burma under their leader Tai Mao prince Chao-lung Sui-ka-pha. They carried with them their own Tai culture, marriage, rites and ritual and burial system which was different from the local people.

According to the Ahom tradition as recorded in the Ahom Chronicles, the origin of the Chak-long marriage dates back to the period when Ahom progenator Lengdon married Nang Hun pha. To begin with Lengdon sent his messenger to Mo-lau-Khri to the girls family with a gift and expressed Lengdons interest for their daughter for marriage. When the consent is given then it is followed by finding out an auspicious day by examining *Ban-Cheng*, invitation and other related ceremonies. The ritual that was observed in this wedding according to norms set up by Goddess 'Ja-Sing-Pha' are called Chak-long. As per legends these ritual were then carried from heaven to earth by their grandsons Khun lung, Khun lai who was sent to rule on earth. Since that time marriage by the ceremony of Chak-long has come into vogue among the Ahom.

Pre-wedding Ceremony

Ceremonial Bathing

For ceremonial bathing or *noani* of the bride and grooms at certain stages of marriage is an important part of marriage in Assam. The Ahom kings and nobles once performed their marriage by chak-long for 7 to 5 days. But now a days people performed this for 3 days only.

A wooden or bamboo platform is erected of bamboo and banana plantation which is quadrangular in shape. The bamboo posts are again decorated with banana sheaths. The platform is also covered with banana sheaths. Then a pira (tool) is placed at the centre of the platform for the groom or bride to sit and bath. Under the bathing platform are buried fowls eggs a pair of betel-nuts, one coin, one needle and one sickle to ward of evils. It is symbolized as auspicious bath in the present of close relatives and mother.

Joran

Joran[3] prior to the main ceremony the 1st day is called *Joran* diya according to tradition the groom's family sends *Joran* with mother and other relatives. They carried gifts, gold and silver Jewellery, wedding apparels. One of the most important articles are silver pen knives, a silver lime box, a betel-nut. Also the earthen pot filled with mango twig having five leaves planted in each of the pot. Other articles turmeric and black pulse are sent for the bathing ceremony. In the brides house with the presence of people, the bride is given the gift of *Joran*. The women sing songs. While coming back they carry one of the earthen pot, one set of knife and lime box and one set of dress for the groom presented by the brides parents. These article is also to touch by the bride.

Na Purusar Saul Khowa

In the second day, a ceremonial feast is observed which is known as *na purasar saul khowa* or offering oblation to the nine ancestors who were believed to be came down to earth to take their offering and to bless them. In this function nine elderly persons are invited to have feast with *lok-lao* (rice-wine) rice, fish, meat, vegetable, etc.

The bride and the groom in their houses respectively offered betel nuts, and other present and bowing down and seek blessing for future life.

Rik-khon

Another important ritual performed in the 2nd day is Rik-khon, 'Rik' means call, 'khon' means longevity. In this ceremony 2 or 3 priests would take 2-3 *Jakoi* (fishing equipment made of bamboo) and go to the nearby pond or river and worship the river deity Khao Kham offering betel nut, egg, rice, for the long life of the bride and bridegroom. The fish caught here is then wrapped and brought home. The fish is then kept over the head of the groom/bride by the saying prayer for long life. Then the fish is cooked and served to the bride or groom.

Deo-ban

A day before the wedding Deo-ban[4] is performed at the couples houses for their happy future. This is the ritual of offering prayers to the Ahom gods— Lengdon, Langkuri, Jan Sai hung and Jashingpha. The ceremony is held primarily at the grooms home and the offerings of betel nuts, 12 eggs, a small quantity of rice, luk lao, honey, singkora flower, 12 thuria tamul (a piece of areca nut inside a betel leaf) are sent to the bride's house. In honour of the expired ancestors of the family a platter is offered. After this priests worship god Phura by lighting seven earthern lamps in seven banana sheath.

Ap Tang

In Ap tang[5] ceremony bride take bath with mixed medicated water prepared by the priest. While pouring water on the bride or bridegroom one should stand on a sieve and to look at a tree full of branches and leaves and pour the water on the head by uttering the name of the Phra Tara. After changing clothes the bride or the bridegroom should take a sickle, retreat 3 steps and draw three sacred lines on the ground with it in the name of "Phura Tara", then should leave the place saying "O ills and evils! do not come hither across the lines".[6] After this five or seven persons should be invited to light refreshment and bride or groom bow down with them in respect.

Ganthian Khunda

Ganthian Khunda is a ceremony performed in the 2nd day at night by women. Ganthian is a sacred knotted plant with fragrant root.[7] The root is pounded on a stone slab by the mother, sisters and other women. After the paste is made the women gives mark in the forehead of the bride. The function, which is full of merriment is very specific ceremony of the Ahom community.

Doiyan Dia

On the very Chaklong marriage day, at the dawn this ceremony is performed by a group of women, mother of the bride and three young girls.[8] The women holding two betel leaves with the two hands deep the upper ends in curdled milk, contained in the vessel, anoint the cheeks, arms and feet by three times.[9] In this ceremonial occasion women sing song.

On the Marriage Day

On the marriage day a ceremonial bath takes place where bride is poured holy water collected from river. After the bath, bride is duly dressed up and sits on a mat in front of an altar with multicoloured figures of lotus petals drawn on it. Small size banana trunks are planted on the four corners of the altar. These are tied round with thread chipped with mango leaves. Before leaving for the brides house he bows down his parents, relatives and gathering people. Bridegroom adorned with traditional cloth and leave with his best friend to be constantly accompanied him is called Doradhora.

At the bride place at the centre of the pandal an altar with the figure of a lotus is made for the chak-long ceremony.

Huaguri-tola

Huaguri tola is the first reception of the groom in front of the brides wedding gate. This means collect luck or fortune with auspicious *ulludwani*[10] when the bridegroom arrives this led up to a *pira* (small tool). At this stage women generally throw rice on the group of the bridegroom as a token of hearty welcome and wishing prosperity. It is also called *dora-adoora*. The women and mother of the bride come out to the gate carrying the holy water pot with the flaming earthen lamp on tray to receive the groom. A little girl is then wash the feet of the groom.

after this mother of the bride welcome him by sprinkling with the mango leaves the holy water of the pot on him and then on herself repeatedly 3 times and fanning him three times with a hand made for. At the end she gives affectionate kisses to groom on the cheeks. Then the groom is led and sometimes carried by brides brother or uncle to the *pandal*. He sits there facing east with the altar. Left side is reserved for bride and to the left of the brides seat is for father or guardian of the bride. Officiating priest sitting facing the south.

Chak-long Ceremony and Sacred Mandala

For performing chak-long most important part is *mandala* an octagonal shape lotus design structure is guarded by four banana plants. Seven different colours are used to decorate the *mandala* with 101 earthen lamps put at different crossing points all facing the east direction seven different colours are used the match in the *mandala* like white, black, blue, green, purple, red and yellow. The lotus has 16 petals of large size. The *moral* from the centre point gives way to 16 points criss-crossing each other and make 96 points in total. At the centre there are 2 concentric circle one smaller within a larger one. The space between the circle are divided into four equal parts by four straight lines whose length is limited by the circumstances of the two circles. One larger lighted earthen lamp is placed at the centre, that is within the innermost circle with the wick pointed to the east and four such lamps of smaller size are placed in then same position within the four parts into which the space between the inner and outer circle is divided. This lotus figure is accepted figure illuminated with 101 lamps, each containing mustard oil poured

Figure 41.1: 101 Earthen Lamps of Chak-long Marriage Ceremony

into it and a wick to burn. All the lamps pointed to the east, are lighted just before the bridegroom takes his seat bowing down to the illuminated altar.

A few betel-nuts platters covered with kerchief is placed ahead hear the *moral* as a token of respect for father and elders of the family.

In the meantime bride is dressed up exquisitely with wedding dress specially made for the occasion, gold ornaments and covering her face coming out and seated on the left side of the bridegroom after bowing down to the altar. When all are seated in an orderly manner ceremony begins with priest sprinkling spiritual water over everyone with a prayer by the priests. Than bride and bridegroom holding oblatious of flowers and rice with folded palms and uttering the following prayer 1st

O' phra ban naoi chak-long
Ci cim, heu tim.
(O God let our marriage be happy)

Then the oblations are thrown to the altar. Then brides father gifts the groom with a gold ring which he puts on the ring finger of the groom then father of the bride gives *sampradan* (offering the bride to groom) by placing the right thumb of the bride on the left thumb of the groom holding them in that position utters thus O! God of heaven, in presence of you, I am offering my daughter to the bridegroom and to addressing the groom in presence of God, I offer you my daughter keep her with love and affection.

Figure 41.2: Chak-long Marriage Ceremony of the Ahom

Then the couple stands up and exchanges garlands of 101 flowers with uttering the *mantra* addressing to each other. Thus, the bride addressing the groom with the garland in her hands says "I adore you with this garland of 101 flowers of 101 ideas and choose you as my husband". Thereafter the bridegroom too puts garland of 101 flowers to the bride and accept her as wife. At this point women shower flowers and rice on their heads. priests then blessed the bride and groom. That is followed by telling the history of their forefathers. Ahom priest recounts the family trees of great deeds of forefathers to newly wed couple. Then the bride and groom are joined by a scarf or cloth as a link at one end of the bride and at the other end with the scarf of the groom and this is called *legna granthi* or 'conjugal knot'. Then, they jointly prayed to God, deities many more times uttering prayers holding flowers and rice and throw the oblation to the central light of the altar and the *morala*. Then, the assembly blesses the pair with a chorus of voice wishing their happy life and shower flower to them. Then at the end of the joint prayer, a *Hengdan* and a cloth girdle with an amulet is given by bride to groom. The bride gives the *Hengdan* or traditional sword to the groom to protect the country, family and property and groom accepts the sword in hand and promises to protect the country and family in presence of all. The bride is also given a cloth girdle with an amulet. The bridegroom solemnly promises to conquer the enemies by wearing them.

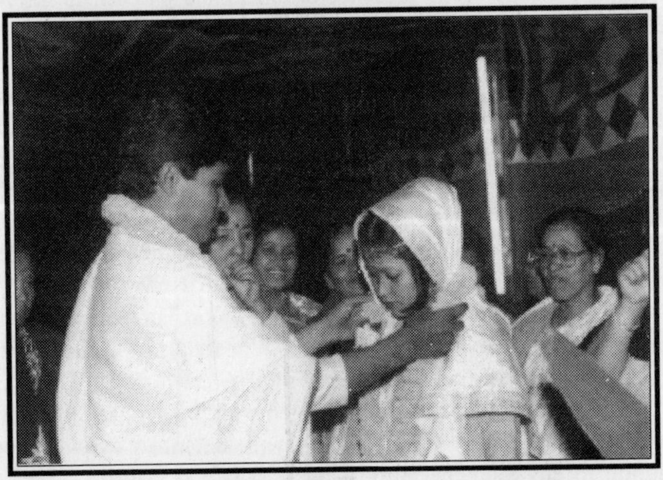

Figure 41.3: Groom Offering Garland of 101 Flowers

After this vows are taken and the priest advice and wishes to God for blessing the newly wed couple, the essence of which is to lead a noble life, caring for each other and their families, devoted to God. The advice to the newly married couple is also seen among the Chinese and Hindu marriages and Palaung of the Shan States.

Here ends the ritual of *Chak-long*. After this couple exchange gold rings, silver boxes and knives put inside a rice heap. This bridges the union between the two souls. Next step is playing dice and cowries by the couple. Then, they are treated with a mixture of sweet foods. Thus, the formalities of marriage are concluded and blessing are given by the parents and bride start her journey for new house. When they arrive, a warm welcome is given in the gate of the house by the relatives of the groom. Then on entering the bedroom the couple prayed five deities for granting a happy and peaceful life. The newly wed bride visits her parents after 8 days of marriage with husband on invitation. a feast is arranged in honour of the couple. This ceremony is called *ath mongola.*

Conclusion

The most significant part of the *Chak-long* marriage is its ritualistic part which leads to protection of the family and the country. For royalty marriage is performed at the bridegroom's house, where entourage was sent to bring the bride to the palace. For common people, chak-long is customarily takes place in the bride's house as mentioned above. It is also a socio-religious ceremonies with 101 earthen lamps which signify to make a promise in the presence of elders and parents. In the Ahom marriage there is no *homa* ceremony, nor ritual of *saptapadi*[11] like Hindu marriage. Chak-long marriage is a social duty, its binding being social and mutual. It is unlike to *Vivaha-Sanskara* of Hindu marriage and not in dissoluble life after life. Despite Ahom came under the influence of Hinduism in the seventeenth century and incorporate many Hindu ways of life even then they still followed some custom, and this form of marriage festival has been still performed without any break. Many of the customs and rituals of chak-long bears semblance of traditional Assamese weddings pertaining to different communities, but there are some aspect which are definitely Ahom. Though certain Hindu elements have been seen in the Ahom marriage ceremony, it has maintained a South-East Asian pattern.[12] *Chak-long* ritual has been revered down the ages, a lot has changed with time, since culture is not static, it changes in a given environment in human activities or his adaption to environment. Amidst this *Chak-long* manifests itself as a popular cultural milieu of the Ahom. It is really remarkable that while the Ahoms have adopted many local customs and cultures during their eight hundred years socio-political existence in Assam, they still carry forward their age old cultural elements like *Chak-long*. In the present context it is important and significant to note how the Ahoms have successfully preserve this basic cultural heritage in the view of the global cultural force. Besides *Chak-long* is an epitome of the unity in diversity of India in greater perspective. It is a contribution of the Ahoms towards enriching the diversified cultural heritage of India.

NOTES AND REFERENCES

1. Westermark, E., *History of Human Marriage*, London, 1921.
2. Barnes, Harry Elmer, *Social Institution*, New York, 1942.
3. Joran is a Tai Ahom word which means living together. Gogoi, P., *Tai Ahom Religion and Customs*, Guwahati, 1976.
4. 'Deo' means God and 'ban' means pray, sun, meaning prayer to the tutelary God above.
5. 'Ap' means to wash the body, 'tang' means with mixed varieties of things.
6. *Tai Ahom Religion and Customs.*
7. *Tai Ahom Religion and Customs.*
8. 'Doi' means curdled milk and 'yan' means to apply.
9. *Tai Ahom Religion and Customs.*
10. Chetia, Satyanath, *Tai Ahom Marriage*, Guwahati, 2005. Gohain, Dr. Brindra Kumar, *Tai Ahom Janagosthi Aru Tai Parampara*, Guwahati, 2009.
11. *Saptapadi*, the rite of seven steps. The bride is to make seven steps, while the groom recites. In every step, both of them utter *mantras*.
12. Terwiel, B.J., *The Tai of Assam*, Centre for South-East Asian Studies, Gaya, 1980, Vol. I.

42

FESTIVALS OF THE TIWAS OF NORTH-EAST INDIA
An Overview

Mowsumee Bordoloi Hazarika

Introduction

The North-East part of India is the home of many diversified, small, but culturally rich ethnic groups. Since, time immemorial this valley of the Brahmaputra, the mighty river which flows through this part of India has attracted many migrating ethnic groups of different origin. Various tribes belonging to Indo-Tibetian, Mongoloid, Austro-Mongolian origin has migrated to this valley of North-East India and has made its fertile and verdant land their homeland. The aboriginal people residing in the Brahmaputra Valley which mainly traverse through the State of Assam of North-East India are the Boro, Dimasa, Karbi, Mising, Tiwa (Lalung), Garo, Deuri, etc. These groups with their colourful socio-cultural identity and magnificent way of life creates an unparalled diversified culture, reflecting unique and rich tradition. Among these groups the 'Tiwas' living in the State of Assam and its neighbouring State Meghalaya depicts a rich and vivacious heritage of cultural identity. This ethnic group belonging to the Tibeto-Burman branch of the Indo-Chinese Mongoloid tribe, has contributed immensely to the formation of the grand nationality of Assamese people as well as for the evaluation of the present day culture and language of Assam. The socio-cultural contribution made by the Tiwa and other ethnic groups of North-East India has not only enriched the way of life of the people of this region, but also contributed substantially for the integrity and peaceful co-existence of the various groups of diversified identity. The North-East India depicts a Anthropological museum of cultural assimilation and socio-cultural synthesis in which an integrated unity has emerged keeping the individual identity intact.

The Origin of the Name Tiwa

Different section of people belonging to the Mongolian tribe living in the North-Eastern part of India have two ways of determining their nomenclature.

1. The people of other tribes living with their tribes address them with names based (and derived) on their culture, character patterns, dwelling places/abodes, lifestyle, etc.
2. The people of the tribe themselves choose a name based on their geographical location and occupation.

Thus, it is seen that the people of "Non-Tiwa" tribes addressed the people belonging to the Tiwa tribes as "Lalung". But, on the other hand the people of this tribe, who speak the tiwa language, identify themselves as "Tiwa". The origin of the word "Lalung" has no scientific evidence, but the word "Tiwa" denotes a 'riverbank' or 'the banks of a river'. Therefore, "Tiwa" means the people residing on the banks of a river.

Abode

The original people of the "Tiwa" tribe resided on the banks of the Hwang Ho and Yangtze Kiang river of China. Thereafter, they shifted to the Brahmaputra Valley in search of food as they were mainly agriculture based. After many years they travelled through the east and south-east routes of North-East India and finally settled down in the hilly and valley regions of this area. According to an ancient myth, the Tiwa tribe of Mongolian origin established their own kingdom named "Hilali" in the south of Bhutan, from where they had migrated to North-East India. But there is no written history of this tribe. The Tiwa's of this region lived forming small kingdoms out of which some were independent and some were subordinate tribes. The great Tiwa tribe was formed by the '*Panchoraja*' (a kingdom of five kings), the '*Satoraja*' (a kingdom of seven kings) and the '*Datioliya Raja*' (the king of the small and neighbouring states) of Nagaon and Morigaon Districts of State of Assam.

Social System

The Tiwas of Assam stays in a well-knit social structure. Most of the Tiwa people live in the hilly region while some of them live in the plain area. Due to the greater degree of secluded dwelling which is free from surrounding influence, the Tiwas of the hilly region are more radically inclined and they tend to stick to their traditional values more in comparison to the Tiwas living in the plain areas.

(i) The Tiwa people worship Lord Fa Mahadeu (Lord Shiva). The sacred place where they worshipped is called 'Nabar'. The Tiwas also use the 'Nabar' as a meeting place for the senior members of the families where they perform the worship and other social activities.

(ii) 'Samadi' or 'Dekechang' is the main learning place of the Tiwas youths (Pathai). The 'Samadi' is one of the most significant social custom of the Tiwa society. There is a steering committee to control the 'Samadi' which is called 'Pathaikhel'. In 'Samadi' the Tiwa youths are given practical wisdom by their seniors and this learning process prepare them for their future life. It is a compulsory social norm for the youth of Tiwa to stay at 'Samadi'.

(iii) There are many sub-sections among the Tiwas. Although they belong to the same ethnic Tribe these sub-group differs in social customs and rituals, etc. As for example, although all of them speak the basic Tiwa language the subtle variation in way of speaking, tone, etc. are apparently visible in many sub-tribes.

(iv) Tiwas have developed different social *strata* i,e, different class of people (*Kul*) among themselves. Marriage is not possible among these different classes or Kuls in Tiwa society.

(v) Each class of these groups (*Kul*) of Tiwa society worships different gods which substantiates this social division. Each family of a particular group offers *Puja* (worship) once in a year to their respective adored God observing customary rituals which may include animal sacrifice. This annual rituals are not only perform for the well being and prosperity of a particular family or a group of Tiwa people, but also is observed for the overall prosperity of the whole village. Generally, these community rituals are done in the month of February and March with the help of the designated priest known as 'Deuri'. An agrarian society, the Tiwas worshiped their lords with prayers for good harvest and healthy crop as well as to protect the community from natural hazards, sickness or epidemic and bad omen, etc.

(vi) 'Govia' (a married man staying with the in-laws) system prevails in the Tiwa society. In Tiwa society the bride and the groom has full authority to choose their life partners without the interference of the society or their parents. However, same Kul marriage is not allowed in Tiwa society.

(vii) Tiwas, particularly hill dwellers, practices 'Jhoom' or shifting cultivation. They produce mainly paddy and other crops like potato, ginger, tamarind, sesame seed, etc. for their own consumption. Sometime they exchange these products or sale these mainly to procure some of their alternative requirements like salt, edible oil, etc.

(viii) The Tiwas people prefer boiled and steamed food. Local fish dehydrated in sun light is one of their delicacy. They preserve dry fish and other food items in vacuum tubes made of bamboo. Fresh bamboo shoot as well as dried bamboo shoot used to flavour pork and fish dishes are their most desirable food items.

(ix) Tiwa people are very skillful and produces colourful hand woven clothes for both the male and female members. The male Tiwas wear 'Tagla sola' (jacket), Thana and Phali (Gamosa, a cotton towel) and the ladies used Kachang (Mekhela, long skirt), Phaskai (worn over blouse), Nara (colourfully designed cotton waist band), etc.

(x) The Tiwa women wear variety of self-designed ornaments made of Gold, Silver and different jewels. During the time of festival both men and women wear jewellery.

(xi) Tiwa people are culturally very rich and are particularly fond of music. They are proud inventor of many musical instruments like Khram, Khrambaro (drum), Big drum, Thakari, Pangchi (flute), Kamna (gagana, string instrument played by mouth), Muhuri (Chambal), etc. They have their own musical identity and produces great folk music and dance forms which are well adorned by all other tribes and people of the Brahmaputra Valley.

(xii) At the time of death of an individual in Tiwa society the whole village came together showing unique camaderiship in performing the rituals. The funeral process in Tiwa society is known as 'Karam'. Generally, they perform 'Karam' of a deceased individual at the household of a leading villageman. Sometimes, they club a group of dead person's rituals together in order to reduce cost and burden of the individuals.

Festivals

Cultural uniformity among the tribes of North-East India and Assam are wildly visible and there are a great deal of similarity in the way of life and the cultural activity of the different tribes living in the area. Since, most of the South-East Asian countries are agro based and hence, the lifestyle and cultural expression of the people of this region bears a lot of similarity. As agriculture became the focus and source of their social life, the process in which these people plan their activities has a lot in common and the festivals and rituals evolving from these practices also bears similarity to a large extent. Agriculture-based festivals and traditional customs have a important role in the development of civilization and cultural evolution.

Bisu or Bihu

Among the Tiwas there are two types of main agriculture-based festivals known as Bihu and Bishu and Chagra or Chagramisava. Bihu, in fact is a common festival observed in the whole State of Assam with slight variation visible by different tribes. The Tiwa people form a village committee for performance of the these festivals which is known as 'Khel'. The 'Khel' constituted with the old people of the village is known as 'Poroi Hari' or 'Buhra Khel'. While performing Bihu the 'Pathai Hari' meaning the 'khel' of the young ones is also associated with the Poroi Hari since Bihu is their main festival. One of the significant aspect of the Bihu is that this festival is observed by the Tiwas only on Tuesday and Wednesday. It is worth noting that Wednesday is the most auspicious day for the various tribes of this region.

After harvesting when the foodgrains are produced and stocked in the respective household stores the Magh Bihu is celebrated in the month of January and subsequently with the advent of the Spring in April the Bahag Bihu is celebrated which involves much merry making. Rituals like setting up of Bhelaghar (Thatched structure made in the field) and burning of the same during Magh Bihu, worshipping the most important animal used for cultivation, the bullock and cow during Bahag Bihu and worshipping forest God prior to bullock worshipping are practiced by the Tiwas. Further, during the festival time they worships their adored God by sacrificing white bird (chicken, duck, pigeon), etc. praying for the well being of the family members.

Changramisava or Chogra-Miswa

There is another main Spring festival of the Tiwas which is similar to

Bihu and is known as 'Changramisava'. After harvesting the Changramisava is celebrated for three days. The interval between two cultivation period is utilized by the Tiwa for this merry making with songs and dance, etc. After harvesting period is over this festival is observed in February and March. The word Changra means year (Chan) and Kara means the end which has led to formation of these word Changramisava. During these festival the young and middle aged people dance for eighty four (84) hours continuously in three days and three nights. This dance is not perform in the open field, but is performed in the household of the village head. The participant are treated with 'Ju' or 'Su' (wine), dry fish and sweet sticky rice, all local delicacies.

The Changra songs are of erotic nature. No ladies participate in this dance. The male dancers surrounds a bonfire and sing Pisugeet (Bihu song) with the help of local instruments like Khram, Pangchi and Thorang, etc. The basic theme of these songs are erotic description of the glory of the female body which in real sense is a symbolic aspiration for making the earth fertile and capable of producing seeds. Although these songs are erotic in nature, it is the belief of the Tiwas that the ritual will make the earth fertile with the blessing from the sky. This dance is one of the remarkable dance in the world.

Wansyua

One of the Tiwa groups known as 'Amkhawali' performed another festival known as 'Wansyua' or festival for making rice powder. This is celebrated after the interval of five or six years in a day between Tuesday and Thursday in the months between May to July. A Ural (drum for crushing rice) is set up in the courtyard of the village headman and villagers crush rice grains dancing to the tune of musical instruments. After this Tiwa cake are made from this rice dust and is offer to the king as a token of respect. During this festival the whole village dances and sings and the atmosphere takes a festive mood.

Barat Puja

Another important festival celebrated by the Tiwa is 'Barat Puja'. Significance of this festival is that it is jointly celebrated by neighbouring villages and mainly considered important for the females. It is celebrated in the month of Kati (November) in *Purnima* (full moon night). Ladies take a important part in this festival. The women are very careful with their rituals while observing these festival because they consider any lapse in following the rituals will bring bad omen to the community.

In this festival one virgin young girl is properly washed and kept in fasting for the period of the *puja*. The ladies who take care of her, known as 'Aayati' shall also have to fast and maintain righteous way of living along with the young virgin during the festival period.

The preparation of 'Barat' *Puja* starts before one month of its commencements. All the arrangement for the *puja* are being done under the guidance of the village heads. Each group among the invited guests of different village brings one 'Palanquin' for 'Barat' *puja* complete with colourful decoration. In the Palanquin 360 earthen lamps are alighted. The main *pandal* is decorated by lighted torch, where the young girl dances along with the devotional song sang by the women (Aayati). One of the remarkable aspect of this dance is that the dancers uses mask symbolizing Tiger, Lion, Elephant, Monkey, Deer, Bird, etc.

On the next day of the Barat *puja* symbolic Peera (low stool) Yuj (fight) begins and the winner girl of this fight awarded by the king. During the Peera fight the Aayatis splashes sacred Tulsi (basil leaf) water on the participants which is considered very sacred. After the *puja* all the offerings to the girl are placed in a Sungari (decorated peera) and merged in the river. At the end of the festival the participants returned singing songs and carrying the young girl (Barat Kuwari) back. The festival ends with a great feast.

Junbeel Mela

Historic Junbeel Mela which had originated around the fifteenth Century has been a meeting ground of the different communities. According to historical record during that time people from hills came down to meet their relatives in the plains. Till the fourteenth century, the hills tribal people frequently created disturbance among the people of the plains of these areas and looted their belongings. To overcome this, the Ahom King during fifteenth century organized melas in certain places in the border areas of the kingdom to ensure commercial and cultural amity between the hills and plains. The tradition still continues in the Junbeel Mela. The people from hills of Meghalaya, Karbi-Anglong come down with products like ginger, lac, indigo, mats and they barter it with items like traditional dry fish, cake, rice powder from their brethren in the plains. With the necessary food item collected from the plains people and with this the hill tribals then celebrate their *Magh bihu*. People used the barter system to carry on their trade as currency was not in vogue then. Since then this age old custom which is practiced even today in the *Mela*.

Another important event is community fishing in the Junbeel lake is a significant aspect of the *mela* from which it got its name. This is an important component part of the festival which is conducted subject to permission by the Gobha Deo-raja. It plays a big role in fostering the spirit of friendship among different communities. This year too this *mela* is organised for 3 days from Jan 17th to 19th, 2013 organised by the Gobha Deo-raja, Junbeel mela samiti on the eve of Tiwa Magh Bihu with great enthusiasm and excitement.

The *Mela* is followed by *Rajdorbar* (royal court) of the Gobha kingdom at the *Mela* ground in which 14 *rajas* from various kingdoms other dignitaries also attend the *Rajdorbar*, Deepsing Dea-raja, the ceremonial king of Gobha kingdom takes the leading role in holding the *Mela*.

The example set by this *mela* apart from providing a common platform for different communities, but also carrying forward the legacy to strengthen the bonds of goodwill among the people of the hills and plains. The *Mela* is of ethnic and socio-cultural importance as this becomes a meeting ground of different hill tribes of Assam and the people of the plains.

Conclusion

Thus, it appears from the above that the "Tiwas" from NE India are one of the most culturally developed ethnic tribes of Mongoloid origin. The rituals and festivities of the tribe bears special significance. It is not easy to reflect adequately the various festivities and rituals performed by this culturally rich tribe. In the modern day scenario, like any other socio-cultural groups, the cultural identity of the Tiwa tribe is also influenced by the wave of globalization. The influence of all pervading mass culture of western origin has also made its inroads into the rich heritage of the 'Tiwa's'. Many unique elements of its cultural identity have undergone rapid metamorphosis during recent times. This silent cultural aggressive, however, has not only eroded the strong cultural edifice of the Tiwas, but this also holds true for the cultural heritage of many similar ethnic groups. Due to this reason, a concern has developed to protect the socio-cultural identity of these groups. Even, UNO has given due consideration in this regard. The UNO decide and declared in 1994, 9th August, every year as World indigenous people day to protect their culture, language, religion and heritage urging to grant them certain rights the primary which is the right of self-determination. The need to preserve and develop the varied elements of the culture of these groups in terms of religion, food habits, attire, etc. is a matter of growing concern today. Further, these smaller ethnic groups has contributed immensely for the formation of larger cultural groups to which they are an integral part and thus the threat faced by them may affect a larger cultural entity. The new generation has a significant role to play in this matter and only with their awareness and patronage these rich elements can be preserved and made to co-exist with the modern day global atmosphere.

REFERENCES

Anil Kumar Baruah, *The Lalungs* 1989, Guwahati.
Edward Gait, *A History of Assam (1905)*, 1994, Guwahati.
G.C. Sharma Thakur, *The Lalungs* (Tiwas) 1985, Guwahati.
Krishnaram Mili (ed), *Tiwa Sanskritir Rehrup*, 2009, Guwahati
P.C. Bhattacharya, *Asamar Janajati*, 1999, 4th Edition, New Delhi.
Padma Pator (ed), *Janajati Samaj Sanskriti*, 2008, Guwahati.

43

TIHAR AND BHAI TIKA OF THE NEPALESE OF ASSAM

Ranjan Kumar Bhatta

Introduction

Tihar, the festival of lights is one of the most dazzling of all Hindu festivals. *Tihar* is broadly associated with *Dipawali* and *Lakshmi Puja* followed by *Bhai Tika (Bhatri Dwitiya)*. It is the second biggest festival of Hindu Nepalese. It is a five days festival, starting from the *Kartik Krisna Trayodashi* upto the *Kartik Shukla Dvitiya*, which comes soon after the *Dashain* (Durga Puja) festival. Nepalese celebrate *Tihar* according to their customs and traditions, which is to some extent different from that of other Indian Societies.

In this festival, Nepalese worship Goddess Lakshmi, the Goddess of Wealth. The five day festival is considered to be of great importance as it shows reverence to not just the humans and the Gods, but also to the animals like crow, dog, cow and ox, who maintain an intense relationship with the humans, which is the characteristic feature of this festival unlike other festivals where only gods are worshipped. The most important specialty of this festival is the ritual of brothers being worshipped by sisters (*Bhai Tika*) with wishes of long life and prosperity of brothers.

Tihar is also known as "*Yama Panchak*", which literally means — five days of the underworld lord, *Yamaraj*, who is worshipped in different forms in these five days of festivities.

Nepalese worship Goddess Lakshmi on the third day of the festival. Goddess Lakshmi, the wife of almighty Lord Vishnu was formed from the ocean and she has all the wealth of the seas. People believe that Goddess Lakshmi sits on a full-grown lotus and her *steed* is the owl. On the third day of the festival at the stroke of midnight she makes a world tour on her owl looking how she is being worshipped, and hence, bestows her blessings.

There is a story, which tells why this revelry is celebrated so widely. Once there was a king who was living his last days of life, his astrologer had told him that a serpent would come and take his life away. The king did not want to die so he has asked the astrologer if there was any way to escape from death. The king was advised to sleep with lit oil lamps all around his bed and decorate the palace with oil lamps on *Lakshmi Puja* day. So, Goddess Lakshmi would talk to the serpent not to take his life. It did happen, the serpent was convinced by Goddess Lakshmi. The serpent took the king to *Yamaraj* and told him that it was not yet the king's time to come to the underworld. So *Yamaraj* opened his ledger and in it the kings remaining age was written zero, but the serpent cleverly put seven before zero. Thus, the king lived for seventy more years. Since then onwards *Tihar* is widely celebrated worshipping the underworld and Goddess Lakshmi.

Another legend related with *Tihar* is that Lord Shri Rama returned to Ayodhya after killing Ravana and releasing his wife Sita from captivity. The delight of his subjects knew no bounds and they celebrated this occasion of Lord Shri Rama's return to the kingdom after 14 years, by dancing and singing, going from door to door. Moreover, the entire kingdom of Ayodhya was decorated with oil lit lamps, to mark the return of their adorable king Lord Shri Rama.

Methodology

In this study descriptive survey method has been adopted to study the *Tihar* festival. An attempt has been made to study, describe and interpret the fact related with *Tihar* of Assamese Nepalese with participant — observation method.

Findings

The respondents of various age groups and qualification in the survey among few members reveals that, in preparation for *Tihar* every home is cleansed and beautifully decorated, white-washed as an invitation to the mother goddess, so that, she may visit and bless the house with good fortune. The market is filled with shoppers seeking gifts, luxuries, sweets and enormous supplies of temple offering for the god, as well as foodstuffs for the family feasting. During this festival all the houses in city and villages are decorated with various types of unblemished lights, oil lamps, magical electrical lights, candles, decorations and rangoli made of different colours. Thus, during the night the entire city or village looks like a sparkling diamond. Delicious foods and sweets are prepared in every home, so *Tihar* is also called festival of sweets. One special item that is prepared during this festival is *Gumayeka Roti* or *Sel Roti* (a type of *roti* deep fried in oil looking like a bangle). In other words this festival is meant for life and prosperity.

It is observed that the festival of *Tihar* is divided into 5 (five) days of celebrations, which are mentioned as follows:

1st Day *Kag* (Crow) *Tihar*
2nd Day *Kukur* (Dog) *Tihar* or *Khiche Puja*
3rd Day *Gai* (Cow) *Tihar* and *Lakshmi Puja/Kali Puja*
4th Day *Goru* (Ox) *Tihar* or *Govardhana Puja/Mah Puja*
5th Day *Bhai* (Brother) *Tihar* or *Bhai Tika*

1st Day Kag (Crow) Tihar

The first day of the festival is called *Kag* (Crow) *Tihar* — worship of Crows. On this day *puja* is offered to crow, which is believed to be the henchman of the underworld Lord, *Yamaraj*. People bath in the early morning and cook delicious foods for them as well as for crows. Although crow is regarded inauspicious, it is worshipped and each member of the family offers delicious food to crows in a plate made out of leaves (*Tapara*). The crows descend in large numbers to partake the offerings. The cawing of the crows symbolizes sadness and grief in the Hindu mythology, so the devotees offer the crows food to avert grief and deaths in their homes. In other words, most of the people believe and adore crows for avoiding bad luck and bringing good luck.

2nd Day Kukur (Dog) Tihar or Khiche Puja

The second day of the festival is called *Kukur* (Dog) *Tihar* or *Khiche Puja* — worship of Dogs. On this day, people adore the very loyal and best friend of humans, i.e. dogs and are specially treated. The dogs are worshipped and ornamented. By offering red *tika* on the forehead and flower garlands around the neck and are fed with delicious foods. People request the dogs to guard their homes and other domestic animals from enemies. According to Hindu mythology, dogs are another henchman and loyal guard of the Lord of underworld, *Yamaraj*. Additionally, the dogs are also considered as the stallion of the terrified God Vairab, god of annihilation. Thus, the dogs are worshipped on this day. *Kukur Tihar* is also observed as *Narak Chaturdashi* remembering the victory of the God Krishna over the demon of filth, *Narakasur*. People wake up before the dawn and go to nearby rivers, take a dip and light oil lights and let them float and take away by the river. Doing this they believe they will be in safe side from going to hell.

Figure 43.1: Worship of Dog during *Kukur Tihar*

3rd Day Gai (Cow) Tihar and Lakshmi Puja/Kali Puja

The third day of *Kartik Krisna Amavasya* is called *Gai* (Cow) *Tihar* or *Lakshmi Puja* — worship of Cows. On this day, people worship cow. The cow is regarded as the representative of goddess Lakshmi. After bath, people prepare delicious foods. They ornament cows by *tika* on their forehead and colours all over cow's body. Mustard oil is applied to their horns and hooves. They offer flower around the neck, offer sweets and delicious foods to cows. Again, people clean their houses with extra labour on this day and wipe various part of their house with *Rato Mato* (red clay) and cow dung. Not only this, people sprinkle a drop or two of her urine in their body. Hindus regard cow's urine as very pristine and is used to sprinkle in order to purify in events like funeral, name giving day, and on other holy occasions. On this day, the *Raksha Bandhan* which they had tied on their wrists in "*Janai Purnima*" (Sacred thread changing ceremony on full moon day) is tied on cow's tail. It is believed that if one does so, the cow will help to cross the "*Baitarani River*" (an imaginative river that separates hell from heaven).

Figure 43.2: Worshipping of Cow during *Gai Tihar*

In the evening, people decorate their houses with flowers and garlands and erect gates with plaintain in front of their respective homes to greet Goddess Lakshmi. They illuminate their paddy fields, main streets, cowsheds, interiors of their houses with rows of mustard oil lights (*diyo*) and even electric lights.

Nepalese, make a line using red clay and cow dung from outside to inner section of the home where goddess Lakshmi is going to be worshipped. *Lakshmi puja* is done by a female member of the family. She uses her hand covered with red clay to make a symbolic foot-print on the floor entering the home and makes a trail leading to the Puja room. People believe goddess Lakshmi will enter the home through this line on this night.

After these decorations, a cauldron filled with paddy/uncooked rice and putting valuable things like money, gems, jewelleries, etc. in a box where from generation to generation money is put every year worshipping goddess Lakshmi, on the top of the heap of paddy or rice. It is garlanded with flowers, goddess Lakshmi is worshipped and offered various fruits and sweets to her. After worshipping goddess Lakshmi in their traditional rituals gambling starts in every household. This is a festival when gambling is not illegal.

On this day young girls start roaming around by singing *Bhaili* (a special song of girls singing during *Tihar*). The groups of girls and women who sing them are called the *Bhailinis*. The groups come one after another to every house throughout the night to sing and dance. After the singing and dancing is over they pray to god for blessings into the household. In return, the host offers *sida* or *dakshina* (donation) including money, paddy, rice, fruits and *Selroti* (special kind of Nepali bread) decorated in a *nanglo* (a kind of round winnowing fan made of bamboo) to them, on which a burning *diyo* is also placed.

Sample of Bhaili song is as follows:

	Rendering in English
Bhailini ayim angana	(Bhailini came to your yard)
Badari kundari rakhana	(Keep your yard neat and clean)
Aunsi baro gai tiharo bhaili	(Today is the new moon day, Cow *Tihar* and we play *Bhaili*)

The *Bhailinis* not only sing *bhaili* songs, but also sings and dance varieties of songs of merriment like *Madale Nritya* and *Maruni Nritya* (a special form of folk drama prevailing in the Nepali Society of Assam) in the yard of every household.

4th Day Goru (Oxen) Tihar or Govardhan Puja/Mah Puja

The fourth day is called *Goru* (Oxen) *Tihar* or *Govardhan Puja* — worship of Oxen, bulls and male calves. Nepali people on this day worship the Oxen, bulls and male calves with *tika*, garland and then delicious meal is fed to it. On the other hand people who follow lord Krishna perform '*Govardhan Puja*'. People make an emblem of the Govardhan Hill with cow dung and put some grass on it, on the main post of their cow shed and worship it with seasame, sandal-wood paste, *aksweta* (uncooked rice mixed with curd), flowers, curd, milk, resin, etc. wishing increase in the number of heads of cattle. This puja symbolizes the act of lord Krishna when he lifted the Govardhan Hill and saved millions of people and cows from floodwater. According to *Vishnu-Purana*, the people of Gokul commemorated a festival in honour of Lord Indra and worshipped him after the end of monsoon season every year. Lord Krishna, during his young age, once prohibited the people from offering prayers to Lord Indra. Lord Indra got angry and sent a torrent rain to sink Gokul. Hence, Lord Krishna lifted the Govardhan Hill and held it as an umbrella for the people and saved millions of people and cows from floodwater.

Figure 43.3: *Govardhan Puja*

On this day people belonging to Newar community perform '*Mah puja*' which literally means worshipping oneself. They worship life by doing *puja* on themselves. They make special kind of *Mandala* (Manda in Newari), decorating with various flowers, sweets, fruits, *Mala* (Garland) and *Ita* (special kind of thread made to burnt as symbolizing the life span of oneself). People also accept *Shagun* (dish consisting egg, fish, fruits, meat, sweets, etc.) by the elder female members of the house. The process is meant to purify one own body. Moreover, on this day the Newar New Year also starts.

In the evening, young boys start roaming around door to door by singing *Deusi* or *Deusure* (a special song of boys sung during *Tihar*). The leader of the *Deuse* group is called the *Bhatyaune* (prime mover). He narrates some mythological stories in musical rhythms suitably in sentences so that after each part of the sentence he sings, his companions say *Deva Shri Ram* or *Deu Shri Ram* or *Deu Sire* in chorus. Hence, the songs sung on this day is known as *Deusi* or *Deusure*. The *Deusi* groups offer blessings in musical verse and hence, in return, people offer *sida* or *dakshina* (donation) to them, as offered to the *bhailini* groups on the previous day.

A sample of Deusi song is as follows:

		Rendering in English
Jhilimili Jhilha	*Deu sire*	(Twinkling Twinkling. Dev Sri Ram)
Ke ko Jhilimili	*Deu sire*	(What is Twinkling? Dev Sri Ram)
Phulako Jhilimili	*Deu sire*	(It is the twinkling of flowers. Dev Sri Ram)
Rato Mato	*Deu sire*	(Red mud trail. *Deu sire*)
Chiplo Bato	*Deu sire*	(Slippery trail. *Deu sire*)
Larddai Parddai	*Deu sire*	(Slipping and Sliding. *Deu sire*)
Ayeka Hami	*Deu sire*	(Finally, we made it to your home! *Deu sire*)

The singing goes on

....	*Deu sire*
....	*Deu sire*

Blessings given by Deusurey groups are as follows:

Yo Gharma Laxmi	*Deu sire*	(In this home Goddess Lakshmi. *Deu sire*)
Sadhain Aun	*Deu sire*	(Let always come. *Deu sire*)
Gai Goru le	*Deu sire*	(Let cows and bulls. *Deu sire*)
Gohali bharun	*Deu sire*	(Fill the cowshed. *Deu sire*)

5th Day Bhai (Brother) Tihar or Bhai Tika

The final day of *Tihar* is known as *Bhai Tihar* or *Bhai Tika*. This festival is also known as the festival of brothers and sisters. Nepalese celebrate this festival with lot of enthusiasm and gaiety. Sisters invite brothers to their house on this occasion with flowers and betel-nut. They begin the rituals applying oil and combing the hair of their brothers. Before putting *tika*, the sisters offer *puja*, at first to a deep, *kalash* and Ganesh and then to *Yamaraj* and *Yamuna* (sister of *Yamaraj*, after which they make a *pradaksina* (circling round) of their brothers for three times dropping oil and water on the floor from a copper pitcher. An *okhar* (walnut) or a betel-nut is treated as a symbol of *Yamraj* and *puja* is offered on it and at the end it is smashed and thrown away. Putting of *Tika* starts with placing a banana leave already cut into a vertical line shape placed on brother's forehead held by one of the sisters hand, then they apply *tika* base (made from rice paste). Then the sisters put *Tika*, on their brothers' forehead into the linear vertical shape which is then decorated with spots using seven colours (*Sapta-rangi Tika*). A towel is wrapped on the brother's head and sisters garland their brothers with long lasting flowers or *Makhamali* (Globe amaranth) wishing their brothers security from the cruel clutches of *Yamaraj* (God of Death). They pray to Lord *Yamaraj* for their brother's long and prosperous life. The sisters offers *Sel-roti*, fruits, nuts, clothes and sweets to their brothers.

The brothers also put a round *tika* on their sisters' forehead and gift them with clothes and other valuables. Brothers bless their sisters with a happy life. The sisters on this day feed their brothers with varieties of delicious foods and meal.

People who do not have brothers or sisters of their own observe this festival by adcpting a brother or sister from near or distant relations.

Conclusion

The most exotic and dazzling festival comes to an end after these five magnificent days of worship and honour to the goddess Lakshmi and the underworld kingdom. In other words this festival is meant for life and prosperity. It is a celebration of the triumph of light over darkness and of hope over despair. That the festival is celebrated by people from diverse faiths is a significant affirmation of the great Hindus traditions in the world. Nepalese all across Assam celebrate *Tihar* in their neighbourhood with many cultural activities. Apart from celebrating *Tihar* in each and every Nepali family, *Tihar* is celebrated by various organizations and committees. as a common celebration for all. These organizations and committees raise funds from various sources and organize various activities like — Cultural functions, Seminars, competitions among the children, etc. These kind of celebrations are fun-fair, where various competitions like — *Sel Roti* preparing competition, Traditional Dress competition, *Deusi-Bhaili* competition, *Madale Nritya* and *Maruni Nritya* draws the attraction of the general public. Moreover, during *Dashain* — *Tihar* celebrations swings made of bamboo and coconut rope (*linge ping*) is erected because there is a tradition to swing at least once in these festivals. The *linge ping* which is erected during *Dashain* is dismantled after the *Tihar* celebrations are over.

From the above account, it is clear that the purity and originality of *Tihar* is not yet lost. The age old traditions are still prevalent. *Tihar* is a knot of cultural interrelationship among the Nepali people of Assam. They exchange greetings and celebrate the festival in perfect cultural harmony. *Tihar* being the common festival of poor and rich, entertainment and merry making is the only thing that counts. Family and religion are of paramount importance, and are constantly reflected throughout the culture.

The religion, culture and traditions of the Nepalese of Assam are powerfully interlinked and one can visibly sense and visualize the influence of religion on the culture and traditions of the people. The traditions, customs and usages of the Assamese Nepalese have remained more or less in tact, but now if these practices are not put down in writing, there is every possibility that these will be forgotten and consigned to archives only.

REFERENCES

Upadhyaya, Dr. Jamadagni (ed.), *History and Culture of Assamese Nepali*, Deptt. of Historical and Antiquarian Studies, Assam, 2009.

Subba, T.B.; Sinha, A.C.; Nepal, G.S. and Nepal, D.R. (ed.), *Indian Nepalis: Issues and Perspectives*, Concept Publishing Co. Pvt. Ltd., New Delhi, 2009.

Upadhaya, Bisnulal, *Assamese Nepali Haru*, Tezpur, 1984.

Jaisy, Shyam Raj, *Assamese Nepali Haru Ko Aitihasik Pristhabhumi*, B.K.P. Digboi, 1990.

Sinha, A.C. and Subba, T.B., *The Nepalis in North-East India: A Community in Search of Indian Identity*, Indus Publishing Company, New Delhi, 2007.

Gyamtso, P.T., *The History, Religion, Culture and Traditions of Bhutia Communities*, ISBN No.: 81-86230-75-0, New Delhi.

www.google.com

http://guru.com.np/tihar.htm dtd. 1.11.2012 time: 9.03 PM

http://www.visitnepal.com/nepal_information/tihar.php dtd. 02.11.2012 time 7.45 PM.

http://www.nepalhomepage.com/society/festivals/tihar.html dtd. 02.11.2012 time 8.45 PM.

http://www.weallnepali.com/hamro-nepal/tihar

http://nepalvista.com/tihar

44

TRADITIONAL DANCE DRAMAS OF THE KHAMPTIS OF ARUNACHAL PRADESH
An Ethnographic Note

Rashmirekha Sarma

The Khamptis are an indigenous group of Arunachal Pradesh belonging to the greater Tai-Shan civilization. They migrated from Bor-Khampti or Mung-Khampti-Lung in the Irrawaddy valley of Burma and settled around the Tengapani River in 1751 (Dutta Chaudhury, 1978:44). They mainly inhabit the Lohit district of Arunachal Pradesh, though a small fraction also lives in parts of Assam as well as East Siang district. The word *Khampti* means "a land full of gold" (*Khamp* means gold and *ti* means place). The Census of India, 2001 recorded the population of the community as 11,503.

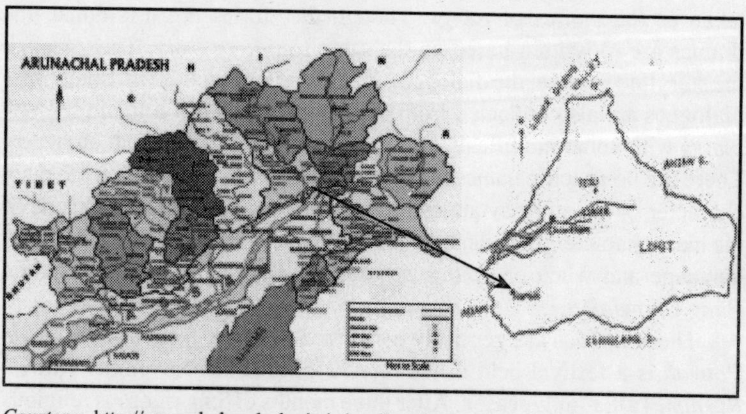

Courtesy: http://arunachalpradesh.nic.in/pgallery.htm

Map 44.1: Lohit District and the Area of Fieldwork

The Khampti language, belonging to the Tai family, is known as 'Khamp-Tai' language and is one of the very few languages of Arunachal Pradesh, which has its own script. The Khampti people are believers of Hinayana Buddhism. Their main festival is Poi-Sangken, celebrated for three days in April.

The Dance Drama of the Khamptis

Arunachal Pradesh is immensely rich in all forms of the performing arts, maintained and enriched by different indigenous groups, though the only significant theatrical performance among the indigenous groups of Arunachal Pradesh is the dance dramas of the Khamptis (Sarkar, 1974:xiii-xvi).

The Khampti dance drama is called *Kapung. Ka* means dance and *pung* means drama. The whole word means the story depicted through dance. *Kapung* reflects the rich culture of the Buddhists in this territory and unfold the myths and tales of moral values. The Khampti people generally mention dance dramas only as *pung. Pungs* are performed to educate people through entertainments and it represents the socio-religious and socio-cultural features of the society.

Religion, classical literature and mythology are the source of origin of all *pungs*. There are two traditional themes for the dance dramas of the Khamptis. The first source is the *Jataka* stories of Lord Buddha (the stories of 550 previous births of Lord Buddha) which is the popular and dominant theme. The second source is the two great Indian epics, the *Ramayana*, the *Mahabharata*, and some part or stories of these two are taken as the stories of *pungs*. Though the stories are traditional, the dramas are re-written based on the same source or story. Thus, though the storyline is same, the dialogues are different in each *pung*. Sometimes dialogues are also collected from old pungs, which are suitable for new *pungs* with some modification to suit the taste of the present audience. There are no specific names of the *pung*. The *pung* is named on the main character of the story by attaching the word "*pung*" before the name of the main character. For example, Rama is called *Choulamang* in Khampti language and when one *pung* is based on *Ramayana* then it is called *Pung Chowlama*.

These dramas are generally performed after the festival of *Potwah. Potwah* is a festival held in the months of October-November (*Kartik Purnima*) after rainy season. After three months of long rigorous religious practices involving learning the teachings of Buddha and following the lessons of Buddha, the festival is celebrated. During these months or just after these three months, the Khamptis donate *stupas*, statues of the Buddha, etc., and it is to celebrate these occasions that *pungs* are organized.

Traditionally, it is performed in an open place. The performers form a circle around one or two banana saplings planted in the middle of the ground where they plan to have the performance. The orchestra sits with the performers. The audience also sits in a circle around the performers.

The performance is a combination of dialogue, music and dance. Dialogue is narrated in chanting style. The tonal dialogues of *pung* have three categories.

1. *Kham-poy* which is the sound for respect and serious matters.
2. *Kham-chakheng* which is the sound for excitement.
3. *Kham-pali*, which is the sound for romantic, pleasant, fun or playfulness.

After the dialogues, the instrumental music starts and with the music, dance is also performed. There are no particular forms of dance. The dance movements exhibit the emotions that the dialogues express. The playing styles of musical instruments also express different moods of the situation like sorrow, anger, happiness, etc. *Kongpat* (big drum), *Kongtail* (long narrow drum), *Paiseng* (cymbal), *Yammong* (Gong) and *Ting* (instrument with one string) are the main musical instruments.

After the harvesting season, from October onwards, the performances of *pungs* start and it culminates in January-February. To perform dance dramas, *pung* troops are organized. A big *pung* troop consists of 35 to 40 members whereas the small troops have 10 to 15 members. These dance dramas are performed every year though not in the same villages. Not every village can organize *pung* every year as it is expensive. The troops first perform in their own village and then perform in other villages on invitation. Sometimes, *pungs* are also invited by individuals. The host family has to provide hospitality to the *pung* troop. Sarkar (1974, 50-51) mentioned that the troops are invited by the affluent villagers to perform *pung* in their houses and they are paid for their performance. The invitation to perform *pungs* in other village is known as "ful-paan". In "ful-paan", an amount of money is given as token honorarium. There are no fixed amounts of money to be paid for inviting the troop. The master artist or other performers believe that performing in *pungs* is like offering prayers to god and getting the blessings. Therefore, the performers do not demand money. At present *pung* troops are paid an amount of ₹2,000 to ₹10,000 as per the capacity of each village. On special occasions, for example, the donation of the statues of Buddha, the honorarium is higher and it ranges from ₹ 10,000 to ₹ 20,000. Still, everyone related to *pung* performance admits that it is impossible to practice *pung* as a full-time job because the amount they receive for the performance is not enough to sustain for a whole year. That is why all the performers are part timers. Traditionally, these *pungs* are overnight performances.

Before performing the *pungs*, they rehearse for almost one month. Rehearsal is significant, because no other community of Arunachal Pradesh rehearse before the performance of their dances or dramas. It is done spontaneously. For rehearsal, the villagers invite a master artist or performer. The master artist is a distinguished person of the society who can choreograph and teach dance, write screenplay, teach dialogue delivery and can play all musical instruments. He is invited to teach for 10 days, 15 days or for one month. He instructs local villagers about the form of dialogue delivery, dance style and steps, how to play musical instruments properly, etc. Moreover, he also creates the screenplay and dialogues from the stories of *Jataka* or modifies the old script of *pung*.

In *pungs*, everyone can do everyone's job. For example, the master artist who creates the screenplay also directs the drama or makes the costumes or mask; the dancers also can play the musical instruments, etc. Moreover, many of the local villagers who act on *pungs*, are also the craftsman who make the musical instruments. There are 10 to 15 master artists in all the Khampti villages at this time. However, traditionally women cannot perform in *pungs* and female roles are played by man in female attire.

The knowledge of the *pung* is traditionally transmitted from one generation to the next among the Khamptis. Unlike the other indigenous groups of Arunachal Pradesh, the Khamptis have an organized style of transmission of the knowledge of *pung* with the help of Buddhist monasteries. Almost every Khampti village has a Buddhist monastery (*Vihara*) that has played a significant role as cultural centre for the villages. Most of the Buddhist monks are eminent scholars of Buddhist literature and *Kham-tai* language and they always help the villagers to organize the pungs.

The Khampti language is known as *Kham-tai* and the script is known as *Choung* or *Kyang*. The villagers, who are selected to perform in *pungs*, must have some working knowledge of the spoken and written form of the *Kham-tai* language. To learn their language and the teachings of Buddha, traditionally the Khamptis have a policy of "stay and learn" in their village monasteries where they learn the formal form of their language to study the Buddhist literature. In this policy, the boys or men stay in the monasteries (*Viharas*) for a stipulated time. The time frame could be anything, though it generally ranges from three months to six or seven years.

Changes on *Kapung*

Culture is always changing and it is a very gradual process. Adaptation and change happens over time and then allows the old ways to coexist with or alter the new ways. In the process people are made aware of the changes. They have the power to decide what elements to alter and what not, and what will coexist with new things. With the introduction of the modern education system and the arrival of the new medium of entertainment, *pungs* have witnessed some changes. Almost all informants admit that *pungs* have changed quite evidently in the last 20 years.

Kongpat

Demon Mask

Yammong (Set of Gongs)

Figure 44.1: Image Photographs of a *Kapung** and Some Musical Instruments and Mask

* Photographs of *Kapung* are taken out from a video, originally captured by Sanjay Mien. The name of dance drama is *Pung Kung-Cheti-Kongmu* (The virtue of Pagoda Donation). The video film is presented by the "Tai-Khampti Heritage and Literature Society".

Courtesy: Sanjay Mien, Photo: Rashmirekha Sarma.

The *pungs* are now mostly performed in stages, rather than in open places. Though limited to performances in national or international stage, the Khampti women have now started to perform in *pungs*. The duration of the *pungs* has been reduced to three to four hours from the traditional full night performances. Some parts of the traditional *pungs* are removed reducing the period of performance. Not many changes are observed in musical instruments. Costumes have become elaborate with increased ornamentation both in costume and ornaments worn. Dance steps have become more complex and elaborated. Same dance steps were repeated four to five times in earlier performances, though now this repetition is reduced and rather, dialogues are given more importance.

Pungs have their own religious and moral outlook and as stated by many master artists or performers, these are acknowledged as a kind of ritual of veneration. Though the frequency of *pung* performance has decreased, the importance and effects have not reduced. Again, many NGOs or educated Khampti persons have stepped in the field to revive and to popularize this old form in a new and modified style without altering the subtlety of tonal dialogues or dance movements. Though many traditions of Arunachal Pradesh are faded away, all these reasons indicate the *Kapung* or traditional dance drama will definitely survive for future generation.

REFERENCES

Barua, S., "Khampti" in Singh, K.S. ed., *People of India: Arunachal Pradesh*, Vol. XIV, Anthropological Survey of India, Seagull Books: Kolkata, 1995.

Barker Chris, *Cultural Studies: Theory and Practice*, London: Sage, 2003.

Batsayan, Kapila, *Traditional Indian Theatre*, National Book Trust: New Delhi, 2003. Translated in Assamese by Dutta Birendranath, *Paramparagata Bharatiya Natya: Bahumukhi Dhara*, New Delhi: National Book Trust, 1996.

Bhattacharya, Ananya, "Heritage and Creative Enterprise" in *International Journal of Intangible Heritage*, 2011, Vol. 1:6-12.

Census, 2001. Government of India, accessed in 10.07.2012 from http://www.censusindia.gov.in/Census_Data_2001/States_at_glance/state_profile.aspx

Dutta Chaudhury. S. ed., *Arunachal Pradesh District Gazetteers: Lohit District*, Shillong: Department of Information and Public Relations, Government of Arunachal Pradesh, 1978.

Dutta, P.C., "Arunachal Pradesh: From Tradition to Modernity", *Resarun*, 1981, VII (1 and 2): 14-16.

Elwin, Verrier (1957), *A Philosophy for NEFA*, Reprint. Delhi: Isha Books, 2009.

Ellen. R.F. ed., *Ethnographic Research: A Guide to General Conduct*, London: Academic Press, 1984.

Gobo, Giampietro, *Doing Ethnography*, Translated by Adrian Belton, London: Sage, 2008.

Goldbart, Juliet and David Hustler, "Ethnography", in *Research Methods in the Social Sciences*, edited by Bridget Somekh and Cathy Lewin, 17-23. New Delhi: Sage, 2005.

http://ccrtindia.gov.in/theatreforms.htmAccessed on 29.04.2012

http://lohit.nic.in/people.htm Accessed on 29.04.2012

Mudgal, Subha. December 31, 2011. *Globalization and India's Performing Arts*, Accessed on 11.09.2012 from http://www.thehindu.com/opinion/op-ed/article 2761382.ece

Namchoom, Chow Bilaseng, *The Tai Khanpti of Lohit: On the Trail to the Land of Golden Pagoda*, Accessed on 29.04.2012 from http://easternpanorama.in/index.php?option=com_content&view=article&id=1627:the-tai-khampti-of-lohit&catid=75:october

Pandey, B.B., *Folk Songs of Arunachal Pradesh (Adi)*, Itanagar: Directorate of Research, Arunachal Pradesh, 1996b.

Phukan, Jogada, "Spiritual Belief and Practices Among the Arunachalees: A Glimpse Into The Process of Converzation and Its Effects", *Resarun*, 2000, 26: 82-87.

Ray, Sanjoy, "Tai-Phake Language, Literature facing extinction threat", *The Assam Tribune*, November 3, 2009.

Sarkar Niranjan, *Dances of Arunachal Pradesh*, Directorate of Research, Arunachal Pradesh: Itanagar, 2009.

Sarkar, Niranjan, "Preservation and Promotion of Folk Dances of Arunachal Pradesh", *Resarun*, 1980, VI(1): 8-11.

UNESCO (United Nations Educational, Scientific and Cultural Organization), *The Convention for the Safeguarding of the Intangible Cultural Heritage*, 2003. Accessed January 11, 2011.http://www.unesco.org/culture/ich/index.php?lg=en&pg=00022"art2

UNESCO (United Nations Educational, Scientific and Cultural Organization), "Investing in Cultural Diversity and Intercultural Dialogue", *UNESCO World Report*, 2009. Accessed May 25, 2010. http://unesdoc.unesco.org/images/0018/001847/184755e.pdf

UNESCO ICH Kit, Kit of the Convention for the Safeguarding of the Intangible Cultural Heritage. Accessed April 20, 2010. http://www.unesco.org/culture/ich/en/kit/And http://www.unesco.org/culture/ich/index.php?lg=en&pg=00252

Yin, R.K., *Case Study Research: Design and Methods*, 4th ed. Vol. 5 of the *Applied Social Research Methods Series*, London: Sage, 2009.

45

RELIGIOUS PRACTICES OF THE MISING PEOPLE OF THE MAJULI ISLAND

Binita Pegu

According to an Anthropological Survey of India report, Assam is a land of more than a hundred communities consisting of tribe and castes, and formed on the basis of ethnic identity, caste, religion, language and geographical locations. Among these communities the Mising forms one of the plains tribe of the land.

The Mising were earlier called Miri, and all records of the pre-independence times mention them as such. Belonging to the Mongoloid stock of the population, they are mostly found in the districts of upper Assam — Lakhimpur, Dhemaji, Dibrugarh, Tinsukia, Jorhat, Sibsagar, and to some extent Sunitpur.

The Misings originally dwelt in the hills of present Arunachal Pradesh, and they were akin to the Adi tribe of the state. It is said that the ancestors of the Mising tribe of Assam came down from their hill abode as a result of the clash between them and the Adis. It is not known when the Misings came down to the plains as a community. Early British records always put them on the slope of the hills when they had to refer to them. But, as known from the Assamese chronicles, they had some contact with the plains people as early as the medieval times. According to Gait, the Misings were once inhabitants of Tibet from where they slowly came down to the lower hill districts now covered by the territory of present Arunachal Pradesh. From there they came down to the plains (*A History of Assam*, Reprint, Guwahati, 1981). After migration to the plains they settled down in the areas of the Brahmaputra, Subansiri, Dihing and Debang valley.

It is not possible to trace exactly the history of migration of the Misings in the Majuli Island. But it is almost certain that they did not inhabit this area long before,at least before the early nineteenth century.[1] The Mising ealier called Miri, who form about 37 per cent of the total population strength in Majuli, are the best advanced of the tribes in the island. With 57,760 population according to Census of 2001, they form 84 per cent of the total tribal strength. They are found over almost the entire island, although they are concentrated in its northern belt. Jengraimukh in north-eastern Majuli being their cradle, its hinterland consists of Daphalakata, Jakaibowa, Rangachahi, Kalitapar, Patharichuk, Ratonpur, Chetadarchuk, Phutukichapori, Baraguri, Naganachuk, Bargaya, Dhapak, Boralimara, Baligaon and so forth.[2]

The traditional religion of the Misings is called animism by the foreign missionaries and the conventional anthropologists. Their underlying principle is belief in fear and dread of the Super natural power.[3] The traditional religion practices of the Misings are based on three major belief systems; first about the creator of the universe, second, existence of spirits around human habitates and third about of human soul. The Misings believe that the universe was created by a supreme heavenly power defined as 'Sedi' Ba:bu' (SEDI, the Father) and Melo Nanc' (MELO, the Mother) consider themselves as the progenies of the Sun (Do:nyi, Anc, i.e. Sun Mother) and the Moon (Po:lo Abu, i.e., the Moon Father). These deities are held to be omnipotent, omnipresent and always benevolent to mankind. Therefore, on every occasion of social and religious functions, the Misings offer prayer first to these deities. In fact, no auspicious function starts without the names of Sedi Melo and Do:ni; Po:lo.[4]

The present religion of the Misings is the synthetic product of animism and Hinduism. That religion among them is known as Kewalia or Kathanghati or Nishamlia. Inspite of the mixture, they are worshippers of Uyu or spirit. The name of the Do:nyi (the Sun) Po:lo (the Moon) is recited in every ritual.

Festival

Some of the main *Pujas*-cum-festivals of the Misings are Po:rag, Ali-ai-ligang, Taleng Uyu (*Pujas*-cum-festival concerned with agriculture), Dabur, Ashi Uyu, Yumrang Uyu (*Pujas* for the deceased) and Dodgang, Urom Apin (*Pujas* for ancestors or ancestor —worship). Thus, the above *pujas* can be divided into three broad headings, e.g. group *puja*, self or personal *puja* and *pujas* due to causes.

It has been mentioned earlier that the Misings are the worshippers of numerous Uyus (Spirits). In this context the MIBOO (the priest) plays a significant role among them. He is supposed to know the Uyus responsible for all evil happening of the Misings. The Miboo usually offers chickens in the name of Dopun-Dorum (an imaginary spirit having three heads), and after some ritual activities the Miboo knows the measures for the remedy of the sufferer. Later, according to the direction of the Miboo, the family offers pig, fowl, apong (Rice beer), etc. to the spirit for remedy.[5]

Sedi and Melo

Sedi and Melo are conceived by the Misings as the earliest earth beings representing Male and Female creations. The predessor of Sedi-Babu is said to be Pundolando, who in term has emerged out of Tapapumang which means something like vast expanse of the mist.[6] The people believes that out of the marriage of father, Sedi and mother Melo, the Ditem (earth), the Adi-ditem (hills), the Neinengan (trees), the Payi-Pettang (birds) and the Ruki-Merang (ants and insects) were created. It is thus seen that all animate and inanimate objects of the universe were created by Sedi Melo, the super God.

Sedi or Kedang is the earth and Melo or Taleng is the Sky. Immediately after the earth sky had emerged, there was life of any kind in the earth till Pedong Nane descended and gave birth to livings beings.[7]

Dony and Polo

The Misings also consider themselves as the progenies of the Donyi (Sun) and the Polo (Moon). The sun is called Donyi Ane, i.e., Sun mother and the Moon is named Polo Abu, i.e., Moon father. So, by faith the Misings are worshippers of Donyi (Sun) and Polo (Moon).[8]

There are two beliefs regarding the birth of Donyi-Polo. The first one is that Donyi and Polo were twine sons of Pedong Ane who had luminous eyes. The second beliefs, which is supported by the majority of the Misings is that Donyi Polo were female and male casmic principle and direct descendents from Sedi Melo. Besides the people regarded Donyi and Polo as the custodian of law, truth and believe that nothing can be kept concealed from their luminous eyes. Even today, at the beginning of melting or a social gathering blessings of this luminous spiritual couple are invoked as the custodian of law and truth.[9]

Taleng and Uyu

It is a primordial worship of community. Taleng Uyu means Gods of heaven. There are two kinds of Taleng Uyu. One is perform in jungle under a thunderbolt struck tree and other is performed in front of Kumsung (Granary). A black young Female pig is also slaughtered, Fried rice, rice powder, banana, etc., are required here. In this worship, Gods are prayed to protect their paddy from harmful insects, wild animals, drought, flood, etc.

Rakpu Dono Uyu or Yumrang Uyu

God of foliage is the Rokpudone (poultry eater), he is also known as Yumrang Uyu. That the omnipotent and ever living God manifests in green wood as possessed — spirit is the central point of this celebration. Thus Asi Uyu spirit that live water and Dopun Dorum who is believed to be a three heated demon are performed by them. The Misings are the worshippers of numerous uyus (spirits) and the Miboo (the priest) plays a significant role among them.[10]

Death and the Attendent Ceremonies

Among the Misings all the dead bodies irrespective of age, sex and nature of death are buried. Every village has a common burial ground. The grave is called "Ago". The demise of one who has gained honour is announced by ringing a bell "Lenang" Dead body is taken out to the courtyard not by the usual door, but by a special door made in the back side wall. The corps is bathed and kept in a Log-coffin called 'Rung Kung' after being wrapped in 'Empoo' (a bamboo mat 1.5 meters long and 1 meter wide). After the death the Misings observe a four tier purificatory ceremony namely 'Tilani' on the 3rd day, 'Sushi' or pyade, on the 6th day, 'Mahekia' on the 30 day and 'Daha' after one year or so, one can postpone the final ceremony, i.e. Daha maximum for a period of 3 or 4 years. Two or three families can jointly observe this function.[11]

There are various festivals performed by the Misings such as Ali-aye-Legang, Po:rag, Dobur, etc.

Ali Aye Ligang

Ali-aye-Ligang is the prime and national festival of the Misings. It is the ceremonies beginning of forming activity of the village folk. It is observed as a festival in connection with agriculture. Ali-aye-legang means sowing of roots and fruits (Ali-roots; Aye-fruits; Legang-sowing). Ahu-paddy was the staple agriculture produce of the Misings people. Ali-aye-legang, makes the advent of Ahu season. However, in the annual open session of the Mising Bane Kebang, 1956 it was decided that Ali-aye-legang would be celebrated uniformly on a fixed date on the first Legang Longe (festival day) that is Wednesday on the February Month.[12]

Po: Rag

Po: rag is one another biggest socio-religious festivals of the Misings people. It is animistic rite held on a community basis. At the end of harvest time the rite is held. It is a festival of proper accompanied with elaborate and expensive arrangement continuously for three days. Po: rag is a huge feast in which more then thousand guest and invites are intertained for 3 days. The Merimbir-Yame (young boys and girls) the association of the young people of the village bears the responsibility of making the festival a success. Generally, Po: rag is celebrated after an interval of 2 to 5 years. Because of its expensive and elaborate arrangement, Po: rag is generally in a Murong (a public hall). One of the backbones of their social system is the Murang system, unique in many ways.[13]

Dobur Uyu

One of the important rituals of the Misings is the Dobur-uyu. The women are debarred from participating in it. During the performance of Dobur-uyu, traffic and business transaction with neighbouring villages is with held for a day by constructing gates on both sides of the main entrance lane of the village. On the same day, the villagers approach house demanding dues (Aje-ng). The families offer apong (rice beer), pig, fowl and rice which they collect in the outskirt of the village. Dobur-uyu is performed once a year. This ritual is one of the examples of ritual performances of the Misings.[14]

The Mising carried their hill culture till they came to the Majuli Island, so much so that many of them till the early part of twentieth century did not know the Assamese language, and the male members used bow and arrow for hunting and defence. But during the last one hundred years the Mising have undergone significant changes in their socio-economic life. Almost all of them are now used to Assamese language beside their tribal tongue, have acquainted themselves to the Brahminical way of life, change their dress and ornaments, and above all, have adopted to habit of settled agriculture and habitation.[15]

While the Misings migrated to the plain, the Donyi-Polo (Sun and Moon) was their faith and great religion, but as time passed, they came into the shades of many other faiths and religion. In the fifteenth century, Neo-Vaishnavism emerged in Assam. The Mising, like many other tribal groups of region, came under influence Neo-Vaishnavism.[16] Srimanta Sankaradeva brought the Neo-Vaishnavism movement in the Assam.[17] They did not accept it totally in the beginning, but gradually incorporated. Some of its beliefs and practices are found in their own system of religious functions.

Vaishnavism of the Mising People of Majuli

Among the most populous of the Mising villages of the Majuli Island are the Bargaya, Daphalakata, Jakaibowa, Rangchahi, Kalitaper, Ratonpur, Patharichuk, Chetadarchuk, Putukichapori, Baraguri, Naganachuk, Dhapak, Boralimara, Baligaon, and so forth. Some of the people of the villages are practice both Vaishnavism, Christian and their own tribal religious beliefs. Being located within the proximity of the Satras, and more particularly, being in the mids of the Vaishnava culture of the Majuli Island, people of the Bargaya village are largely influence by the Satras. As a result, their religious beliefs and practices have become a conglomeration of both Vaishnava and ethnic tribal religious system.

The Neo-Vaishnavism of Srimanta Sankaradeva and his disciples had some impact on the Misings also. Sankaradeva converted a group of this tribes under the leadership of Paramananda Miri as Guru into his newly propagated '*Sanatana Dharma*' which teaches the doctrine of unconditional love of God and advocated the aspects of mono-ethnic adoration. Paramananda Miri from the Misings was one of the foremost and favourite disciples of Sankaradeva.[18] He was from Ratonpur village of Majuli Island.[19] Following his foot steps the Misings began to adopt Ek-Saran Bhagawati Dharma or *Sanatana Dharma* in addition to their traditional religion. They were mainly influence by Guru vice Sankaradeva, Madhavadeva, Gopaldeva, Jodumonideva, Krishnadeva and Sunandadeva according to the passing generation of the Vaishnava Gurus.

The Brahmins of Assam have extend great on influenced the rural Misings. The adoption in Hinduism led to the emergence of the Bhakatiya Cult, which is an admixture of both the Misings role of Vaihnava-cum-Tantricism. The role of Vaishnava Brahmins, preachers and satras played a great role in attracting tribes to Hinduism.[20]

Christianity Among the Misings of Majuli

From the mid nineteenth century century the Christian missionaries visited the island and attempt to spread Christanity among the inhabitants here. But, while the caste section of the society did not come nearer to the missionaries due to the impact of the Satras and its Vaishnava heritage, there was no Mising village as such to be approached. However, the missionaries attempted in Sadiya where there were some Mising inhabited foot-hill territories. In the year 1836 American missionary Rev. Nathan Brown came to eastern Assam to preach the Gospel amongst the people of the locality in the surrounding Himalayan foothills and set-up a missionary camp at Sadiya.[21] It is not known to what extent they were successful in getting converts to Christianity from among the Misings. But that they continued their attempt and established their camps in subsequent times among the Misings of North Lakhimpur (1834) and at Pathalipam near it (1895) was fact.[22]

In the third decade of the twentieth century Christian missionaries succeeded in spreading their faith among the Misings. It may be recorded that in the years between 1921-1930 thirty eight members of the tribe opted to embrace Christianity as their religion.[23] The current of conversion became more stronger after independence. Since then when India became a secular state spread of the faith became easier comparative to the earlier times. Christian missionaries now undertook certain innovative means such as establishment of training camps and schools in the remote Mising villages and enrolling the younger generations to the Church and the theological colleges. Thus, the missionaries entered the areas of Majuli, Lakhimpur, Dhemaji and other remote and isolated areas.[24]

Parama Pegu was the first Misings person who got converted to the Christianity in the year 1978. This school boy belonged to a poor Mising family of Jengraimukh. He was, it is reported, brought by a missionary of the Catholic Church and educated at their own expenses. Following Parama Pegu, a few others accepted Christianity in the village of Kumarbari Lakhimi Gaon, in the heart of the Jengraimukh township area. In recent years a good number of Mising families of this area had been converted into Christianity. It is here that the missionaries have established schools and charitable institutions for spreading education. The most famous school the missionaries have established here is the Saint Paul High School which was established in the year 1987. Since then the school became a centre of Christianity with a Church built within its campus, and families of the locality beginning to take it as their most revered place. During the late seventies and early eighties of the 20th quite a few number of Mising people converted to the Christianity.[25]

According to Gopal Doley, who is an ardent supporter of Christianity, and who himself is a worker of the faith, Christianity becomes popular among the Misings of Jengraimukh because it is a religion where sacrifice of animals is prohibited. As against this, he pointed out, the ethnic belief of the Misings involves much killing of animals and birds, and the religious practices here are costly due to necessity of a large number of animals and birds for offering. Sri Padma Pegu, a noted Christian convert since 1986 and a teacher of Namoni Chapori High School, is a similar supporter of the faith. It was also observed during our field work that the hatred and distinction maintained towards the tribal people by the Vaishnava society of Majuli is working in the mind so the people to accept Christianity where such hatred and caste disabilities are absent. On interesting aspect to be noted in this regard is that those who have converted themselves to Christianity, among them the prevalence of superstition like witchcraft and magic are absent. Among them literacy rate is also high. But, they do not celebrate any ethnic festivals and customs like other members of the community. Thus conversion seems to be a threat to the Mising ethnic life and culture of the Majuli island.

NOTES AND REFERENCES

1. D. Nath, *The Majuli Island Society: Economy and Culture*, Delhi, 2009, p. 49.
2. *Ibid.*, p. 48.
3. R.N. Mosahary, an article entitled, "Traditional Religion of Boro's of Assam", published in *proceeding on NEIHA*, 8th session, Kohima, 1987, p. 508.
4. Dr. D. Doley, *The Misings their History and Culture*, 1998, p. 75.
5. Jatin Mipun, *The Misings (Miris) of Assam*, Delhi, 1987, p. 26.
6. S.R. Payeng Kakati, *Miri Jatir Buranji*, Dhemaji, 1935.
7. N.C. Pegu, *The Misings of the Brahmaputra Valley*, 1981, p. 143.
8. Lakhinath Pegu, "Religious Beliefs of the Misings", in D. Nath, ed., *Religion and Society in North-East India*, Guwahati, 2011, p. 143.
9. N.C. Pegu, *op. cit.*, p. 144.
10. Jatin Mipun, *op. cit.*, p. 26.
11. J.J. Kuli, ed., *History and Culture of the Misings*, Guwahati, 1998, pp. 115f.
12. Lakyeswar Doley, an article in titled "Mising Jatir Utsav Ali-aye-ligang Aru Dharmia Porampora, Ati Somu Abhas", Published in *Doksiri* (ed.) by Jostshna Doley Pegu, Guwahati, 2005, p. 47.
13. N.C. Pegu, *op. cit.*, p. 82.
14. Jatin Mipun, *op. cit.*, p. 26.
15. D. Nath, "Misings Society in Transition" in the *Proceeding of Annual Conference of the North-East India History Association*, vol. Ix, 1988, p. 257th (Indeswar Pegu).
16. L.N. Pegu, an article entitle "Impact of Hinduism and the Religions on the Misings Religious Belief" Published in Souvenir *Doksiri*, Guwahati, 2005, p. 95.
17. Dr. S.N. Sarmah, *The Neo Vaishnvite Movement and the Satra Institution of Assam*, Kolkata, 1966, p. 13.

18. Maheswar Neog, *Sankardeva and his Times Early History of the Vaishnava Faith and Movement in Assam*, Guwahati, 1965, p. 370.
19. L.N. Pegu, *op. cit.*, p. 94.
20. N.C. Pegu, *op. cit.*, p. 324.
21. M.S. Sangma, *History of the American Baptist Mission in North-East India*, Delhi, 1987, Vol. 1, p. 4.
22. *Ibid.*
23. D. Nath, *The Majuli Island: Society Economy and Culture*, p. 94.
24. *Ibid.*, pp. 95f.

46

BREAKING THE PATRIARCHAL MYTH
A Study of Naga Customary Laws

Rituparna Patgiri

The north-eastern part of India is well-known for its diversity of communities and their varied cultures. The seven sisters are made up of many communities with complex socio-economic, political, cultural and religious relations. Talking about socio-economic relations, gender relations are an important facet of that. It is generally held that the gender relations are much more egalitarian in nature in the North-east compared to the rest of the country. The purpose of this article is to contest this proposition with the help of an example from the region. The State of Nagaland is comprised of many tribes and is thought of as one of the more gender egalitarian States of India. However, this essay aims to break that myth with the help of certain instances.

In order to arrive at my argument, I intend to use data from some secondary sources like the Nagaland State Human Development Report of 2004 and certain personal observations that I made during my stay in Kohima, the capital of Nagaland. In this context I would like to mention that I am thankful to North-East Network (NEN) for giving me an opportunity to visit Kohima and aiding my understanding of the city.

According to the Nagaland State Human Development Report of 2004, Naga women are more empowered compared to women from other Indian States. Some of the areas of strength for Naga women are high literacy rates, low maternal mortality rates, a rising sex ratio and a quality of life in general which is better than the national average. The school enrollment rates for girls in Nagaland are higher than the national average although it is still not comparable with the most literate states in the country. This reflects on the potential of Naga women to attain better educational qualifications and hence, better economic and social status.

Women traditionally get married within their own tribes, a practice which is still common today. Men customarily paid dowry to the family of the bride at the time of marriage in the form of livestock as bride price. This practice is different from most parts of India, where the bride's family pays dowry to the groom's family. Rooted in this tradition and governed by a general culture of care, the value of the girl child has continued till today. There is no prevalence of female foeticide in Nagaland. It is in this context that Nini Meru, Secretary of the Nagaland Board of School Education said, "A Naga woman, to me, enjoys more privileges than most other women elsewhere".

However, such state reports do not reveal the real picture of the condition of ordinary Naga women. The perception that Naga women are more empowered compared to women of other states is a myth and has acted as a shield in preventing attention from being drawn to their problems. They do not own property rights, hold no stake in land, have no inheritance rights and are marginalized in the decision-making process. The biggest victims in the ongoing separatist conflict between Nagaland and Government of India have been women. Their concerns always go unheard. The State government is unfriendly to women and the State Womens Commission has been reduced to a mere rubber stamp body. The Village Development Boards (VDBs) are equally unfriendly to women and talk about women's participation only on paper and do not implement it in reality.

In this regard it is essential to look at the dichotomy between customary and constitutional laws because this dichotomy forms one of the central bases for women's oppression.

Evolution of Customary Laws

Customary laws change when they are codified and the formal system that has a written document as its base recognizes them. That is what has happened in the North-East. After bringing the tribes of the region under its control, the British administration recognized their customary laws through the Scheduled District Act of 1874. The Assam General Clauses Act, 1915 protected tribal customs and practices by restricting the application of Provincial Laws in the Hill areas. The Montague-Chelmsford Reforms 1919 made similar provisions. The 1930 Indian Statutory (Simon) Commission recommended that tribal customary rights be protected. The Government of India Act, 1935 accepted it and divided the hill areas into Excluded and Partially Excluded areas and stipulated that no Act of the Central or Provincial Legislatures would apply to them unless the Governor in his/her discretion so decided. It empowered him to make regulations for peace and good governance in these areas. The Sixth Schedule of the Constitution of India recognizes this evolution and accepts their role in the Naga, Khasi, Garo and other Hill areas that the British "excluded". Later it was applied to the Karbi-Anglong and North Cachar Hills which were granted District Autonomous Councils in the 1970s. The Boros have been granted a Territorial Council in 2003. The Tiwa (Lalung) and Rabha are also demanding it. Constitutional amendments have recognized the role of customary laws in Nagaland (Article 371A) and Mizoram (Article 371G). The North-East has witnessed an ongoing interaction between tradition and modernity. The Sixth Schedule thus symbolizes the ongoing interaction between the informal system of the tribal communities of this region and the formal system represented by the Indian State.

Customary laws have a gender dimension in the sense that they clearly define the roles of men and women. The tribes combine kinship based political organization with well-defined laws and procedures for punishment of offenders through traditional courts. Thus, most of them accept the authority of the customary laws that are well synchronized with their religious beliefs. Many values have changed, but not the customary laws around resource sharing, maintenance of ethnic identity or regulation of marriage. Both the tribal customs that favour women and those that discriminate against them are based on the central pivot of women as homemakers and men as providers and protectors. Their myths and beliefs legitimize these practices and taboos (Vitso, 2003:58). Angami men claim that they want to preserve the identity of their tribe and, therefore, prevent girls of their tribe from marrying non-Angamis (Fernandes and Barbora, 2002a:161). Women are allowed to attend village meetings in case of a conflict involving a relative or a family member, but are not allowed to speak.

Naga customary laws are very clear cut in the sense that they emanate from a patriarchal value system. Hence, women in Naga society are deemed inferior. According to different books published on customary laws like the *Ao Naga Customary Laws* (1980), daughters are always regarded as subordinate members of the family and have no property rights. The Tribal Research Centre of the Department of Sociology of Nagaland University published a pamphlet which stated the obvious fact that in all tribes of Nagaland the status of women is inferior to that of men. Thus women's secondary position is substantiated by writings of sociologists and anthropologists and they agree on the term 'inferior'.

There is no place for her in the clan, village, etc. and the village council is constituted only by men.

The Nagas had an act called Rules for the Administration of Justice and Police in 1937. The British government had made the village councils integral parts of administration. They were given powers to handle criminal offenses. After independence, laws were made like Article 371(A) and the 73rd and 74th Amendments. However, the Panchayati Raj Institutions (PRIs) did not apply to Nagaland. The State government said that the Nagas already have these institutions. Thus, the village councils in Nagaland had the same powers and roles as *panchayats* in other states as specified by acts like the Nagaland Village Council Act, 1978. The constitution of the village councils should consist of members chosen by villagers in accordance with customary laws. There is no mention of male members. Women living in villages are also members of villages. They are not only Nagas, but also citizens of India. Thus to be a member of a village council, an Angami must be a citizen of India. However, there is no mention of being a male citizen. In other parts of India, in PRIs members are elected for five years and 33 per cent seats are reserved for women. But this is not the case in village councils. The most interesting aspect is that like PRIs even village councils receive funds. So, village councils cannot exclude women in the pretext of being traditional bodies. Traditional bodies do not receive funds from the government. Thus, being citizens of India, Naga women deserve all rights. In order to understand the functioning of customary laws, it is crucial that we analyze the specific structures of Naga society.

Social Organization

There exists in the Angami society the moiety[1] system consisting of clans and lineages that are localized and maintain their distinct identities in their structure and functions. In most Naga villages, social groups are divided into Khels (an Assamese word for an exogamous group that corresponds most closely to the Angami word *thino* and the Ao word *muphy*). Individuals are tied through kinship related obligations because property management is associated with lineage. Each clan has its own labour pool for rendering help to individuals, particularly during house construction. The village is an alliance of several clans. Peer group or *peli* is another source of help to individual families in the agricultural season. Every Angami village has its own myth of origin and a traditional village council. Capi, the traditional court of the Angami villages, continues to be influential in the maintenance of social, political and juridical order. Each clan has representatives in it. In Naga societies, both boys and girls take their social identity from their father and are placed in his agnatic group and familial unit. In some interior areas it is still common to have girls get married off at the age of 15 or 16.

Crimes against women have significantly risen and even cases related to domestic violence have come out in the open. Domestic violence is often considered to be a private matter and most cases go unreported. Most often, severe offences like rape are trivialized by resorting to customary laws. There was a particular rape case when even after the rapist and victim both admitted that it was a rape, it was ruled by the Cepi that it is against the customs and traditions of a tribe to create a fuss against another tribe. Hence, a fine was paid by the girl's tribe to the boy's tribe. In the Angami tribe, when a rape is committed above the main road, it is not considered to be a rape as the accused man could not have pulled a woman to the road and she must have come willingly. Because customary laws are unwritten, they can be interpreted differently. During the past five decades Naga society has been a witness to severe conflict and violence. Insurgency has taken a heavy toll, with women bearing the brunt of the consequences. Often, women themselves have been victims of violence and conflict and many of them also had to take care of their families single-handedly. The survival, health and growth of the society were almost entirely entrusted to their care. They have been not only victims of violence, but also charged with additional responsibilities of supporting their families and communities to cope with the adverse impact of violence. Naga women have played a pivotal role, individually and collectively, in helping their communities survive and in enabling human development across Naga society.

Political Structure

In every Khel, some male members are assigned to look after the administration of the village and settle disputes. The political infrastructure from the Khel moves to the village level where the village councils draw their powers and responsibilities from the people, through their support and consensus drawn from tradition. State elections in Nagaland began in 1964 and since then, till the 2007 State Legislative Assembly elections, less than 20 women have contested and none of the women candidates have ever won. The only woman who had made a notable entry into politics was Rano Shaiza, who was the first and only lady from Nagaland to become a Member of the Parliament when she was elected to the 6th Lok Sabha. Thus, when one looks at the national and state political scenario, women have a long way to catch-up with mainstream politics which is dominated by men. In the villages, customary laws are used instead of Constitutional laws. In this set-up, women have no role or voice representations of any kind. The Village Councils are especially strong as they have the back-up of the Government too. The Nagaland Village and Area Councils Act, 1978 was enacted to empower the traditional village institutions and village courts guided by customary laws. Under this Act, no women were part of the council as members were chosen keeping in mind customary practices. The Village Councils are vested with full power and authority to deal with all internal administration of the village. They also act as village courts with both civil and judicial duties and have the power to maintain law and order. However, this act does not talk about women's representation, but only that of villagers.

The Nagaland Municipal Act, 2001 delineates the responsibility of urban governance to elected representatives of the towns. There are three Town Municipal Councils — Kohima, Dimapur and Mokokchung. There are also 16 Town Committees and Urban Station Committees. These Councils and Committees are given the responsibility of developing and maintaining the basic amenities and general infrastructure of their respective towns. However, even in this area, women have basically very less involvement. In relation to this issue, the Nagaland State Assembly had passed the Nagaland Municipal (Amendment) Act, 2006 whereby 33 per cent of seats in the civic bodies were reserved for women.[2] When the Government of Nagaland decided to implement 33 per cent reservation for women in Mokokchung Municipal elections, there was a hue and cry raised by the men folk saying that it is against the customary laws. A bandh was also called by the 'All Wards Union Mokokchung Town' on September 4th, 2008 in protest against the 33 per cent Women Reservation in the ensuing Mokokchung Municipal Council elections. In reaction to this, the various women bodies, led by the Nagaland State Women Commission met the state governing bodies. They had demanded that the Government and Deputy Commissioners appoint women *dovashis* and *gaonburas* so that they can articulate women's concerns better. It will also give women the power to make decisions. Customary courts are the places where most people go to seek justice and as such the failure to appoint women *dovashis* lie with the State government.

Reservation is not a new word to the Naga dialogue and has been in use since ages. Provisions in the Constitution of India not only grant equality to women, but also empower the State to adopt measures of positive discrimination in favour of women for neutralizing the cumulative socio-economic disadvantages faced by them over the years. Apart from the original Constitutional provisions of universal suffrage, of special significance is the 73rd Constitutional Amendment Act of 1992 that ushered in the Panchayati Raj system all over the country. According to the Act, the Gram Sabha will comprise of all the adult members registered as voters in its area. One third of the elected seats in the Panchayats are reserved for women, so are a third of the posts of chairpersons. By reserving a third of the seats for women at all levels, it ensured their participation in the decision-making bodies of their society and ensured that they led the grass-roots level political institutions from the village to the district level. However, in town councils and municipalities, there was no reservation for women as the government passed the municipal act in 2001 without it.

This provision has been made to preserve the identity of Naga people by allowing them to live with their distinct religious, social practices, customs, traditions, etc. They have been given the opportunity to administer civil and criminal justice as per their customary law. Article 371A is silent about the share of participation of Naga men and women in the local administration. There is no mention about reservation for Naga women representatives in the local administration. Article 371A has no role to play in the matter of providing reservation for women representatives in the Village Council or local body. This provision is for a mighty and lofty purpose to preserve the distinct identity of the Naga people for which it has been made incumbent upon the Parliament to have the approval of the Nagaland State Legislature before any Act is implemented or enforced in the State of Nagaland. The Parliament thus does not have any say in the matter of providing reservation for women. Much of North-East comes under Schedule 6 of the Constitution of India. PRIs do not become automatically extended.

According to Article 13, anything inconsistent with the fundamental rights will not be applicable even if they are customary laws all over India. But it says nothing about personal laws. However, under Article 371(A), Nagaland's customary laws cannot be challenged. Thus, Naga women get entrapped in a vicious circle of patriarchal interests and law becomes a cog in the wheel.

A writ petition was filed in the Guwahati High Court by a Naga lady challenging the Municipal act which forced the government to amend it in 2006. According to the Court order, in September 2008, after extensive deliberation, 82 wards were reserved for women and in 19 town councils and municipalities, elections were supposed to be held in January 2009. But it did not take place as the State government in November 2009 cancelled the elections on the pretext of the ongoing peace process and because of objections from the Nagahoho, the apex tribal association of Nagaland. This forced the women's associations to hold meeting after meeting. Thus, in May of 2011, all the presidents of the women's associations unanimously decided to file a writ petition in spite of scarcity of funds and a Joint Action Committee (JAC) was formed. The JAC comprises of two representatives from each tribe to facilitate communication.

All in all, five hearings were held in which the other tribal associations like the Nagahoho tried to shift the blame and said that they were not against gender equity. The Government came up with numerous excuses like Article 371(A) for not implementing reservation. The judge, however, directed the Government to hold elections immediately and strictly implement women's reservation in the town councils and municipalities. He ordered that Constitutional laws overrule customary laws. The State Election Commission was forced to send a lawyer to the court and the judge made an observation that a government official cannot be the State Election Commissioner. Although the State government made an appeal, it was rejected and it has been directed that elections take place by the end of April, 2012. The JAC has been empowered by the tribal associations and it has decided to scan the profiles of the women candidates and has also made it mandatory that the contestants must be living in the ward itself from which they are contesting elections. Most of the women will be independent candidates and not members of political parties. The contestants will be well-trained too.

Economic Organization

The lower status that these customs indicate for women is reflected in inheritance laws. The Angamis follow the patrilocal or neolocal rule of marriage. In either case the girl enters the boy's house and is deprived of her property rights in her ancestral home. Women cannot inherit immovable property, though the father can gift it to them. If he gives it to her as a gift during his lifetime, it remains hers till her death, however, after his death it reverts to his heirs. A widow remains in her husband's family only as a guardian of honour of the family, but cannot inherit his property. A man with only one daughter may give his property to her. Her daughters may inherit it. If the transfer of the property is not done during her lifetime, at the event of her death, the property would go back to her father's heirs.

Even in the industrial and agricultural sectors, women farmers or entrepreneurs are not encouraged. Since, they do not own property, banks do not grant them loans at affordable interest rates as they have problems in mortgaging property. Only rich women farmers have flourished in ventures like floriculture and horticulture. Most of the schemes are Central Sector Schemes (CSS) which means that the funds come to the States and they carry them out. It is very difficult for the Central Government to keep track of what is going on in a district of a particular state. Therefore, it is the responsibility of the State governments to carry out developmental practices with properly.

Health

Women's health is in bad shape and government schemes like the Janani Suraksha Yojana (JSY) are inadequate in dealing with the peculiar nature of women's problems. There is scarcity of labour rooms, lack of beds and no proper mode of transport to the hospitals as many ambulances are driven by the doctors themselves. It is thus, very important to carry out a community monitoring of National Rural Health Mission. (NRHM) There is preferential treatment in payment of JSY if a boy child is born. HIV AIDS is also a major issue of concern for women's health as some of the most affected and infected are women in the state.

Conclusion

It is no surprise that women's issues receive secondary priority. State government officials have been constantly opposing any move made to enhance women's position. For example, Nagaland's Chief Minister Neiphiu Rio spoke of the rights of the Nagas under Article 371-A of the Constitution with special reference to land and its resources. According to the provisions of the article, land and its resources belong to the people and no Act of Parliament can infringe upon this article, which gives special status to the Nagas. The article is a special safeguard to protect and preserve the Naga way of life, to acknowledge the people as owners of land and its resources. The Nagaland Government and various organizations have voiced concern over infringement upon the article by the Centre. Rio said the article confers authority to the Assembly to make the final decision on these issues. It makes the Nagaland Assembly the custodian of the Naga people's rights and interest.[3]

In fact, some analysts consider Nagaland to be a 'sovereign' state because of Article 371(A). Nagaland Minister for Planning, T.R. Zeliang objected the introduction of the Nagaland Lokayukta Bill. Supporting his stand in opposing the Nagaland Lokayukta Bill, 2012, he observed that the bill has to comply with all the rules of procedures. He said that the Bill does not meet the requirement of Rule 67(ii) and also did not fulfill the requirements of the statement of object and procedures under Rule 65 clause (i). He also reminded the House that Article 371(a) was extracted from the 16-point agreement and enshrined in the Constitution of India and termed Article 371(A) as the current guardian of Naga's right. He said that the Nagaland Lokayukta Bill was totally unacceptable and not in tune with the Naga way of life and opined that the present method was better.[4]

The State government admitted 'faults' in amending the Nagaland Municipal Act of 2001 in 2006 when it inserted 33 per cent reservation for women. Chief Minister Neiphiu Rio said the amendment was made out of ignorance. Criticizing Naga women, Minister for Urban Development Shurhozelie Liezietsu, emphatically told the State Assembly that no Act of Parliament can supersede Article 371(A) and that it supersedes all other acts. "*This is a supreme law to supersede all Parliamentarian laws*", he said, adding that some people were trying to grab political power. He urged members to take a stand against the reservation policy stating that Article 371(A) recognizes uniqueness of social practices of the Nagas. "*We cannot go against the people who have sent us here*", he said.[5] And of course by 'people' he meant the men folk of Nagaland.

The masculinizations of the National Women Commission and State Women Commissions have diluted their powers and as such they have not been able to work with ease. They must be provided with proper infrastructural facilities, power and status to facilitate women's development. A Commission can be strong only when its members are strong. Every issue is peculiar and has its own requirements which must be addressed differently. One cannot compare Nagaland with any other state. Gender equality is no exception and requires a collaborative effort from both men and women. Men must not think that domination is a women's issue and does not concern them. Patriarchy is deeply entrenched in the customary laws. Since, it is customary laws that are at stake, the issue is contentious and must be handled with utmost sensitivity. However, since women constitute half the population, they must be equally represented at all levels without any excuse. We should have a look at the resources that an average woman has at hand. Constructive use of the media, especially the radio and FM, can go a long way in making people aware about the need to achieve gender equity. Ultimately, it is common women who form the fulcrum of Naga society and so it is crucial that they make full use of their human potential.

NOTES

1. If a society is divided into exactly two descent groups, each is called a moiety, after the French word for *half*.
2. *The Morung Express*, Vol. III issue 230.
3. *The Telegraph*, 29 June, 2011.
4. *The Times of India*, 17th March, 2012.
5. *The Telegraph*, 21st March, 2012.

REFERENCES

Fernandes, Walter and Sanjay Barbora, *The Socio-Economic Situation of Nagaon District: A Study of Its Economy, Demography and Immigration*, Guwahati: North-Eastern Social Research Centre, 2002a.

Vitso, A., *Customary Law and Women: The Chakhesang Nagas*, New Delhi: Regency Publications, 2003.

47

CULTURAL ASPECTS OF THE KHAMTIS OF NORTH-EAST INDIA

Prafulla Borah

Introduction

India is a land of diverse cultures and traditions. Each region of the country has a unique culture which is also prominently visible in its various arts forms. Almost all the region of the country has their specific festivals, folk music and dance-drama which prove to be a wonderful way of expression of their community and its arts tradition. In India, the north-east India is one of the most ethnically and linguistically diverse region. The region has a high concentration of tribal population. Each tribe has its own distinct tradition of art, culture, dance, music and life styles. The numerous fairs and festivals celebrated by these communities and their friendly nature are irresistible attractions for the visitors. Considered to be an ethnographical paradise for the study of tribal history and culture, the north-eastern region is a meeting ground of various ethnic groups, having diverse cultural heritage. The heritage of the region is reflected in pre-historic and megalithic remains, Brahmanical monuments, fort and fortifications, Buddhist antiquities in the form of monasteries and stupas, coloured dances, religious festivals and rituals, traditional arts and crafts, oral traditions, indigenous faiths, beliefs system, etc. Festivals are an essential part of the socio-cultural life of the people and most the festivals of north-eastern regions are connected with agricultural and celebrated with ritualistic gaiety either to thank God for his providence or to pray for a bumper harvest. The festivals highlight the regions rich indigenous culture with folk-songs, tribal dances, food and craft. Each tribe has its own distinctive way of dressing, jewellery designs and dance. They all have their separate festivals grouped with tribal songs in their own language. After all, the entire region is a land of diversified culture, which reflects a chain of festivals of different tribes throughout the year. The perfect fusion of heritage of tribes and sub-tribes has made North-East India the home of the most colourful festivals. Different sister states of the Seven Sisters and one brother state of North-East celebrate different festival, either to commemorate the new year, religious celebration or cultural festivals. The simplicity of life of the people is reflected in their celebration.

About the Khamtis

The Khamtis are one of the tribal groups mostly concentrated in the Lohit District of Arunachal Pradesh and Lakhimpur district of Assam in India as well as in Myanmar. They belong to the greater Tai race. According to Dutta Choudhari (1978) they migrated from Bor-Khamti or Mung-Khamti in the Irrawardy Valley of Burma (now officially known as Myanmar) and settled around the Tengapani River in 1751. Later a section of them settled to different places in Sadiya, Lakhimpur, Dibrugarh, etc. The word Khamti means 'a land full of gold' (*kham* means 'gold' and *ti* means 'place'). The Khamtis are very far in advance of all the north-eastern frontier tribes in knowledge, art and civilization. T.T Cooper says in 1873 "To speak of the Khamtis as a tribe is to do little justice, for there is that about the word tribe which conveys the idea of wildness and want of culture, very far from forming a characteristic of the Khamtis, for form some of their social laws even civilized nations might take a lesson". The community had its own script and the people speak Khamti dialect which belongs to the Tai family of language. Assamese and English are used for written communication. The Khamti men and women can be identified by their dress. The men commonly wear a tight-fitting cotton *chyn* (jacket) and a cotton or silk *fanoi* (lungi). The lungi has a chequered pattern combination of green, red, violet and black. They also put on a turban. A man of a higher status wears the Burmese *pasto* (a piece of multi coloured silk). The female dress consists of a *sein* (black skirt), *khenyao* (long-sleeved jacket), *longwat* (embroidered waist cloth) and a white turban. The last two are generally worn by married women.

The Khamtis belong to the Theravada or the Hinayana sect of the greater Tai-Burmese tradition. Each village has a *chong* (monastry) also known as *Buddha vihar*. The *vihar* is adorned with images of Lord Buddha. The community has two types of priest. The first is called *chowsra* (principal monk) and the second is called *chau-mun* (ordinary monk). The priesthood or monkship is not hereditary. Anyone can become a *chou-mun* (ordinary monk), but to become a *chowsra* (principal monk) one has to study Buddhist philosophy through Pali literature and have minimum 10 years of experience. The monks reside in the monastery and receive *som* (food) from the villagers known as *dana* in Sanskrit literature. The monks give religious teachings to the villagers and perform birth, marriage and death rituals of all the families rich or poor. The Khamtis are devout followers of Buddhism and there is tinged with traditional beliefs and practices. The Khamti society is divided into classes having distinct social status. The highest position is occupied by the chiefs or hereditary village chief (in Khamti *chowfa*). The priests who are second to the chiefs and position are very influential. Below them there is the class of free men who form the bulk of the population. The slaves of the past were at the bottom of the social structure.

Objectives of Study

(i) The main objective of the study is to show the existing of the belief of Therevada Buddhism among the Khamtis through their festivals.

(ii) To study the existence of the traditional art of dance-drama even in the present phase of modernization.

(iii) To study the developing the prospects of tourism in the area by promoting the cultural activities of the Khamtis.

Methodology

This research article is the form of an explanatory study in analyzing the potentiality from North-East Indian states (more particularly among the Khamtis) which will maintain a bright prospect of cultural development in terms of tourism industry. The present study is based on secondary data collection. The secondary data was collected by various published sources like books, journal, magazine, reports, publications, etc. The study is also relying on primary sources such as interviews with individuals and community leaders.

Festivals of Khamtis

The Khamtis observe a number of Buddhist festivals which are tied to the lunar calendar of Buddhism. These festivals are *Sangken* (the New Year), *Paya Puthikam* (*Buddha Purnima*), *Neova* (*Vassavasa*), *Kathing poi* (robe offering ceremony), *Wa-Ok Sitang, Wan-Lu Poi, Maiku-Sum-Phai* and others. The festivals celebrated by the Khamtis have a reference to the Buddhist culture and religion. It is seen that Buddhist festival is used for performing tourism and for harmonizing the entire ethnic group since everyone present in this festivals to participate in cultural shows, traditional games and sports, festival food, etc. The Khamtis have also beautiful *Viharas* which are called *Kyong* or *Chang* and these *Viharas* attract tourist's attention due to their height among the other houses of the village and due to their pattern of Burma-like roofs. The festivals of the Khamtis discuss following:

(i) *Sangken (the New Year)*

According to the Khamtis traditions, *Sangken* is a New Year festival with religious piety and boisterous fun. It is celebrated on the fifth month of the Buddhist calendar, which falls in April. In this festival, otherwise known as water festivals, the image of Lord Buddha is brought out and kept in a small makeshift house (*Kyangfra*) built by the villagers and washed ceremoniously with great devotion. The festivals continues for three or sometimes four days when everybody offers food items to Buddha and prays for peace, harmony, prosperity, happiness and seeks blessings to avoid occurrence of misfortune in the coming year. This celebration is a mixture of religious piety and boisterous. To celebrate this festival, men, women and children sprinkle water on each other out of fun. On this day all the Khamtis village were agog, in festive mood and the sprinkling of mud and water on each other was a common scene among the travellers. Though the festival falls in the month of April, but the villagers make their preparation for this festival a month ahead. The stating of dramas, singing and composing of songs and dances, wearing of new clothes, etc. are the features of this festival.

(ii) *Paya Puthikam (Buddha Purnima)*

Paya Puthikam or *Buddha Purnima* or the full moon of May is commemorated as the day on which all Buddha's attained Enlightenment and on which the present Buddha, Gautama, was born, attained Enlightenment and died. In addition to the central ritual of any *uposath* and observance of the precepts — the day is marked by watering the bo-tree, the tree under which Buddha had his enlightenment. During the time of festival, the people listen to *ahimsa* discourse from monks, recite *Panchashilas* and religious song is sung, followed by a mass prayer and community feast.

(iii) *Neova (Vassavasa)*

The three months from the full moon of July (*Asadha*) to full moon of October (*Aswina*) is call the Buddhist *vassavasa*. During this period the full moon day are considered very auspicious. In the beginning of the rainy season on a full moon day, the festival *Neova* is celebrated. The festival arresting falls on a full moon day of *Aswina*, when the villagers give alms of food and fruit to the monks and feed the poor people. In addition to its monastic importance — monks may not travel for that period — it is a solemn season for laymen. Marriages cannot be performed, plays and other forms of public entertainment are forbidden and pious Buddhists attempt to observe the *uposatha* as frequently as possible during this time. Therefore, together with New Year, the full moons that mark the beginning and the end of vassavasa are occasions for the two most important holy days in the Buddhist calendar.

The religious significance of *Asadha* is enhanced by the fact that it marks the beginning not only of *vassavasa*, but of two seasons; the rice production and monsoon seasons. The villagers now pass from an economically slow to an intensely busy period, planting and transplanting rice and the climate has changed from oppressive heat and drought of the dry season to welcome rain and relative coolness of the monsoon.

(iv) *Kathin Poi (Robe Offering Ceremony)*

The *Kathin poi* festival is celebrated on the full moon day of October-November, villagers prepare robes for the image of Lord Buddha and monks, especially by the womenfolk and this work has to be finished within the night. During the one-month period from the first waning moon of October to the full moon of the month of November, Khamtis busy with celebration of *Kathin poi* festivals. Scripturally based, this festival consists of the public offering of yellow robes to monks. Needless to say, these and all other public offerings are accompanied by a large feast for the monks. Although individual monks are supplied with robes through-out the year faithful, those offered during this season fall into a special category; they are given collectively rather than individually and to an entire chapter of monks rather than to an individual monk.

(v) *Wa-Ok Sitang*

The *Wa-Ok Sitang* festival is organized on a full moon day of *Kartika* to remember meditation; Buddha's disciples did for three months during the rain. In this festival, villagers prepare artificial desire giving tree (Petesa) with pickiest of foodstuff hanging from the branches and give these as gifts to the monks in recognition of their sacrifice and piety.

(vi) *Wan-Lu Poi*

The *Wan-Lu Poi* is similar to Magh Bihu and on the day, villagers prepare stacks of wood and light bonfire and food is offered to the monks.

(vii) *Maiku-Sum-Phai*

Another festival of the Khamtis is *Maiku-Sum-Phai*, which, in Khamti mean putting of wooden stack into fire on *Phalguna Purnima* and as per the tradition, the people organize the festival to offer warm to the monks to get happy and prosperous year and the festival is a farewell to the winter. During this festival the Khamis built a very beautiful *Mezi* and it is somewhat different from *Magh Bihu Mezi* among the Assamese society and at the same it attracts the tourist very much due to its exceptional style.

Dance-Drama of Khamtis

The Khamtis have many dance-dramas through which they unfold some stories or depict mythical events bearing ethical lessons. These dramas are generally staged during the religious festivals of Potowah, Sankian or Khamsang, constituting the entertainment part of the festivals. In Khamti, the dance is called *ka* and the dance-drama is called *kapung* (*ka* means dance and *pung* means story) and actually means story depicted through the dance. There are always a few aged persons who were good dancers in their youth and their help is sought at the rehearsal of a drama starts about one month before festivals. This may be done in the monastery or in any house of their choice. At the time of rehearsal, which is generally done after dusk, they do not wear the costumes. Women do not take part in the drama. The female role, if any, is played by a man in the drama, in woman's costume. After the performance the party is given a remuneration of seven, fourteen, twenty-one, twenty-eight or forty-two rupees — always an amount divisible by seven. The purchase with this money the costumes and masks used in the dramas. The following are the dance-dramas of Khamtis —

Ka Fifai Dance-Drama

The *Ka Fifai* drama is woven round the theme of the traditional belief that ghosts appear and kidnap girls or men and trouble them. The participants in the drama consist of a man, his daughter who is kidnapped, the ghost who does the kidnapping, the Ministers of the State who make preparations for war against the ghost, the King of the State in which the girl's father is a subject and the king's men who go out to capture the ghost.

The drama opens with a man and his daughter walking in the garden. The ghost appears and captures the girls and immediately the man greatly aggrieved rushes to the king's court to inform him of the incident and to beseech him to rescue his daughter. The King's anger is aroused at this news and he calls for his Ministers and asks them to prepare for war. The king's men go in search of the ghost and bring him before the king who severely warns him never to do such thing again. The ghost frightened bows before the king and with this ends the drama.

Ka Muhchu Dance-Drama

This drama unfolds the story of a hunter who unwittingly kills a saint. The hunter, armed with his sword, bow and arrow, first invokes the saints to bless his hunting trip. Then he stealthily enters the jungle to seek his chase hither and thither. Spying something he hears it and shoots it, but on drawing closer he realizes his dreadful mistake, for he finds that he has a saint, who sits in meditation under a tree. Filled with sorrow, the hunter who is himself a pious man begs the saint's forgiveness. The saint consoles and advises him. The hunter leaves with bowed and repenting.

Ka Kongtukai Dance

It is dance depicting cock-fight. The two dancers wear breeches and shirt of spotted design and on their head put on masks of cock's head with its crown at the top and the beak projecting over the forehead of the dancer. These two dancers play drums, hung from their neck and dance like two fighting cocks pecking with the beak at each other. Several young men and boys play gongs and cymbals to the accompaniment of the dance.

Chouliuchiyen Dance-Drama

Chouliuchiyen dance-drama is a very popular social drama where a king and his wife are united after long separation and a period of trouble.

Conclusion

The indigenous people (along with Khamtis) in north-east India belong to mainly Mongloid and Tibeto-Burman stock and have preserved their culture, language and way of life even in the present century. The study leads to the conclusion that the Theravada Buddhism became popular among the Khamtis sometimes in eighteenth century A.D. At present in most of the villages, one can notice a monastery and people celebrate a number of Buddhist festivals. So, it proved that the Khamtis are zealous followers of Theravada form of Buddhism. Their dances, festivals, ritual, ceremonies, way of life, monument provide information about their Buddhist cultural heritage. Till today, they are following the essence of Theravada Buddhism in true spirit. On the other hand, the rich flora, fauna diverse topography and ethnic groups have of late, started attracting domestic as well as foreign tourists into the region and recently community based tourism has gained importance. While community based tourism has been used to describe a variety of activities that seek to positively link conservation with economical development, many of the issues involved in the development of a community based tourist area are not clearly defined. There are many concerns about managing negative impacts on local environments, while at the same time sufficiently involving local communities in the planning process to receive just benefits from tourism activities.

REFERENCES

Chatterjee, S.K., *The Place of the Assam in the History and Civilization of India*, Kolkata, 1954.

Choudhury, Amalendu, *Tribal Songs of North-East India*, Kolkata, 1984.

Choudhury, J.N., *Arunachal Panorma*, Shillong, 1973.

Cooper, T.T., *New Routes for Commerce: The Mishmi Hills*, London, 1873.

Daltron, E.T., *Tribal History of Eastern India* (descriptive Ethnology of Bengal), Delhi, 1973.

Duttachoudhuy, S., *Arunachal Pradesh District Gazetteers*, Lohit District, Shillong, 1978.

Elwin, Verrier, *India's North-East Frontier in the Ninetieth Century*, London, 1962.

Gait, Edward, *A History of Assam*, Kolkata, 1967.

Gogoi, Lila, *The Tai Khamtis of the North-East*, Chowkham, 1971.

Kondaniya, *Monastic Buddhism among the Khamtis of Arunachal Pradesh*, New Delhi, 1986.

Magregor, C.R., *Military Report on the Khampti Singpho Countries*, Kolkata, 1987.

Mein Na, Chou, *To the Land of Tai Khamtis of Myanmar*, Assam, India, 2005.

Osik, N.N., *A Brief History of the Arunachal Pradesh*, New Delhi, 1996.

Sarkar, Niranjan, *Buddhism Among the Monpas and Sherdukpens*, Shillong, 1980.

Sarkar, Niranjan, *Dances of Arunachal Pradesh*, Shillong, 1974.

Shakespeare, L.W., *History of Upper Assam, Upper Burma and North-Eastern Frontier*, London, 1914.

Sing, K.S., *Tribal Customary Law in North-East India*, New Delhi, 1973.

INDEX

Abandoned children, 290, 292, 297
Above Poverty Line (APL), 350
Academic Activities, 151
Act of Parliament, 149, 436–37
Activism, 223
Administration of Assam, 272, 305
Administrative Report of Assam, 257
Adult education centres, 198
Ageing society, 354–55
Agrarian society, 394
Agricultural Indebtedness Relief Act, 343
Agriculture-based festivals, 396
Agro-climatic characteristics, 378
Ahom
  culture, 45, 47, 51, 53, 55, 59
  faith, 55
  language, 52, 55
  marriage, 53, 390
  of Assam, 27–28, 32, 383
  practice, 310
Ahom Royal Society, 36
Ahom Tai Mongoliya Rajya Parishad (ATMRP), 34
Alcoholism, 222, 289, 360
Alenpur Tea Estate, 304
Alien land, 247
All Assam Ahom Association (AAAA), 28, 31–33
All Assam Mohan Deodhai Bailung Sanmilan (AAMDBS), 34
All Assam Students' Union (AASU), 365
Angami society, 431
Animal dance, 126
Animism, 314, 420
Annexation of Tibet, 227
Anti tobacco education, 331
Arable land, 307
Art of Assam, 39, 41, 43
Arunabam Tea Estate, 304
Arunabund Tea Garden, 301
Arunachal Pradesh University, 149
Arunachal Pradesh
  Army in, 234
  Government of, 89
  indigenous groups of, 412, 414
  Khamptis of, 411
  Ladakh and, 225
  people of, 128, 283
  social and cultural life in, 127
Arunachal tribesmen, 241
Aryan origin tribes, 106
Assam
  ancient times, 203
  children of, 292
  communities of, 29, 193
  diversified, 183
  far-eastern, 81
  film production, 82
  films, 82
  history of, 215
  land-abundant, 256
  language, 30, 49, 82–83, 106, 129, 197, 284, 379, 423
  mediaeval, 24
  Nepali Society of, 406
  orphanages of, 291–93

post-independence, 221
pre-colonial, 28
pre-Sankarite, 175
religious beliefs and festivals in, 121
rural, 372
tea gardens, 304
Tea plantation in, 298
tribal culture of, 93
tribes of, 105, 124, 187
Assam Accord, 265
Assam Agricultural University Act, 150
Assam Agriculture University (AAU), 150
Assam Ahom Association, 31
Assam Basic Education Act, 323
Assam Chhatra Sanmilan, 216
Assam District Gazetteer, 14, 95, 272
Assam Down Town University, 151
Assam Elementary Education Act, 323
Assam Film Finance and Development Corporation (AFFDC), 82, 84
Assam General Clauses Act, 429
Assam Literary Society, 216
Assam Movement, 265, 267
Assam Pradeshik Mahila Samity (APMS), 333–34, 337–40
Assam Tea Labourers Association, 33
Assam Tribal Development Authority, 199
Assam Tribal Development Corporation, 199
Assam University (AU), 149
Attitudinal development, 159
Authoritarianism, 62

Bamboo dance, 126
Barahi tribes, 47
Below Poverty Line (BPL), 199, 344, 350, 352
Belsiri tea garden, 302
Bengali customs, 94
Bengaluru International Film Festival, 84, 86
Best film award, 84
Best regional film, 83–84, 86
Bhagawati movement, 184
Bhaili songs, 406
Bhakti movement, 10, 61–63
Bholaguri tea estate, 80
Bodo
culture, 119
language, 84, 119
movement, 265
society, 118
Bodoland Territorial Council (BTC), 378
Borbam Tea Estate in Lakhimpur district, 303
Brahmanian customs, 174
Brahmanical culture, 172
Brahmanism, 174
Bride honours, 54
Bride price, 123, 318, 429
British imperialism, 30
British tea planters, 298
Buddhism, 18, 38, 127, 208, 212–13, 441, 446
Buddhist
culture, 442
festivals, 441–42, 446
Tantricism, 19
tribes, 129

Cannes Film Festival, 88
Caretaker-children ratio, 296
Casteism, 61
Central Sector Schemes (CSS), 436
Chaitnaya Movement in Bengal, 64–65
Chak-long marriage, 383, 387–88, 390
Changra songs, 397
Child development, 290
Child marriage, 94, 317, 319, 336, 371
Child Marriage Restraint Act, 336
Children's Home, 290–91, 293, 295, 297
Chouliuchiyen Dance-Drama, 445
Civil society, 28, 357
Civil-Disobedience movement, 100
Classless society, 165
Collective identity, 204, 364
Collectivism, 204
Commercial activities, 359
Communalism, 282, 371
Community/Communities
  advanced, 314
  backward, 324
  distinct, 106
  education, 331
  Hindu trade, 106
  identity, 71
  indigenous, 29
  marginalized, 266
  minority, 32
  Mishing, 381
  Mongoloid, 33
  non-tribal, 316, 377
  Reang, 363
  songs, 180
  tribal, 3, 85, 130–31, 191, 198, 315, 320–21, 341, 363, 430
  underprivileged, 365
  village, 128, 358
Compulsory education, 198–99
Computer-Assisted Language Learning, 142
Contract marital alliance, 254
Criminal activities, 289
Cross-border movements, 268
Cryogenic culture, 288
Cultivable land, 93, 363
Cultural activities, 122, 238, 295–96, 396, 409, 441
Cultural development, 441
Cultural festivals, 440
Cultural identity, 121, 133, 204, 392, 399
Cultural separatism, 35
Customary Laws
  Ao Naga, 430
  Evolution of, 429
  Naga, 428, 437
  traditional, 317
  unmodified, 318
Customary marriage ceremonies, 383
Cynicism, 157

Dalai Lama of Tibet, 127
Dance movements, 413, 417
Dance-dramas, 186, 412–13, 416, 439, 441, 444
Dayang Tea Garden, 302
Deities
  female, 5
  guardian, 38
  sculptured, 68
Destitute Children, 287, 290–91, 293, 297
Devadasi dance traditions, 108
Development indicators, 194

Development initiatives, 366
Development of North-Eastern Region, 204
Development schemes, 343
Development-induced displacement, 356, 358–60, 364
Dhaka International Film Festival, 85
Dibrugarh University (DU), 149
Digital film industry, 87
Digital film, 87
Disadvantaged Children, 290
Dismantling, 356
Distinct identity, 31–32, 115, 132, 265–66, 315, 431, 434
District Primary Education Programmes (DPEP), 198
Diversified identity, 392
Documentary film genre, 90
Domestic communalism, 66
Dynamism, 167, 267

Eaarly marriage, 93, 95–96, 98
Economic activities, 131, 155, 196, 233, 314, 319, 337, 350
Economic development, 113, 194, 196, 199, 223, 240, 322, 357–58, 446
Economic Irrationality of Partition, 285
Educational attainments, 98, 194
Educational backwardness, 94
Educational development, 192, 198
Educational objectives, 335
Egalitarianism, 310
Elementary education, 322–23, 325–26
Emotional development, 287
Employment centric education, 150
Engineering Education, 148
English education, 215
Entrepreneurship development, 155, 196
Esoteric ritualism, 10
Ethnic
  communities, tribal, 258
  festivals, 426
  identity, 35, 258, 263–65, 419, 430
  language, 206
  tribes, 33, 315
Expropriation of land, 359
Eye Asian Film Festival of Mumbai, 89

Factionalism, 221
Fargusab tea planter, 300
Feasting festivals, 49
Female activism, 220
Female education, 97, 335
Festival songs, 72
Festivals of Khamtis, 441
Film and Television Institute of India (FTII), 83–85
Film culture, 90
Film fraternity, 79, 90
Film production, 82
Filmmakers, 79–80, 83, 86–87
  gifted, 86
  master, 88
  off-beat, 86
  prolific, 86
  talented, 90
  veteran, 83
Flamboyant development, 87
Folk culture, 182
Folk songs, 72, 120, 125, 127
Forced marriage, 317
Foreign exchange earnings, 330

Forest land, 254, 359
Formal education, 96, 98
Fragrant tea-gardens, 112
Free land, 58, 308
Freedom movement
Freedom struggle movement, 265, 369–71

Gaandhian movement, 216
Gandhism, 368, 371
Gauhati University (GU), 149
Goddesses of Hinduism, 62
Grazing lands, 264

Haautley Tea Estate, 303
Hazarika, Bhupen, 8, 81–82, 89–90, 162–67
Hazarika Buddheswari, 220
Hazarika Lakhi Kanta, 102
Hazarika Sanjeev, 85
Helem Tea Garden, 301
Heroism, 125, 161
High seismic activities, 365
Hill tribes, 33, 193, 314, 399
Himalayan Environment and Culture, 272
Hindi films, 80, 89
Hindu Marriage Act, 319
Hindu revivalism, 88
Hinduism, Vaishnava cult of, 121
History of Partition, 282
Holy Bardowa dance, 163
Homestead land, 363
Homogenous society, 122
Humanism, 167–68, 177
Humanitarianism, 65, 289

Identity assertion, 28
Identity cards, health facilities, 350
Identity movements, 35–36, 312
Identity politics, 221
Income earning activities, 353
Indian Universities Education Commission, 146
Indigenous
  faith, 439
  language, 84–85
Indo-South-East Asian relations, 213
Indo-Tibetan Border Police (ITBP), 234
Indo-Tibetan borders, 233, 242
Indo-Tibetan Convention, 227
Infant Mortality Rate (IMR), 345–46
Informal education, 157
Inhuman police vandalism, 300
Innovative activities, 218
Integrated Child Development Services (ICDS), 289
Integrated Tribal Development Projects (ITDPs), 344
Inter-marriage, 47
International Agency for Research into Cancer (IARC), 329
International Film Festival of India (IFFI), 79, 84–85, 89
International Institute for Environment and Development, 367
Inter-racial marriage, 82, 122
Irrigated land, 119

Janani Suraksha Yojana (JSY), 436
Japan Landa Imphal, 87
Jayantia and Garo tribes, 124
Jhum land, 130
Joint Action Committee (JAC), 435

Joymoti, first Assamese film, 80

Ka Fifai Dance-Drama, 444
Ka Kongtukai Dance, 445
Ka Muhchu Dance-Drama, 445
Karbi folk dances, 120
Kathin poi festivals, 443
Khadi movement, 218
Khamp-Tai language, 412
Khampti dance drama, 412
Khampti language, 412, 414
Khamti society, 441
Khasi film, 88
Khasi language, 88
Khilafat Movement, 301
Kipat land, 249
Kuki-Chin tribes, 117
Kul marriage, 395
Kuls in Tiwa society, 394

Labour Strikes in Surma Valley Tea Estates, 305
Lakwa tea garden in Sibsagar, 302
Land erosion, 180, 184, 188
Land ownership rights, 132
Land Revenue Administration, 272
Land tenure system, 131–32
Landed aristocracy, 308
Land-grabbing tactics, 85
Landlessness, 357, 359
Language
  proficiency, 134–35
  skills, 141
  teacher, 137
  Lao language, 206
Lao People's Democratic Republic (LPDR), 206
Learner-centred activities, 139
Lingo-cultural identity, 34, 36
Linguistic nationalism, 284
Listening, Speaking, Reading and Writing (LSRW), 135
Literary film, 83
Local tea-tribe, 82
Logical positivism, 79
Loina Tea Estate, 303
Long Range Patrolling (LRP), 235
Low budget film, 89

Mahapursism, 66
Mahayani Buddhism, 53
Mahomedianism, 64
Mainstream society, 199
Majuli
  art of, 181
  cultural significance of, 179–82
  Misings of, 424
  Nuxali of, 187
  Sattras of, 179, 181, 183, 185, 187, 189
Male dancers, 397
Male dominated society, 317, 336
Management Education, 148
Manipur/Manipuri
  culture, 123
  dance, 123
  films, 88
  language, 123, 139
  Loktak Hydel Project in, 363
  Maharaja of, 87
  Mizo Societies in, 321
  social and cultural life in, 122
  society, 124
Manipur Film Development Corporation, 87
Manipur University (MU), 149
Marriage festival, 390
Marriage ritual, 53
Marxism, 167

Mask culture, 181–82
Mass movement, 100
Meghalaya
  Caretakers in, 291
  children of, 292
  hilly areas of, 295
  Khasi-Jayantia hills in, 117
  Lalungs of, 316
  orphanages in, 287, 297
  Social and Cultural Life in, 124
  tribal areas of, 321
  tribes, 125
Meitei culture, 87
Metaphorical film language, 85
Middle class society, 217
Minority movement, 32
Miraculous activities, 6
Mirikajan Tea Estate Darrang, 302
Missionary activities, 97
Mizo society, 317
Mizoram University (MZU), 149
Monotheism, 177
Mughal imperialism, 28
Multicultural society, 284
Multi-ethnic society, 263
Multifarious activities, 383
Musical identity, 395

Naga
  festivals, 130
  separatist movement, 221
  society, 430–32, 438
  grooming tradition, 130
  tribes, 129, 210
Nagaland Board of School Education, 429
Nagaland Municipal Act, 433, 437
Nagaland State Human Development Report, 428
Nagaland State Legislature, 434
Nagaland State Women Commission, 433
Nagaland University (NU), 150
Nagaland Village and Area Councils Act, 433
Nagaland Village Council Act, 431
Narmada Movement, 365
National Adult Education Programmes (NAEP), 198
National film awards, 87
National Institute of Pharmacy Education and Research, 151
National Literacy Mission (NLM), 198
National Policy on Education, 147, 157
National Programmes of Nutrition Support to Primary Education (NPNSPE), 198
National Rural Health Mission. (NRHM), 436
Neo-colonialism, 365
Neo-realism, 83
Neo-Vaishnavism, 8–10, 14–15, 35, 64, 174, 177, 423–24
Neo-Vaisnavite Movement, 14, 29, 66, 175, 426
Nepali's
  domiciled, 264
  foreign, 266
  rich, 267
  urban, 255
  urban White Collar, 255
Non-cooperation movement, 217, 299, 305, 369, 372
Non-formal education system, 326
Non-professional education, 147
Non-tribal culture, 118

North-East Frontier Agency (NEFA), 72, 228–30, 239, 251
North-East Hill University (NEHU), 149
North-East Network (NEN), 428
North-east tribes, 320
North-Eastern Police Academy (NEPA), 241
North-Eastern Region (NER), 111–16, 118, 130, 191, 204, 256, 259, 321, 341, 377, 439

Official Language Act, 284
Oppressive land, 250
Oral culture, 73
Orphan children, 288–89, 291–93

Paddy lands, 284
Pali Buddhism, 212
Panchayati Raj Institutions (PRIs), 431, 434
Pangs of Partition, 285
Parallel cinema movement, 83
Patkar, Medha, 365
Patriarchal society, 93, 97, 335
Patriotic activism, 80
Philosophy of Culture, 61, 63, 66
Phulchera Tea Garden in Sylhet, 302
Political movements, 221
Political nationalism, 215
Population Based Cancer Registries (PBCRs), 328
Pre-colonial culture, 35
Primary education, 293, 322–23
Proselytizing activities, 10
Protest movement, most, 365

Quality education, 150
Quit India Movement, 100–101, 220

Raag Birag, first film, 85
Rajiv Gandhi University (RGU), 148
Rajmai Tea Company Labour Union, 304
Ratna Tea Estate in Sylhet, 301
Ray, Satyajit, 89
Recruitment of Labour for Tea Gardens in Assam, 305
Religion
  Ahom, 35
  animistic, 129
  Assamese, 61
  Brahmanic, 19, 29
  Buddhist, 126, 128
  Hindu, 29, 57, 259
  history of, 8
  jurisprudence, 34
  neo-Vaisnavite, 15
  noblest, 13
  primitive, 23
  principal, 123
  Tai-Ahom, 35
  tantric, 20
  universal, 66
  Vaishnava, 170, 180, 184
  Vedic, 170
Religious
  activities, 12, 319
  faith, 30, 35, 65, 192
  songs, 50, 442
  teachers, 61
  teaching, 441
Retro culture, 71
Revival movement, 35
Revivalism, 35–36
  lingo-cultural, 34

post-Independence, 35
religious, 36
Revolutionary activities, 220
Rituals
annual, 394
community, 394
customary, 394
dam-phi, 49
dead person's, 395
death, 441
gambling, 405
petrified, 62
public, 49
religious, 318
serpent, 74
smartta, 9
social, 13
Tantric, 177
of traditional healing, 6
Vedic, 38
Romantic songs, 50
Royalty marriage, 390
Rural Misings, 424

Sabotage activities, 220
Saivism, 38–39, 42, 51, 106, 108, 170–71, 174, 176–77
Saktism, 17, 25, 30, 56, 170–71, 174–75
Sankaradeva's faith, 8
Sankardeva Studies in Culture, 61
Sankardeva's Bhakti Movement, 63
Sarba Shikha Abhiyan (SSA), 198
Sattra-culture, 109, 189
Sattras of Gormurh, 181
Sattriya culture, 30, 179, 188
Sattriya dance, 66, 108
Schism, 8–9, 14–15
Secessionism, 285
Sema tribes, 129
Semi-feudal society, 85
Separatist insurgency movements, 265
Separatist movements, 103
Shakta songs, 50
Shaktism, 51, 177
Shillong Film Society, 83
Sikkim Manipal University of Health, Medical and Technological Science (SMUHMTS), 149
Singiri Tea Estate in Darrang district, 303
Singpho tribes, 298
Social conservatism, 217
Social customs, 20, 124, 131, 333–34, 394
Social development, 29, 114, 118, 195, 291, 322, 367
Social movement, 356–57, 361, 364–65, 367
Socio-cultural identity, 399
Socio-economic activities, 337
Socio-economic development, 32, 191, 194–95, 199
Socio-religious festivals, 423
Solakia dance, 126
South-East Asian Society, 207
Sparetime activities, 122
Sports activities, 161
State-induced development, 366
State-sponsored film awards, 82
Subversive activities, 220
Sun-worship, 171
Surya worship and Brahmanical culture, 170
Syncretism, 30, 35

Tai Ahom Development Council, 36

Tai Ahom language, 47, 52–53
Tai culture, 383
Tanga tribes, 129
Tantric
development, 18
faith, 121
Tantricism, 17–20, 22–25, 106, 174
Task-based Language Learning, 137
Tea Company Labour Union, 304
Tea estate, 80
Tea Garden Labour Strikes, 298–99, 301, 303–4
Tea garden managers, 299, 305
Tea planters, 298
Tea Trouble, 305
Tea-tribes, 121, 377
Technical education, 145–47, 152–54, 345
Terrorism, 113, 192, 288
Tezpur University (TU), 149
Thai Ahom language, 48
Theravada Buddhism, 209, 441, 446
Tibetan bells, 128
Tibetan culture, 129
Tibeto-Burman tribes, 116
Tiphuk Tea Garden in Lakhimpur district, 302
Tiwa
language, 393–94
society, 394–95
tribes, 361, 393, 399
Tourism Society of England, 111
Tourism, 111–14, 238, 441
development, 113
domestic, 239
Traditional culture, 132
Traditional Dance Dramas, 411, 413, 415, 417
Trans-Asian Railway (TAR), 238, 242
Transhuman pastoralism, 248, 258
Tribal children, 197
Tribal culture, 115, 118–19, 121, 125, 129
Tribal customs, 430
Tribal development, 130, 199, 344, 346–47
imperatives of, 130
Tribal songs, 440
Tribal welfare activities, 344
Tribes and Customary Laws, 314
Tribes
exclusive, 117
girl's, 432
indigenous, 6, 183
matriarchal, 117
mongoloid, 28, 119
patriarchal, 119
primitive, 124
Tripura University (TRU), 149
Tripura University Act, 149
Tripura
Gumti Hydel Project in, 363
Social and Cultural Life in, 126
Tribal communities of, 318
Tripureswari of, 23
Tuli Paper Mill of Nagaland, 363

Ujani Asom Rajya Parishad (UARP), 34
Uncultivated land, 308
Uneconomical land holdings, 342
United Nations Research Institute for Social Development, 367
Universalization of Elementary Education (UEE), 325–26

University Education Commission, 146
Unmarried children, 352
Unpolluted land, 231
Upper Assam Tea Company Union, 304

V

Vaishnava
culture, 424
society, 174, 426
teachers, 175
Vaishnavism, 29–30, 42, 47, 51, 63–65, 106, 170–77, 316, 424
ancient time, 173
prevalence of, 172–73
sectarian, 171
Tantric, 175
Vaisnavite Movement, 8, 62, 65
Value-based
education, 155
society, 65
Vedic culture, 171
Vernacular language, 138
Village dances, 397
Village Development Boards (VDBs), 429
Vivaha-Sanskara of Hindu marriage, 390
Vocational education, 293, 295
Vocational guidance, 293

W

Wage earning activities, 337
Water festivals, 442
Welfare activities, 334
Wet land system, 120
Widow re-marriage, 94–95, 98, 123, 128
Women dance, 125
Women's education, 96–97, 194, 335–36, 371
Women's Missionary Society, 96
Women's movement, 333
World Institution Building Programme (WIBP), 151
Worship
ancestor, 38, 49, 54
bullock, 396
cow, 404
Cow, 405
of dog, 404
of Harihara, 38–39
Hayagriva, 172
Madhava, 171
Matrika, 22
mode of, 65, 171, 177
offering special, 62
primordial, 421
sakti, 17, 22
tantric, 21, 19, 22
Tara, 18
traditional ancestor, 30
Umpha, 48
Visnu, 171, 173, 175–77
yoni, 23

Y

Yimchungi tribes, 129
Yogini Tantra, 19–20, 174–75
Yoginis, 17, 22–23